Psychology of
Language and Learning

COGNITION AND LANGUAGE
A Series in Psycholinguistics

Series Editor: R. W. Rieber

CLINICAL PSYCHOLINGUISTICS
Theodore Shapiro

CRAZY TALK: A Study of the Discourse of Schizophrenic Speakers
Sherry Rochester and J. R. Martin

PSYCHOLOGY OF LANGUAGE AND LEARNING
O. Hobart Mowrer

A Continuation Order Plan is available for this series. A continuation order will bring delivery of each new volume immediately upon publication. Volumes are billed only upon actual shipment. For further information please contact the publisher.

Psychology of Language and Learning

Edited by

O. Hobart Mowrer

University of Illinois
Champaign-Urbana, Illinois

PLENUM PRESS · NEW YORK AND LONDON

Library of Congress Cataloging in Publication Data

Main entry under title:

Psychology of learning and language.

Includes index.
1. Psycholinguistics. 2. Learning, Psychology of. I. Mowrer, Orval Hobart, 1907-
P37.P79   401'.9   79-17959
ISBN 0-306-40371-4

© 1980 Plenum Press, New York
A Division of Plenum Publishing Corporation
227 West 17th Street, New York, N.Y. 10011

Printed in the United States of America

To Linda, Kathryn, and Todd—
whose language learning was
observed by their father and mother
with wonder and delight

Foreword

There are very few psychologists living today who have contributed more to the advancement of psychology, in general, and to the psychology of language and thought, in particular, than O. Hobart Mowrer.

It would indeed be ludicrous to attempt to list the many and varied accomplishments and contributions that Dr. Mowrer has made to his profession over the years. Even the selected essays that are in this volume can only suggest a modicum of his remarkable, vital, and ongoing contribution to the psychology of language and thought. Furthermore, the chapters in this book, which were published over a period of some twenty-five years, clearly illustrate that Dr. Mowrer was concerned not only with basic research, but that he also had an interest in its application. These chapters also point to the fact that although Dr. Mowrer's orientation was primarily that of a "behaviorist" at the onset, his constant attempts to revise knowledge in this field and broaden its scope make it virtually impossible for us to classify him as a *behaviorist* in the narrow meaning of that term. The chapter on mental imagery, for example, written only a few years ago, serves to illustrate this point. In addition, the Autism Theory of Speech Development (see Chapter 4), one of Dr. Mowrer's most important contributions that is all too often overlooked in today's literature, integrates the concepts of hope and fear into an already rich theoretical framework of language learning, giving both shape and power to the Second Signal System— the mediating structures through which the stimuli of the physical world are filtered.

Hobart Mowrer has had truly a distinguished and a creative career. As a behavioral scientist, his current output is still, beyond doubt, both imaginative and practical and very often candidly outspoken. The heuristics he has developed in this book are worthy of the most careful attention. It is our expectation that this work will help the reader to understand more clearly the present level of development in the field of the psychology of language and thought, as well as to come to understand how we have arrived at where we are today.

R. W. RIEBER

Preface

The papers (originally published between 1945 and 1961) which are reproduced as Part I of this volume consist of what may be termed "missing links" between I. P. Pavlov's First Signal System (ordinary conditioning) and his Second Signal System (full-fledged language, including predication). Because the author undertook these studies from the standpoint of the psychology of learning rather than primarily as a student of language, it will not be surprising that the attempt to establish connections between Pavlov's two Systems proceeded, so to say, from the ground up. This series of studies thus provides the conceptual background for and articulates with the exciting contemporary research now being carried on, for example, with chimpanzees by the Gardeners at Reno State University and at the Yerkes Primate Laboratories in Atlanta, and with other studies predicated on the continuity of communicative processes between lower animals and man.

The reader should, however, be informed that two major papers from the period covered in Part I are not included here. The first, entitled "The Psychology of Talking Birds," was originally published as Chapter 24 of the author's *Learning Theory and Personality Dynamics* (New York: Ronald, 1950) and was republished by the Ronald Press (in its Social Science series, No. P-257). And another paper, "The Psychologist Looks at Language," which could equally well have been entitled "Predication: Formation and Function," was originally published in the *American Psychologist* (1954, *9*, 666-694) and was republished in a volume edited by L. A. Jacobovits and M. S. Miron entitled, *Readings in the Psychology of Language* (Englewood Cliffs, N. J.: Prentice-Hall, 1976, pp. 6-50). These two papers are omitted in the present compendium partly because of their ready availability elsewhere, partly to save space, and also because their basic hypotheses appear in both Part I and Part II. The reader interested in the more detailed and technical aspects of these papers is referred to their original versions.

Although the author did not publish in the mainstream of psycholinguistics during the 1960s (because of preoccupation with other matters), he was nevertheless aware of some sort of strange revolution, instigated by Noam Chomsky, that was sweeping over this field but which he was unable to follow in detail or comprehend. However, in 1969, he was invited to address the New York Academy of Sciences, and, deciding that this would afford a good opportunity to update his knowledge in this area, produced a monograph entitled *"Psycholinguistics Revisited—or, Why All the Chafing over Chomsky?"* This document, which appears here as Part II of this book, summarizes many of the ideas advanced in Part I and sets forth new material designed specifically to refute the Chomskian postulates.

Although, as already indicated, the author discontinued publication during the 1960s of the kinds of studies reproduced in Part I, he wrote at some length on a phenomenon generally neglected in the field of communication, namely, the flagrant and frequent abuse of language known as deception or lying. Virtually no discipline, with the exception of religion (and it has its own problems with mythologies and debatable metaphysics), has given this problem any sustained, systematic attention; and this is all the more surprising because of the very substantial evidence that lies and guilty secrets can become pathogenic (i.e., a major source of identity crisis—Erik Erikson's useful substitute for the misleading term "neurosis"). A number of the papers pertinent to this problem are reproduced here as Part III. Such material received only scant attention when first published because deception and guilty secrecy were then common in both high and low places in our society, and were even regarded, in many quarters, as a form of cleverness and a legitimate means of manipulation. Perhaps one of the main reasons that psychotherapy, in the hands of members of the various mental health professions, has often been so nontherapeutic is that this matter of truthfulness, integrity, and unambiguous identity has been neglected or even denigrated. (For two striking exceptions, see H. F. Ellenberger's article "The Pathogenic Secret and Its Therapeutics," *Journal of the History of Behavioral Science,* 1966, *2,* 29–42, and F. J. Schwab's book, *The Agony of Honesty—Guidelines for Self-Improvement,* published by the Exposition Press, New York, 1971.)

Part III of this book consists of only six articles; but, space permitting, three more relatively long papers could have been added: "Communication, Conscience, and the Unconscious," (*Journal of Communication Disorders,* 1967, *1,* 109–135); "Psychoneurotic Defenses (including Deception) as Punishment-Avoidance Strategies," *Punishment and Aversive Behavior,* B. A. Campbell & R. M. Church, Eds.,

Appleton-Century-Crofts, 1969);   and "A New Theory of Schizophrenia," Anonymous (*Journal of Abnormal and Social Psychology*,
1958, *57*, 226–236.) The thesis that there is often a connection between
deception and personality disorder is also elaborated by the author in
The New Group Therapy (Princeton, N. J.: Van Nostrand, 1964) and
Morality and Mental Health (Skokie, Ill.: Rand-McNally, 1967).

This volume, in substantially its present form, was completed in
1970 and forwarded to Professor R. W. Rieber, who, because of his
favorable disposition toward it, had kindly agreed to seek a New York
publisher. Under date of October 11, 1972, he wrote as follows: "I have
looked through your manuscript *Psychology of Language and Learning*
and, quite frankly, I would like to see it in print. However, I have had
no success with publishers that I have shown it to and I have gotten no
satisfactory rationale from them, just polite and flattering refusals. Some
use the jargon of "not enough market potentiality" and others say that
they "are not the right publishing house."

But Dr. Rieber and I remained in contact, and on June 7, 1976, he
and I had lunch together in New York City, and it was at that time that
he gave me the Big News: Chomsky's house of cards had fallen, he and
his questionable speculations no longer dominated the field of psycholinguistics—had, in fact, been largely discredited—thus leaving the field in
disarray but more open and free, once again, for the discussion and
publication of non-Chomskian views and empirical research. In late
April (28–30) there had been a conference at the New York Academy of
Sciences, one session of which was devoted to "Historical Aspects of the
Psychology of Language and Cognition," and this meeting had
apparently confirmed an already existing reality, and was, in effect, a
kind funeral for the Chomskian concepts and cult (cf. Evelyn F. Segal's
1972 mimeographed paper entitled, "Chomsky's Anguish"—San Diego
State University).

"Now," said Rieber, "is the time to reconsider the publication of
your book, and I think I have a publisher for you," as indeed he had.
Moreover, at about the same time, between 1972 and 1976, we had
"Watergate" and the publication of a number of remarkable books, by
Dan Rather, Bernstein & Woodword, Jimmy Breslin, and T. H.
White, who, among others, have demonstrated in a most dramatic way
the longrun impracticality and personal hazards of deception, in
politics, industry, and "private life." I am sorry to say that it was, on
the whole, journalists and not clinical psychologists who first identified
and raised their voices regarding "the cancer that is growing on the
Presidency;" and the Congress that had to instigate presidential
impeachment proceedings is now in process of examining its own

"ethics." But psychologists have not been altogether insensitive to these events. For example, an editorial in the January, 1976, issue of the *Canadian Counselor* illustrates a trend. Here we read:

> It appears to me that we are shifting away from an emphasis on the counselor relating to clients in a special way that will release the clients' potential so that they can "do their own thing." . . . I do not wish to launch into a discussion of the skills and knowledges that I consider important [in counseling] but rather point out that such skills and knowledges plus values and moral norms are becoming the focal point for many counselors.

Brief mention should also be made of the fact that the approach to language development favored in this compendium as a whole ultimately presupposes the occurrence and functional utility of mental imagery and certain other cognitive phenomena. This is a point of view systematically, but not completely, elaborated in the twin volumes I published in 1960, *Learning Theory and Behavior* and *Learning Theory and the Symbolic Processes*. This position was not sympathetically received by the then very numerous radical behaviorists among psychologists, but since then there has been a general swing toward the postulation of more and more "intervening variables" (between S and R, stimulation and response) as essential to a complete and adequate science of psychology in general, and language theory in particular. This development, which has been documented in a large and growing literature, makes many of the papers in this book much more congruent with the prevailing zeitgeist than they were at the time of publication (e.g., see Carol McMahon's paper, "Images as Motives and Motivators," *American Journal of Psychology,* 1973, *86,* 465–490).

A final word now, about the need for some "connectives," to give cohesion and unity to this book and to articulate it, in a concise but solid way, with the contemporary scene in psycholinguistics. To facilitate the first objective, some time during 1970, after I had assembled and organized the papers constituting this volume, I wrote brief "prologues" designed to provide a transition from one paper to the next and to integrate the volume as a whole. Recent political events have made the papers in Part III arrestingly contemporary, without further comment. However, the papers in Parts I and II need, in addition to the prologues, some further commentary to update them and establish their ongoing relevancy. As the years since these papers were assembled have passed, I have collected and have a large cardboard box full of reprints, monographs, and books in the field of language genesis and process which have seemed sound and significant to me—despite Chomsky's disrupting influence—but I must admit that I have not read very much of this material, and, without an enormous amount of time and study, cannot give an accurate and reasonably comprehensive account of the present state of the best scientific and scholarly work in this field. Therefore, I have fallen back on two expedients: (a) I have asked Professor Rieber, and he has kindly agreed, to write a Foreword for this book in which he explains the reasons for his continued interest and "faith" in the documents here assembled, and makes other remarks that seem appropriate against the background of his current and comprehensive knowledge of the field of psycholinguistics; and (b), with the concurrence of Dr. Rieber and the publisher, I have added, as Part IV, a section entitled "Epilogues," consisting of three somewhat disparate but pertinent contributions: Chapters 14, 15, and 16.

After this book had gone to press, the writer chanced upon a remarkable, and to him previously unknown, 1128 page compendium, entitled *How Animals Communication* and edited by T. A. Sebeok (Indiana University Press, 1977). By this time it was, of course, too late to make detailed and systematic reference to this work, but readers of the present volume should know about it should they perhaps wish to examine it. This book contains 38 chapters covering a pervasive range of subject matter, but with a preponderant emphasis upon innate rather than learned behavior. The closest approximation to the concerns of the present volume comes in Chapter 37, by R. S. Fouts and R. I. Rigby (pp. 1034–1054), entitled "Man–Chimpanzee Communication." This chapter is an excellent review of relevant research done up to the date of publication, but it does not include any reference to the singular results achieved by Francine Patterson with gorilla subjects (see acknowledgment below). Nevertheless, *How Animals Communicate* is a stupendous achievement, which should be more widely known than it apparently is. Also, an announcement of the publication of *Psycholinguistics—An Introduction to Research and Theory* (second edition), by Hans Hörmann (Springer-Verlag, 1979), has just come to the author's attention. Although the book itself has not yet been examined, the contents suggests considerable affinity to the present volume. The last three chapters, more than the earlier part of the book, deal with the psychological aspects of language and look particularly interesting.

Of special interest and value is a book edited by Thomas A. Sebeok and Donna Jean Umiker-Sebeok, entitled *Speaking of Apes—A Critical Anthology of Two-Way Communication with Man* (New York: Plenum, 1979). Some of the highlights of theory and research covered in this volume are to be found in Joan Bazar's article, "Catching Up with the Ape Language Debate" (*The Monitor*, American Psychological Association, January, 1980).

Origins and Evolution of Language and Speech (New York: New York Academy of Sciences, 1975) is a monumental volume containing 75 papers and edited by Steven Harnad, Horst D. Steklis, and Jane Lancaster. This work is somewhat dated and marred by acceptance of the assumption that "the Chomskian revolution in modern linguistics has radically altered our conceptions of the nature of language," but it is still a notable scientific and scholarly achievement.

Acknowledgment is gratefully made to Professor Rieber, editor of the Plenum Cognition and Language Series, for his role in the publication of this book and for the Foreword he has written. He has been both friend and wise counselor in his undertaking. The publishers of the journals in which most of the chapters of this volume originally appeared have also been most gracious in granting permission for their reproduction here. Inspiration for the sketch which appears on the front of the jacket of this book comes from a photograph on page 452 of the October, 1978, issue of the *National Geographic*. It is part of a fascinating article by Francine Patterson, entitled "Conversations with a Gorilla," and is a dramatic breakthrough in bridging the gap between mind in man and in "lower" animals. Although adumbrated by other related studies that are cited in this book, Ms. Patterson's achievement is in some ways as dramatic as the education, and socialization, of Helen Keller who, before she learned to comprehend and produce sentences, was, in fact, "just an animal"—and a very incompetent one at that. It is not too much to say that Ms. Patterson has forged the *mental* "missing link" between man and other anthropoids, just as the Leckeys appear to have finally found the true evolutionary line of ascent. Anyone who has not read Francine Patterson's report of this epochal achievement has in store a rare intellectual treat.

By an odd combination of circumstances, the passage of time has thus made the contents of this book more, rather than less, pertinent than they were a decade ago, and we anticipate that this compendium will have a favorable reception.

O. HOBART MOWRER

June, 1980
University of Illinois
Champaign-Urbana

Contents

PART IV: EPILOGUES   211

From the First to the Second 'Signal System'

E. B. Holt once remarked that in the course of organic evolution the advent of the conditioned reflex, or associative learning, "brought mind into being." By this he meant that organisms whose responses occur, and occur only, to specific, "physiologically adequate" stimuli are little more than organic machines, but that when, as a result of the temporal association of some initially neutral stimulus with the one which inevitably produces a given response, the originally ineffective, neutral stimulus itself becomes capable of producing this response, a momentous forward step has been taken beyond mere mechanism, toward *mind*. In other words, when an originally inert stimulus precedes, with some regularity, what I. P. Pavlov called the "unconditioned" or "unconditional" stimulus for a particular response (or "reflex"), and thus becomes capable of eliciting this response *in advance* of the "unconditioned," "physiologically adequate" stimulus, a great new principle of biological adaptation comes into existence. An organism with this capacity is, as we say, able to respond to *signals*, and thus not only gains in natural adaptability, but also acquires the rudimentary basis for the development of interorganismic communication and language.

In the first few chapters of this book, we shall be dealing with a number of situations in which the groundwork is being prepared for the next monumental step forward in the evolution of mind, that is, the emergence of linguistic predication ("sentences") concerning what Clark Hull has termed "the not here and not now," that is, the step from spatial and temporal concreteness to *abstraction*. Chapter six in this section offers an hypothesis, one not without considerable empirical support, as to how the phenomenon of predication evolved, out of the nexus of simpler learning and signaling processes. In order to denote and discriminate these two levels of adaptation or "minding," Pavlov introduced the felicitous expression, "first and second signal system."

1

Language and Learning:
An Experimental Paradigm

There is no mystery as to how either human beings or lower organisms learn the "meanings" of events ("signals") which regularly precede other events. The principle here involved is associative learning or "conditioning." And it is equally understandable how it is that lower animals make certain stereotyped signals (gestural, auditory, visual, olfactory); they do so reflexly, automatically, instinctively, given the appropriate stimulus circumstances. But the signals which human beings most often use are sound-producing responses called words, which are not at all reflexive, but conventional, that is, learned, as a function of the particular system of words, or language, which the infant hears in use around him.

The question to which this first chapter addresses itself is: How does a child learn to make the response which will reproduce a specific auditory stimulus (word) it hears others making? One common, but manifestly unsatisfactory, assumption is that children learn to reproduce the words used by the society into which they are born by the process of trial and error. This process is much too slow to account for the prodigious speed of language learning, once it is well under way. Another common hypothesis is that children learn to speak through an "instinct of imitation." But, in this context, imitation remains an unanalyzed phenomenon, and is therefore unsatisfactory for explanatory purposes.

In the paper which follows a suggestion is made as to how the process of making conventional signals can be greatly facilitated, in both animals and infants, which does not presuppose either trial-and-error learning or an "instinct of imitation." A more satisfactory explanation of word iteration will be suggested in later chapters, but the present study is a step in the right direction.

This paper was published jointly with Peter Viek in the Harvard Educational-Review, *1945, 15, 35–48.*

An eighteen-month-old child leaned forward, grunted, and groped for a small dish of butter which sat on the table before her. The child's mother, seated nearby, said, "Mary, say, 'butter.'" The little girl said something roughly approximating "butter," and was given a small amount of this substance in a spoon.

Anyone who has observed small children in a normal home environment knows how frequently parents and others are likely to use the procedure just described as a means of facilitating the acquisition of language, but the writers are unaware of this procedure's having been previously analyzed in the light of modern learning theory. It is the purpose of this paper to offer such analysis and an experimental paradigm.

Conditioning and Teaching

Conditioning, or associative learning, is generally recognized as a process whereby it becomes possible to elicit by a new, formerly indifferent stimulus a response which originally could be called forth only by means of another, so-called unconditioned stimulus. Pavlov (1927), Hull (1929), and others have commented upon the biological utility of this form of learning as a means whereby living organisms are able to acquire anticipatory responses, of both an avoidant and an appetitive nature, and thereby greatly increase their chances of survival. And Bertrand Russell (1927), Ogden and Richards (1923), Bloomfield (1914), Korzybski (1941), and other students of logic and language have pointed out the connection between the meaning, or understanding, of words and the conditioning process: a word (symbol) as heard or seen is the conditioned stimulus, the thing which the word symbolizes (the referent) is the unconditioned stimulus, and the meaning which the word has for the subject (its reference) is the conditioned response. What we wish to add is simply that conditioning plays an important role in teaching children those habits which are involved, not alone in the understanding, but also in the *use* of words.

Russell has clearly differentiated between words as understood and words as used and has suggested that the understanding of a word is a matter of conditioning, whereas skill in using a word, as a means of influencing the behavior of others, is acquired on the basis of trial-and-error learning. That the untutored exploratory babbling of infants sometimes leads to the production of sounds which are responded to as meaningful by parents is well known. As a matter of fact, if parents listen carefully and respond consistently to certain word-like sounds which infants spontaneously make, the latter can learn to use a limited number of such sounds (ma-ma, pa-pa, ba-ba, etc.) amazingly early (at three to six months of age). This observation controverts the common assumption that a child must "understand" words before he can use them. We have repeatedly seen infants use words long before they began to respond meaningfully to these same sounds as made by others.[1] However, the fact remains that if language had to be acquired solely on such a trial-and-error basis, learning to speak, in a really fluent manner, would be an agonizingly slow and inefficient process. Normally the acquisition of speech proceeds relatively rapidly once it is begun, a circumstance which makes it sufficiently apparent that trial-and-error is superseded or at least importantly supplemented by some other mechanism.

The all-too-facile traditional explanation of language development is that it is "due to imitation." Miller and Dollard (1941) have shown how inexact, even mystical, are the ways in which this concept has often been employed, and these writers have succeeded in deriving from basic learning principles many of the behavioral phenomena often characterized as imitative. There is no doubt that, at later stages, children model their speech as well as other actions upon the behavior of others, both through self-conscious copying and unconscious identification. Important as "imitation" may thus be, it nevertheless fails, no less than does the trial-and-error hypothesis, to give us a completely satisfactory

---

[1] The same observation holds for infantile gesturing. The reason it is generally assumed that a child must "understand" the meaning of a word before he can use it is that most parents respond to the word-like sounds made by their offspring only when these sounds are uttered with adult, dictionary connotations. Thus, "mama" is the symbol used by adults (and older children) to refer to a particular person in the household and normally serves as the subject of a sentence: "Mama is gone," "Mama will bring us a present," etc. It is not surprising that the ability to use the word "mama" in this relatively sophisticated manner usually does not develop until the second, sometimes the third or even the fourth year of life. But if the attendant adults will at first interpret "mama" as "I am uncomfortable," and will do something about this discomfort, the average child can learn to use this word and at least a few others within the first half year of life. The same is true of the use of gestures. However, in saying that a child can thus learn to "use" words, or gestures, at such an early age, we should point out a certain ambiguity in this term. Words have two major types of use: the first we have just described; the second involves, not mere signaling of wants and desires, but the communication of "ideas," or "knowledge." In order to use words in this second sense, a child must indeed first "understand" these words. Whether there is any practical advantage in helping a child learn to "use" words in the first of these two ways, as an intermediate step to the second type of usage, is a problem for further research and analysis. We mention it in some detail only because of its theoretical interest.

account of speech development: neither approach sufficiently acknowledges the active tuitional roles which parents and other adults continually play in this connection.

When the senior author began teaching courses in education, he was unable to decide how the word "teaching" ought to be defined. If one interprets it to mean the process whereby one individual influences the learning of another, the term becomes so broad as to be useless, or at least equivalent to "social interaction." But how can it be used in a narrower, more exact sense? Various writers have attempted to define teaching as the "guidance of learning," "helping others learn," etc., but it remained for a student[2] to suggest a more satisfying and precise definition, namely, that teaching is the process whereby one individual enables another to learn something (solve a problem) more quickly than he would on the basis of his own trial-and-error behavior.[3] With this definition in mind, we quickly see that Mary's mother was engaging in an unmistakable act of teaching when she commanded Mary to say "butter."

How likely a small child is to say "butter," or even "buh-buh," on a purely trial-and-error basis at a time when the child wants a particular edible substance cannot be precisely estimated (cf. Thorndike, 1943), but the chances are obviously slight. On the other hand, if a child who has learned to say "butter" on command is given this command while wanting butter, and if the child obeys this command and gets some of the desired substance, only a few repetitions of this procedure will be required for the child to learn to utter this word whenever he wants butter. In this way the child is enabled to acquire the habit of using the word, "butter," far more directly and quickly than he could ever do on the basis of unaided trial-and-error.

Schematically, we may say that once the response, "butter," has become attached (conditioned) to the command, "Say, 'butter,'" the latter can be used as a sort of ladle, or handle, for transfering the butter-response to another stimulus (butter-want) to which it is initially very unlikely to occur. Once this "transplantation" has been carried out a few times, the butter-response "takes root" and becomes firmly con-

[2] Ms. Barbara Lyndon.

[3] Linton (1936), Ford (1939), and others have defined human culture as an accumulation of ready-made solutions to problems which are transmitted from generation to generation. Language is the prime vehicle of culture transmission (teaching), but language, as a social invention, is itself a part of culture and has to be transmitted, as a prerequisite to the child's more formal "education." Teaching is likewise a social invention which, together with language, makes culture possible.

nected to the butter-motive, because of the reinforcement which occurs when the butter is received and the butter-want reduced.

This analysis leaves unanswered the important question as to how the child initially learns to say what he is commanded to; this problem must ultimately be considered. First, however, let us exemplify the process just described by a simple laboratory paradigm.

The Paradigm

How likely is an untutored laboratory rat to leap into the air when hungry? Without, for the moment, attempting to be very precise, we can be sure that such a response is relatively unlikely to occur. On the other hand, if a rat is placed on a metal grill and given an electric shock, the response of leaping into the air is almost certain to occur fairly promptly. Our problem, then, let us assume, is to get this jumping reaction "transplanted" from the latter situation, in which it is readily elicited by shock, to the former situation, so that it will also occur in response to hunger. How can this be done?

The foregoing discussion provides the clue. If we can get the jumping response conditioned to some neutral stimulus, such as the sound of a buzzer, we can use this stimulus as a means of eliciting the jumping response in a situation in which the rat is hungry and will receive food as a result of reacting in this manner. The jumping response should then become connected to the hunger motive and should occur whenever the rat is hungry, without external prompting of any kind.

The Experimental Group[4]

Using a standard procedure, eight male rats (Lashley strain) about five months of age were trained, with electric shock as the unconditioned stimulus, until they all gave a conditioned jumping reaction 90% of the time when a buzzer was sounded. The rats were then reduced to and held at 85% of their normal body weight. On the first day of the experiment proper, each rat—now reduced in weight and hungry—was put back into the conditioning apparatus (described in Mowrer & Miller, 1942) and treated as follows. If, at the end of 60 sec, the rat had not

[4] The writers are indebted to Mrs. John L. Bakke for assistance in carrying out the experimental procedures about to be described.

jumped, it was caused to do so by means of the buzzer. Following this "forced" reaction, the rat received a small pellet of food.[5] This procedure was repeated until 10 trials had been given; but if at any time during the 60-sec interval between trials the rat jumped "spontaneously," it was likewise given food, and the buzzer was omitted for that trial. In other words, the rat was fed for jumping not only in response to the buzzer (and hunger), but also for jumping to hunger alone, the presumption being that this procedure would lead to an increase in "spontaneous" jumps to the point where their "forced" elicitation would become entirely unnecessary.

How well this supposition was verified is indicated by the solid line in Figure 1. Here it will be seen that by the end of 10 days (100 trials), the eight animals in the experimental group were making, on the average, 7 out of 10 of the required daily jumps on a "spontaneous" basis, that is, were responding to their hunger alone, without external instigation. Unfortunately, this average curve gives a rather poor picture of what actually happened. By the end of the 10 days, six of the eight animals were responding almost entirely to hunger alone, whereas two animals had not yet "caught on," and were still having to be forced to jump by means of the buzzer. Thus, on the 10th day, the number of spontaneous leaps made by the eight animals were 0, 10, 10, 9, 10, 0, 8, and 10. In other words, this type of learning had a certain all-or-none quality. If the experiment had been continued sufficiently long, animals Nos. 1 and 6 would presumably have also solved this problem, but at the end of 100 trials they had obviously not done so, whereas the other six animals had. Therefore, instead of saying that at the end of the experiment, the eight animals were, on the average, about 70% proficient, it is more accurate to say that six of the eight, or 75%, of the animals had solved the problem almost perfectly, whereas the remainder had made no evident progress toward its solution.

[5] If a rat failed to respond to the buzzer within 5 sec, the electric shock was applied, just as in the preliminary training sessions. However, the shock was very rarely necessary, partly because of the high level to which the conditioning had previously been brought, and partly because the giving of food for jumping in response to the buzzer seemed to reinforce this connection considerably, even though this connection was originally established by reinforcement provided by the termination of the shock. Our evidence on this point is not well controlled, but it is supported by Brogden's (1939) finding that a conditioned paw-retraction in dogs which was set up with electric shock as the unconditioned stimulus could be kept alive indefinitely if food was substituted as a means of reinforcement. Cf. Allport's (1940) discussion of habits which are acquired on the basis of one motive's being perpetuated by other motives; also the psychoanalytic concept of "over-determination" (Freud, 1924).

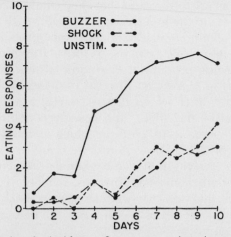

Figure 1. Curves showing the incidence of spontaneous jumping responses followed by eating in the experimental (buzzer) group, control (shock) Group I, and control (unstimulated) Group II.

The behavior shown by the "successful" animals in this experiment, though no different in principle from a dog's "begging" for food by sitting up, or a horse's neighing, or little Mary's saying "buh-buh," was nevertheless very striking. To see a rat jumping into the air as a means of obtaining food (which was supplied from below the grill on which the animal stood) was an arresting experience; and since the genesis of this behavior was carefully controlled and observed, it serves quite satisfactorily to illustrate the hypothesis previously put forward.

Control Group I

It will probably have occurred to the reader to ask: Why condition the rats to jump to the buzzer as a means of "showing" them that this response will secure food? Why not simply force them to jump by means of the unconditioned stimulus, namely, the electric shock, without the intermediary action of the buzzer? It was by no means certain that this method would not prove to be quite as satisfactory as the more complicated method actually employed with the experimental group. However, one could anticipate that the more direct method would involve an important difficulty: namely, that the emotional upset produced by the shock would be so great that it would inhibit the animals from eating when the food was presented, and that they would therefore fail to learn to jump in response to the hunger motive alone.[6]

In order to obtain empirical evidence on this score, we reduced the body weight of eight naive animals, as already indicated, and subjected them to the following procedure. Each animal was put into the experimental apparatus and, after an interval of 60 sec, was shocked until it leaped into the air, after which it was offered a pellet of food. After a few presentations of the shock and food, the animals nearly always began to make "spontaneous" jumps, which were likewise followed by the presentation of food. These jumps were allowed to count as trials. However, it was evident that these animals were responding less to hunger than to another internal stimulus, namely, *fear*. This was indicated by the fact that they showed almost as much hesitation to eat following these "spontaneous" responses as they did following the shock-instigated jumps.

The broken line in Figure 1 shows the comparatively small number of times that the eight animals in this group made so-called spontaneous jumps and then ate the food they thus obtained. As will be seen by comparing the curves for the experimental group and this control group, the use of a conditioned stimulus as a means of "telling," or "showing," the rats how to obtain the food was markedly superior to the use of a stimulus which had intense motivational value rather than primarily "sign function." Although the buzzer undoubtedly aroused some fear (Mowrer, 1939), this emotion was manageable and did not interfere with the eating as much as did the fear produced by the traumatic shock stimulus.

In this group, as in the experimental group, the learning tended, in individual animals, to have an all-or-none quality. On the last day of the experiment, the eight animals in this control group made the following scores: 0, 0, 0, 0, 6, 0, 8, 10. Thus, three out of the eight animals may be said to have solved the problem, as contrasted with twice that number in the experimental group.

Control Group II

A second control group seemed indicated, as a means of determining just how likely hungry rats are to learn to leap into the air for food without any "guidance," or "instruction," whatever. In other words,

---

[6] Estes and Skinner (1941) have shown that fear retards the rate of eating in rats in a free-feeding situation.

this group was designed to determine how quickly they could learn to leap into the air and thereby solve their hunger problem, on a purely trial-and-error basis, without the use of either a conditioned or an unconditioned stimulus to "point out" the solution.

With their body weights reduced in the manner already described, the eight rats comprising this second control group were individually placed in the experimental apparatus and subjected to the following procedure. If a rat did not jump during 10 minutes (ten 60-sec periods), it was simply taken out of the apparatus, returned to its home cage, and fed. If a rat made one or more but fewer than 10 jumps during the 10 minutes, it was given a pellet of food following each jump but again left in the apparatus the full 10 minutes. On the other hand, if it made 10 jumps in less than 10 minutes, it was fed following each jump but was taken out of the apparatus after it had consumed the food received for its 10th jump. This procedure seemed to provide a fair control for our experimental group concerning the question as to how likely our experimental subjects were to solve the problem with which they were presented on an unaided, trial-and-error basis.

The results obtained with Control Group II were somewhat surprising in that the animals in this group showed a greater original tendency to jump in response to hunger alone than we had anticipated. As will be seen by the dotted line in Figure 1, the animals in this group learned, on the average, to obtain food by jumping as well or better than did the animals in Control Group I, with final-day scores of 3, 0, 10, 10, 0, 10, 0, and 0. However, they still fell far below the experimental animals.

Reliability of Group Differences

Inspection of Figure 1 suggests that the results obtained for the experimental group are significantly different from those for the two control groups. In order to test this impression statistically, it is necessary, first of all, to know how many successful responses ("spontaneous" jumps followed by eating) each animal in each group made throughout the 10 days of the experiment. The eight animals in the experimental group made, respectively, the following scores: 1, 48, 70, 70, 2, 63, 95, 61; those in the first control group: 0, 0, 0, 0, 40, 0, 36, 45; and those in the second control group: 3, 0, 60, 54, 0, 20, 0, 0. Thus, the *average* number of successful responses made by the eight animals in the experimental group was 51.250; by the eight animals in the first control group, 15.125; and by the eight animals in the second control group, 17.125. How reliable are the differences between these means? When subjected to "Student's" *t*-test, the differences between the mean for the experimental group and the means for the two control groups both turn out to be significant well beyond the .05 level, which is conventionally accepted as the standard of scientific trustworthiness. On the other hand, the difference between the means of the two control groups is completely nonsignificant, as inspection of the learning curves for these two groups would lead one to expect.

Unfortunately, the applicability of the *t*-test to our data is open to question. We need not go into the details of this difficulty except to say that it hinges upon the fact that in all three groups there appear to be *two* points of concentration of individual scores, rather than one as in a normal distribution. The reason for this bimodality of individual scores is the tendency, already mentioned, for the animals to solve the problem in an all-or-none manner, that is, to make a score either of 0 or somewhere around 40 to 70.

Although this fact renders the *t*-test suspect, it opens up the possibility of applying another statistical technique, namely, the method of Chi Square. Since six of the animals in the experimental group (those with scores of 48, 70, 70, 63, 95, and 61) solved the problem, and two (those with scores of 1 and 2) did not, and since only three of the animals (those with scores of 40, 36, and 45) in the first control group solved it, whereas five (with scores of 0, 0, 0, 0, 0) did not, we can ask how likely one would be to get such a difference in the behavior of the animals in two such groups if these two groups were treated in precisely the same manner, or, what is equivalent, if the two groups were treated differently, but without this difference in treatment's producing any real difference in the animal's behavior. The Chi Square method tells us that the difference between the two groups—for one of which the ratio of successful to unsuccessful animals was 6/2 and for the other, 3/5—is reliable well beyond the .05 level. Since there were also only three animals (with scores of 60, 54, and 20) in the second control group which can be said to have solved the problem, the Chi Square test will naturally give the same value for the reliability of the difference between the experimental group and this second control group.[7]

[7] In theory, this test is designed to ascertain the reliability of the difference between a standard, or known, ratio of some kind (*a parameter*) and an empirically obtained ratio (known as a *statistic*). In our case, *both* of the ratios (6/2 and 3/5) are empirically derived (and therefore subject to error). However, it would seem justifiable to take either of these ratios as the best available estimate of a parameter with which the other ratio could be compared. Somewhat different results are obtained depending upon whether one takes 6/2 or 3/5 as the parameter, but in both cases the obtained *p* value is beyond the .05 level of significance.

The Relative Frequency of "Nervous" Responses

Thus far we have restricted the analysis of our data to a comparison of the number of times which the animals in our three groups
"spontaneously" leaped into the air and then ate the food which was
presented to them as a reward for this performance. The reader will
certainly not be surprised to learn that some of our animals sometimes
made the required response but then refused to eat the pellet which was
offered to them. As can be seen in Figure 2, this type of behavior occurred very frequently in Control Group I (the shocked animals), very
rarely in the Experimental Group (the conditioned animals), and not at
all in Control Group II (the externally unstimulated animals). What do
these results mean?

If an animal failed to eat the food offered following a jump, it was
not because the animal was not hungry. It was rather because the
animal, although hungry, was still more frightened and was more intent
upon reducing fear than the hunger. Here we have a type of behavior
comparable to the so-called "nervous" acts and mannerisms seen so
commonly in human beings, children and adults alike, but so rarely
(save in the experimental laboratory) in animals. There is, however,
this important difference. In the case of our rats which leaped into the
air but then refused to eat the food, we are not in the least mystified: we
know that these animals were afraid of being shocked and were making

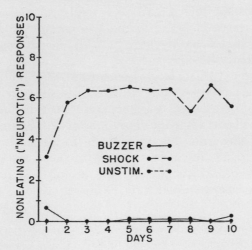

Figure 2. Curves showing the incidence of spontaneous jumping responses not followed
by eating in our three groups.

anticipatory responses which, in all probability, somewhat reduced their fear. On the other hand, the "nervous" movements of human beings are often only a little less mysterious to the person manifesting them than they are to the casual, untrained observer.

In theory we know, of course, that so-called nervous actions, or "symptoms," on the part of human beings are likewise instigated by anxiety (or "nervous tension"); we can also be fairly certain that they, too, are the unintended by-products of some sort of earlier training, or "education." They impress us as mysterious and meaningless only because the time interval between cause and effect in the human situation is often so great that nobody can easily "see the connection." In our laboratory paradigm, this complication and source of confusion does not arise.

Comparing, now, the results presented in Figure 1 and in Figure 2, we see that in the Experimental Group we obtained a good deal of the (by us) desired learning (to obtain food by leaping into the air), and very little undesired, "concomitant" learning (to leap into the air, through fear, but to refuse food). On the other hand, in Control Group I there was much less of the desired learning, and much more of the undesired learning; whereas, in Control Group II, there was a low incidence of both the desired and the undesired learning. The advantage of an intermediary, conditioned stimulus (over an unconditioned stimulus, on the one hand, and, on the other, no external stimulation, or guidance, whatever) is therefore a double one: it produces a maximum of desirable and a minimum of undesirable learning outcomes.

Without wishing to overextend the application of our experimental paradigm, we are nevertheless tempted to observe that schools do not ordinarily care to undertake the education of children until they are skilled in the understanding and use of the exquisitely complex set of conditioned stimuli which we call language. Parents would probably also do well to delay many of the learning tasks they must impose upon their offspring until after speech is well established, concentrating their early tuitional efforts upon the development of this uniquely valuable vehicle for profiting from the experiences of others, instead of prematurely creating for the infant learning dilemmas at a stage at which the only possibility of achieving solutions is through the painful, and precarious, process of trial-and-error (Mowrer, 1941).[8]

[8] It can scarcely be supposed that the ability to "think independently," or "originally," will be much facilitated by confronting the infant with difficult problems before he has learned (through the medium of language) to think at all.

Conditioning, Imitation, and Obedience

In the preceding pages we have seen how useful conditioned responses can be in teaching, i.e., in helping children as well as lower animals solve certain types of problems which would be extremely difficult for them on a purely trial-and-error basis. But there is one rather striking difference between little Mary's mother's teaching her to say "butter," and our experimental paradigm in which rats were taught to jump as a means of showing that they were hungry.[9] In the latter case, the conditioned stimulus for the jumping reaction was the sound of the buzzer, but in the case of the little girl, the conditioned stimulus (as presented by the mother) and the conditioned response (as made by the child) were much the same, namely, the sound "butter." How significant is this difference?

Cowles and Pennington (1943) have reported that they were able to condition rats to squeak in response to a pure tone of high pitch (which symbolized impending electric shock). Some years ago one of us attempted a similar experiment but failed to get the expected conditioning. After reading the report just cited, we again attempted to obtain this type of conditioning, but the results were still negative. If we could have conditioned our subjects to respond to an artificial "squeak" by making a natural one, we might have then been able, by the technique already described, to teach them to squeak ("speak") for food, instead of jumping for it. In principle, there is, of course, no difference between the two procedures, but since we more readily think of the symbolic function of sounds than of other types of behavior, our paradigm would have seemed more like the "real thing."

We now know how it was that our experimental subjects became conditioned to jump when we sounded the buzzer, and we know, at least

[9] It is easy to fall into the habit of assuming that the difference between instrumental and symbolic behavior (i.e., between "work" and "words") is definite and absolute. But this is not the case. If the jumping of our rats had operated an automatic food-delivery mechanism, as well it might, we could scarcely have referred to this behavior as expressive, communicative, or symbolic. It is only because this behavior produced the desired results *through the interpolated activity of another living organism* that we think of it as symbolic. The same is true of orally made noises. The sound "Rex" is ordinarily a symbol, but a clever advertising toy distributed some years ago by a drug company took advantage of the fact that this noise may also be directly instrumental, i.e., has a certain amount of inherent energy capable of performing work. The toy consisted of a little house containing a celluloid dog which jumped out when one loudly called "Rex!" Thus we see that identically the same act may be in the one case symbolic, in the other not. (For further discussion on the definition of a "symbol," see Yerkes, 1943).

in principle, how it would be possible to make them squeak in response to a similar auditory stimulus. But we have not as yet accounted for the fact that little Mary responded to her mother's command, "Say, 'butter,'" by saying "butter" or something roughly equivalent. This, as we have seen, is an essential preliminary to the mother's being able to teach her to use this word meaningfully, that is, as a means of asking for some of this substance when she wanted it, or, at a later stage, being able to make statements about it.[10]

We have already had reason to doubt the adequacy of the imitative theory of speech development as a comprehensive explanation. Let us, therefore, return to observation. When a mother is trying to train a child to say "Bye-bye," what is she likely to do? Not uncommonly, one will observe her gently jostle or tickle him, all the while saying, "Say 'Bye-bye'." We can see that the jostling or tickling would motivate the child to do or say something, but how does he ever happen to say just what the mother is saying? This might occur on the basis of pure trial-and-error, but it would be very improbable, considering the large assortment of other sounds that the child might equally well make. It might also occur on the basis of so-called imitation; but as we have already indicated, it can no longer be taken for granted that imitation is something which children do instinctively, or automatically. In all probability, the child's saying what he is told to say is a subtle form of learned behavior, the circumstances of which are not ordinarily fully identified.

We are indebted to Dr. John Whitting, of Yale University, for what seems to us a crucial observation in this connection. Dr. Whiting has noticed the almost universal tendency for human parents, especially mothers (both primitive and civilized), to babble, jabber, coo, and otherwise *imitate their infants'* own early vocalizations. Thus, if an infant is spontaneously saying, "ba, ba, ba, ba," the mother is likely to make the same sound simultaneously. This means that, although the child starts the performance, the parents gets in at least a few similar sounds before the child stops. In this way the mother's "ba, ba," becomes a conditioned stimulus for the child to utter the same sound. After this learning has occurred, the child is said to "imitate" the mother, but this behavior originates, according to Dr. Whiting's interpretation, in the mother's, and sometimes even the father's, having first repeatedly imitated the child. When, subsequently, the mother holds the child in her arms, agitates him, and says, "Say 'bye-bye,'" the

[10] In a later paper we shall extend the present analysis to include that stage of language development in which children begin to "put words together." Cf. footnote 1.

stage is set for this response (or the closest possible approximation) to occur. If the mother then rewards the child (as she is likely to do by smiles, caresses, and no more jiggling), the response is reinforced, and is likely to occur, not only on command, but "spontaneously," that is, when the child wishes attention or affection.

Soon the child is likely to discover that "doing what mama says" is, in general, rewarding, and will develop an increasingly strong tendency, at least during the years of dependency, not only to do but also to say what "mother says." (This, we can assume, was true in little Mary's case.) On the other hand, if obedience, i.e., following parental commands and injunctions, is not thus rewarding, a sullen, indifferent, or anxious—and linguistically retarded—child is likely to result.

Summary

It is a commonplace that one can do almost anything more easily if told how than if one has to discover the solution independently, on the basis of one's own random (or even well-reasoned) exploratory efforts. On this assumption is predicated the widespread tendency of human beings to try to "profit from the experience of others," to "teach" and "study."

But this passing on of knowledge and skills presupposes, on the part of giver and receiver alike, a still more basic skill—*language*.

Learning to use and understand words is one of the monumentally important events in a child's life. It is the key which for him unlocks the storehouse of man's accumulated discoveries and wisdom, that is, culture. Must the child find this key alone, or do his elders even here attempt to "tell him how"?

Throughout the formal school career of children, much attention is paid to the various language skills, to helping them develop more and more "effective communication." But even before they enter kindergarten, most children have the rudiments of language at their command, that is, they can use and understand, not only words, but also simple (sometimes relatively complex) sentences, and in some instances they can even read and write.

Educators have taken little interest in the teaching and learning of language which goes on in the home, before the child starts to school; yet these are crucial procedures upon which much of the success or failure of the child's subsequent career, in school and out, seems to hinge.

Observation indicates that parents are almost certain to spend a good deal of time with their small children telling them "what to say." "Mary, say 'mama,'" "Johnnie, say 'ball,'" and a thousand other variants of this familiar formula can be heard throughout the day in any well ordered household where there is a baby who is in the early stages of language acquisition. The experimental paradigm with laboratory rats here reported suggests that this practice is indeed well founded, leading to much quicker establishment of the specific stimulus-response "connections," or habits, involved in speech than could possibly occur without such tutelage.

If telling the child "what to say" continues too long, after he has already acquired the rudiments of speech, it can, of course, seriously retard his further development, especially along the lines of self-reliance, resourcefulness, and spontaneity. But in the beginning of language learning, this procedure is extremely useful—provided that the words which the parent commands the child to say prove genuinely functional *from the child's standpoint,* and do not serve merely to gratify the parent's vanity or "power drive."

However, even more basic to language development than the procedure of "telling" children how to solve their early problems of communication is the task of getting them to "catch on" to the utility of saying what they are told to say. Once they find what a wonderful new world words open up to them, they often begin to parrot the speech of parents with almost magical enchantment. But since there is no means of telling infants about the wonders of language before they themselves have language, this discovery must always be an outgrowth of their own experience. The question is: How can we contribute most effectively to their having this experience?

If learning to repeat upon command a particular word uttered by a parent or other older person must thus proceed without benefit of "explanation" or "instruction," it must of necessity come about on the basis of preverbal learning principles, namely, trial and error and conditioning. We still know only imperfectly how this important—and difficult—feat is accomplished, but certain conjectures made in the following pages may provide a basis for further inquiry and analysis.

References

Allport, G. W. Motivation in personality: Reply to Mr. Bertocci. *Psychological Review,* 1940, *47,* 533–554.
Bloomfield, L. *An introduction to the study of language.* New York: Henry Holt, 1914.

Brogden, W. J. Unconditioned stimulus-substitution in the conditioning process. *American Journal of Psychology*, 1939, *62*, 46–55.

Cowles, J. T., & Pennington, L. A. An improved conditioning technique for determining auditory acuity in the rat. *Journal of Psychology*, 1943, *15*, 41–49.

Estes, W. M., & Skinner, B. F. Some quantitative properties of anxiety. *Journal of Experimental Psychology*, 1941, *29*, 390–400.

Ford, C. S. Society, culture, and the human organism. *Journal of General Psychology*, 1939, *20*, 135–179.

Freud, S. A reply to criticisms on the anxiety-neurosis. *Collected Papers* (Vol. 1). London: International Psycho-analytical Press, 1924, pp. 107–127.

Hilgard, E. R., and Marquis, D. G. *Conditioning and learning*. New York: D. Appleton-Century Co., 1940, xi, 429 pp.

Hull, C. L. A functional interpretation of the conditioned reflex. *Psychological Review*, 1929, *36*, 498–511.

Kornorski, J., and Miller, S. On two types of conditioned reflex. *Journal of General Psychology*, 1937, *16*, 264–272.

Korzybski, A. *Science and sanity*. New York: International Non-Aristotelian Library and Publishing Press, 1941.

Linton, R. *The study of man*. New York: Appleton-Century, 1936.

Miller, N. E., & Dollard, J. *Social learning and imitation*. New Haven: Yale University Press, 1941.

Mowrer, O. H. A stimulus–response analysis of anxiety and its role as a reinforcing agent. *Psychological Review*, 1939, *46*, 553–565.

Mowrer, O. H. Motivation and learning in relation to the national emergency. *Psychological Bulletin*, 1941, *38*, 421–431.

Mowrer, O. H., and Lamoreaux, R. R. Avoidance conditioning and signal duration—A study of secondary motivation and reward. *Psychological Monographs*, 1942, *54*, no. 5, 34 pp.

Mowrer, O. H., & Miller, N. E. A multi-purpose learning-demonstration apparatus. *Journal of Experimental Psychology*, 1942, *41*, 163–171.

Ogden, C. K., & Richards, I. A. *The meaning of meaning*. New York: Harcourt, Brace, 1938.

Pavlov, I. P. *Conditioned reflexes*. (Trans. A. V. Anrep.) London: Oxford University Press, 1927.

Russell, B. *Philosophy*. New York: Norton, 1927.

Sapir, E. *Language, an introduction to the study of speech*. New York: Harcourt, Brace, 1921, vii, 258 pp.

Skinner, B. F. Two types of conditioned reflex and a pseudo type. *Journal of General Psychology*, 1935, *12*, 66–77.

Thorndike, E. L. *Man and his work*. Cambridge: Harvard University Press, 1943.

Yerkes, R. M. *Chimpanzees*. New Haven: Yale University Press, 1943.

Intertrial Responses as 'Rehearsal': A Study of 'Overt Thinking' in Animals

The experiment reported in the present chapter was carried out (jointly with Harold Coppock) two years after the one described in Chapter 1, and without any conscious knowledge of a logical relationship between them. Surprisingly enough, however, the second experiment, which pays special attention to the significance and functional utility of intertrial response in an avoidance–learning situation (also alluded to in the first experiment), provides the ideas needed for the development of a truly explanatory or analytical theory of imitation, which, in later chapters, will be referred to as the "autism theory," because of the assumption that "imitation" develops in situations where the spontaneous occurrence of responses is intrinsically rewarding. In short, the idea is that imitation is the learning that takes place when the occurrence or "rehearsal" of a response which has received primary reinforcement is repeated and perfected, during "intertrial intervals," because of the secondary reinforcement which the occurrence of the response now provides (see p. 55, Chapter 4).

This idea is explicitly anticipated in paragraph two on page 29 of the present chapter. Note especially the following sentence: "If a response has been found to terminate a fear-arousing stimulus which has been associated with the UnCS (unconditioned stimulus), then this response might be expected to have fear-reducing, or secondary-reward, value when performed in the intervals between trials." And the reason why this would be true is that in experiments of the kind here under discussion (avoidance learning), the unconditioned stimulus (shock) occurs after varying intervals of nonresponse on the part of the subject, whereas it never occurs immediately after a particular response. Thus, the response, made "spontaneously" (to the fear aroused by the general situation, in the absence of both the conditioned and the unconditioned stimulus) converts the total stimulus situation from a possibly dangerous one to an absolutely safe one. The reward, or relief, thus experienced is, one may say, self-administered. This is why the foregoing explanation of imitation later became known (see Chapters 4 and 5) as the "autism theory," as applied to word learning. But when the present experiment was carried out, its theoretical implications in this connection were not at all seen or appreciated.

The paper here reproduced, written with Harold Coppock, was originally published in the American Journal of Psychology, *1947, 60, 608–616.*

In experiments on conditioning, the investigator is ordinarily attentive to the responses of his subjects to both the conditioned stimulus and the unconditioned stimulus; but he commonly ignores the same responses when these are made in the intertrial intervals.[1] Recently, however, Lamoreaux and Mowrer (1947) have completed a conditioning experiment in which these spontaneous, or interval, responses were carefully recorded and on the basis of which the authors suggest that at least certain forms of so-called conditioning may be thought of as being, or at least importantly involving, simple discrimination learning (Mowrer, 1947).

Many investigators have noted that after a few paired presentations of an initially neutral stimulus and a noxious stimulus, animals begin to "respond," not only when the conditioned stimulus is presented, but also during the intervals between trials.[2] In fact, the subject may at first make many more interval responses (IRs) than conditioned responses (CRs); and only gradually do the former drop out and the latter become

[1] Comparatively few investigators have recorded and commented on the interval responses made by animals in conditioning experiments (Anderson & Liddell, 1935; Garner, 1946; Konorski & Miller, 1937a,b; Moore & Marcuse, 1945; Mowrer, 1940; Mowrer & Viek, 1945; Skinner, 1937; Wolf & Kellogg, 1940). More numerous are the investigators who have been interested in the possible effects of intertrial "rehearsal" in human learning. For reviews of the relevant literature, see McGeoch (1942) and Woodworth (1938).

[2] In this connection, Hull (1943), for example, remarks: "quite naturally, exactly as in the preceding experiments, there is also set up a connection between the various static stimuli arising from the apparatus and the reaction because the former also are active in conjunction with the foot-lifting act and so become connected along with the so-called conditioned stimulus. . . . As a result of this connection the dog will frequently lift his foot when the buzzer is not sounding, just as the rat would sometimes leap the barrier when neither the buzzer nor the shock was acting" (p. 76).

well established. Obviously, in the beginning, the animal does not distinguish between experimental situation with CS and experimental situation without CS. Because of generalization from the former to the latter, both seem dangerous, both arouse fear, and both motivate more or less appropriate behavior (see Mowrer, 1951).

In support of this point of view, Lamoreaux and Mowrer (1947) report the finding that if the safe and dangerous periods are easily differentiated, "conditioning" occurs more rapidly than if differentiation is more difficult. The incidence of interval responses may thus be thought of as negatively correlated with "good conditioning"; all things equal, the more quickly the interval responses disappear, the more quickly conditioned responses, so-called, may be expected to appear.

In the present paper, a somewhat different hypothesis will be briefly described and some experimental data presented which seem to confirm it.

In experiments involving human subjects, it has often been surmised and sometimes demonstrated that learning occurs not only at the time of but also *between* the learning "trials."[3] In the intervals between trials, human subjects, unless powerfully distracted, are likely to "think about" what has gone on before and is to come; and, unless otherwise prevented, they may even attempt at such times to "act out," "rehearse," or "practice" the response or skill which is being learned. It would not, therefore, be altogether surprising if animals showed a similar tendency to "rehearse" between trials the response which is being learned on the trials proper.[4] This was the hypothesis which the writers had in mind in designing the present experiment.

Procedure

Our hypothesis required that we select a learning task the "practicing" of which between trials could be controlled. If we required our subjects (rats) to learn a conditioned response such as free running or jumping (see Mowrer & Viek, 1945; Mowrer & Lamoreaux, 1946) we

---

[3] Perhaps the most extreme statement of this view ever made is William James's familiar remark about one's learning to skate in the summer and to swim in the winter. One is also reminded in this context of the emphasis which certain writers have placed on the concept of "maturation."

[4] Cf. Woodworth's remark that "rehearsal of the performance in the rest-intervals, almost necessarily an ideational rehearsal, may occur sometimes in human subjects, but can scarcely be predicated of the rat" (1938, p. 125). This remark was made à propos of maze learning and was presumably not intended to apply to conditioning.

could not very well prevent them from making such a response between trials; and we could not, therefore, clearly show the effects of this type of behavior upon their "test performance," that is, upon their reactions to the conditioned and unconditioned stimuli at the time of the "trial." As a means of resolving this difficulty, we selected a response to be learned which required for its performance an accessory which, could at will, be introduced into or removed from the experimental situation. This accessory was a small, stainless steel bar; and the response to be learned consisted of merely touching it with the forepaws. Such a response formed a high-resistance circuit (through the subject) between the bar and the grill on which the subject was standing; and by means of a suitable electronic device,[5] it was possible to be quite objective as to when the subject had and had not "touched" the bar. (Actually, either a "make" or a "break" in the connection between the grill and the bar was counted as a response, since it would otherwise have been impossible for the subject to "respond" if, at the time of a trial, it was already in contact with the bar. In practice, however, a "response" nearly always involved a "make" rather than a "break.")

With one group of subjects (4 female and 4 male rats of the Lashley strain, approximately 5 mo. of age), this bar was available at all times, both during and between trials. At regular minute intervals, the CS (a change of illumination) was presented, and if the subject did not touch the bar within 5 sec the CS was followed by a shock (110 V., A.C., through a 150,000 Ω limiting resistance) applied to the grill until the bar was touched. At this point both shock and CS were turned off. If, within 5 sec after the CS appeared, the subject touched the Bar, the CS was immediately terminated and the UnCS omitted.

With a second group of comparable subjects, precisely the same procedure was followed save that the steel bar was not available between trials. It was inserted into the apparatus just as the CS was presented and was withdrawn 5 sec after the rat had touched the bar, regardless of whether the touching occurred as a CR or an UnCR.

Both groups of subjects were given 10 conditioning trials per day for a period of 10 days.

Results

The results thus obtained are shown in Figure 1. As the two curves indicate, the conditioning was, on the average, considerably better in the

[5] This device is a slightly modified version of one which has been described in *Electronics*, September, 1944 (p. 99). We are indebted to Dr. E. B. Newman and other members of the staff of the Psycho-Acoustic Laboratory at Harvard for making the device available to us.

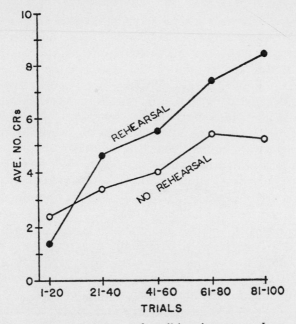

Figure 1. Curves showing the incidence of conditioned responses. In one group the subjects (filled circles) could "rehearse" the CR; in the other (open circles) they could not.

group which could "practice" the bar-touching response between trials than it was in the group which had no such opportunity. On the last 40 conditioning trials (that is, trials 61–100), this difference in the incidence of "conditioning" in the two groups of subjects is reliable at the 1% level of significance. It is also suggestive that among the animals in the experimental group those subjects which made the most IRs also tended to make the most CRs. The rank-order correlation was 0.85. Due, however, to the small number of subjects involved, the reliability is low. (See the parenthetical remarks on p. 27.)

The upper curve in Figure 2 shows the number of "practice," or interval, responses made to the bar by the group of subjects for which the bar was continuously present.[6] The lower curve represents the total time which the subjects in this group spent in contact with the bar. That this line shows only slight change during the course of the experiment is due to the fact that it involves two opposite tendencies: the tendency for the subjects in this group to touch the bar *less* frequently during the intertrial intervals (upper line in Figure 2) and the tendency to touch

[6] Our data for this group as a whole are incomplete; the above curve is, for this reason, based upon records from only six, rather than eight, animals. The lower curve is based on data from all the animals in this group.

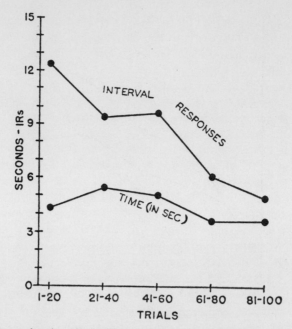

Figure 2. Curves showing the incidence of interval responses and duration (in sec) of those responses. Results are for the "rehearsal" group, it being impossible to obtain such results from the group having no opportunity of "rehearsing."

the bar *more* frequently during the trials proper (upper line in Figure 1).[7] Unfortunately it was not feasible to try to measure separately the amount of time which the subjects spent in contact with the bar during trials and during intertrial intervals.

It should be said at this point that in both of the groups of subjects just described, each make and break of contact with the bar was accompanied by a click, audible to the subject which was made by a telegraph sounder. In a third group of subjects, the same procedure was followed as has been described above for the first group, except that in the intervals between trials the telegraph sounder was disconnected, which meant that the "practice" responses were not accompanied by the click, as they were at the time of the trials proper. It was thought that by withholding the accustomed click when the "practice" responses were

[7] This tendency for IRs to decrease as CRs increase has been reported by Mowrer (1940, p. 514) and is apparently a regular phenomenon in experimental situations where an "instrumental" conditioning technique is used. It is less likely to appear in "classical" conditioning situations, as Anderson and Liddell (1935, p. 351), as well as others, have indicated.

made, these responses might be made less rewarding than they were in the group in which the clicks occurred whenever the bar was touched. There was indeed some indication that this was the case, but the results were inconclusive and for this reason are not reproduced. (It may be noted, however, that in this group, as in the first group, IRs and CRs were highly associated, the rank-order correlation being 0.98).

In this experiment, there are three types of learning: (a) the process whereby the subject learns to touch the bar in response to shock (problem-solving at the level of primary drive), (b) the process whereby the subject learns to be afraid of the CS and of the "total situation" (conditioning, properly speaking), and (c) the process whereby the subject learns to touch the bar in response to fear (problem-solving at the level of secondary drive).[8] The analysis has so far been concerned only with the effect of "practice" responses, that is, responses made to the fear experienced between trials, upon "trial" responses, that is, the responses made to the fear experienced when the CS was presented. What, we may now ask, was the effect of these "practice" responses upon the trial-and-error learning whereby the bar-pressing response was initially acquired as a solution to the shock-problem? Data relevant to this question were systematically recorded, but the results were inconclusive and will not be reproduced.

Discussion

This experiment has implications which seem to be clearly opposed to those of the "discrimination" theory of conditioning, outlined at the outset of this paper. In the second group of subjects, those in which the steel bar was withheld during the intertrial intervals, the trial and the intertrial intervals were more distinctively different than they were in the first group, in which the bar was present continuously. In other words, in the second group the danger period differed from the safety period in that *both* light and bar were present during the danger period and *both* were absent during the safety period. Whereas, in the first group the bar was present at all times; and the light was the sole variable. According to the discrimination hypothesis, conditioning should have been better in the second group than in the first. The results, as already indicated, were the reverse of this. It is not certain, however, that the present experiment was perfectly controlled. Subtle artifacts

[8] Basically there are only two forms of learning, problem-solving and conditioning, but forms (a) and (c) differ importantly in respect to source of motivation. Cf. Mowrer (1945).

may have crept in which we have not detected.[9] At any rate, we are by no means prepared at this point to insist that the "rehearsal" hypothesis is valid and the "discrimination" hypothesis invalid.

As a possibility for further experimentation, it has occurred to us that it might be instructive to study the effect of removing the subject from the experimental situation between trials.[10] Such a procedure would effectively exclude the possibility of intertrial rehearsal and might be expected, therefore, to result in less conditioning than does the more usual procedure of allowing the subject to remain in the experimental situation continuously. On the other hand, the discrimination theory would predict that this procedure would, other things equal, lead to quicker conditioning. Since the subjects would be in the apparatus only during the danger period, the discrimination they would have to make would be an exceedingly easy one, that is, between being in the apparatus and being out of it. One would expect a correspondingly high incidence of responses made by them when inside the apparatus (that is, "conditioned" responses), and a low incidence of responses made by them when outside the apparatus (that is, "interval" responses). Whether such an experiment would crucially differentiate between these two theories cannot at present be said, but it has interesting possibilities.

One of the most intriguing ways of thinking about the results of the present study is in terms of intertrial responses as a form of "overt thinking." Human beings can rehearse, or plan, relatively complicated future actions without doing anything that even remotely resembles the actual performance of such actions. The symbolic equivalent of overt acts, and of their consequences, may be performed completely covertly. In infrahuman animals, on the other hand, it seems likely that "thinking," in the sense of using subvocal and other covert symbols, must be

---

[9] Since the above was written one important possibility has occurred to us in this connection. In our second group of subjects the response-bar was absent during the intertrial (safe) intervals and was reinserted coincidentally with the onset of the conditioned stimulus. Since the reappearance of the bar was shortly followed (if a CR did not occur) by presentation of the UnCS (shock), it is reasonable to suppose that the bar, as well as the specific CS, may have become fear-charged. If this were the case, then the subjects in this group probably had a tendency to turn away from the bar, as something dangerous and therefore to be avoided. This avoidance tendency may conceivably account, at least in part, for the lower incidence of bar-touching obtained in the second experimental group than in the first one.

[10] This, of course, occurs automatically in a maze or a problem-box, in which a "trial" is defined as completed when the subject gets "out." The difficulty is that one has no way of studying the effects of leaving the subject in the experimental situation between trials, without introducing serious artifacts.

severely limited, if it occurs at all. This is not to say, however, that animals cannot "think" overtly. In a previous paper by one of the authors (Mowrer & Ullman, 1945), it has been pointed out that the vicarious trial and error (VTE) of rats at choice points in mazes probably represents a primitive form of reasoning, a procedure in which the subject is acting out, in miniature, the two alternative responses, and anticipating and comparing the potential consequences. There is abundant other evidence that lower animals can react to their own behavior, in terms of what Hull (1930) has called "pure stimulus-acts."

It is not here suggested that interval responses are pure stimulus-acts, at least not in the usual sense of the term. The best known cases of the latter involve acts which are performed as a means of providing cues for subsequent acts. Interval responses can hardly be conceived as having such a function. They may, however, have a somewhat comparable function in this sense, that they provide cues for fear reduction. If a response has been found to terminate a fear-arousing stimulus which has been associated with the UnCS, then this response might be expected to have a fear-reducing, or secondary-reward, value when performed in the interval between trials. As we have seen, there is a tendency for the fear generated during the trials to generalize to the safe-periods, between trials, and it may well be that interval responses have the function of reassuring the subject and reducing "nervousness" at such times. On purely observational grounds, Anderson and Liddell (1935) have remarked that interval responses seem to have this function (p. 351).

A human being, when faced by a recurrent noxious stimulus of some sort, might verbalize the situation as follows: "When that stimulus comes next time, I'll know what to do: I'll do thus and so." As a result of the repetition of this sentence to himself, he is likely to "feel better" (that is, to be less fearful) than he would feel if he did not "know" (that is, could not tell others or himself) how the impending problem could be solved. The rat, unable to compose sentences, but still able to anticipate emotionally the recurrence of the danger situation, does the next best thing: he makes the response which he is predisposed to make when the danger situation actually materializes and which has been effective in dealing with that situation on previous occasions. Presumably, as a result of this kind of behavioral self-reassurance, he accomplishes something comparable to that which the human being accomplishes by means of his symbolic formulations.[11]

---

[11] One cannot, of course, easily eliminate a primary drive in this somewhat magical manner. "Wishful thinking" works best with the secondary drives. .

When one begins to speculate concerning the possible symbolic, or "cognitive," implications, of interval responses, the "rehearsal" and "discrimination" hypotheses are thrown into even sharper contrast. On the basis of the discrimination hypothesis, "understanding of" or "insight into" the nature of the difference between the safety and the danger periods should sharply suppress responses during the former period and sharply increase them during the latter period. On the other hand, on the basis of the "rehearsal" hypothesis, "insight" might be expected to perpetuate the interval responses; at least it would not be expected to suppress them. The insight concept, however, as commonly employed, is so nebulous that it is difficult to know, in any given instance, really what to predict on the basis of it.

From a commonsense standpoint, the "rehearsal" hypothesis may be criticized on the grounds that rehearsal, or practice, in human beings always involves "conscious purpose," whereas, in the foregoing discussion of animal learning, no such factor has been posited. This line of reasoning is likely to be predicated on the assumption that reasoning, planning, and willing are purely "rational" processes and wholly unrelated to motivation. The assumption of the present writers is that behavior, whether overt or covert, "physical" or "mental," is always motivated and, if it persists, does so because it is rewarding, in the sense of being problem-solving. From this point of view, the question of whether "conscious purpose," or "will," is or is not present in any given instance of behavior does not, therefore, appear particularly important.

Summary

In experiments using the conditioned-response methodology, it has been common practice to record the responses made to the conditioned stimulus and to the unconditioned stimulus but to neglect the responses made in the intertrial intervals. In this paper the thesis is explored that these intertrial responses are functionally significant.

One possibility is that they serve as a form of "rehearsal," or "practice," of the response which occurs to the CS or UnCS. An alternative interpretation is that they represent an imperfect discrimination between the "negative" stimulus, that is, experimental situation without CS, and the "positive" stimulus, that is, experimental situation with CS. Experimental findings are evaluated in the light of these two types of explanation.

The "rehearsal" hypothesis leads to a number of suggestions concerning the nature of symbolic action, overt and covert.

References

Anderson, O. D., & Liddell, H. S. Observations on experimental neurosis in sheep. *Archives of Neurology and Psychiatry,* 1935, *34,* 330–354.

Garner, W. R. Symbolic processes in the rat: Spontaneous behavior. *American Psychologist,* 1946, *1,* 275.

Hull, C. L. Knowledge and purpose as habit mechanisms. *Psychological Review,* 1930, *37,* 515.

Hull, C. L. *Principles of behavior.* New York: Appleton-Century-Crofts, 1943.

Konorski, J., & Miller, S. On two types of conditioned reflex. *Journal of General Psychology,* 1937, *16,* 264–272. (a)

Konorski, J., & Miller, S. Further remarks on two types of conditioned reflex. *Journal of General Psychology.* 1937, *17,* 405–407. (b)

Lamoreaux, R. R., & Mowrer, O. H. *Conditioning as discrimination: A study of "spontaneous" responses and their significances.* Unpublished manuscript. Cambridge. Havard Graduate School of Education, 1947.

McGeoch, J. A. The psychology of human learning. New York. Longmans, Green, 1942.

Moore, A. U., & Marcuse, F. L. Salivary, cardiac, and motor indices of conditioning in two sows. *Journal of Comparative Psychology,* 1945, *38,* 1016.

Mowrer, O. H. Anxiety-reduction and learning. *Journal of Experimental Psychology,* 1940, *27,* 497–515.

Mowrer, O. H. On the dual nature of learning: A reinterpretation of "conditioning" and "problem solving." *Harvard Educational Review,* 1945, *15,* 35–48.

Mowrer, O. H. Conditioning and conditionality (discrimination). *Psychological Review,* 1951, *58,* 196–212.

Mowrer, O. H., & Lamoreaux, R. R. Fear as an intervening variable in avoidance conditioning. *Journal of Comparative Psychology,* 1946, *39,* 29–50.

Mowrer, O. H., & Ullman, A. D. Time as a determinant in integrative learning. *Psychological Review,* 1945, *15,* 79.

Mowrer, O. H., & Viek, R. Language and learning: An experimental paradigm. *Harvard Educational Review,* 1945, *15,* 35–48.

Skinner, B. F. Two types of conditioned reflex: A reply to Konorski and Miller. *Journal of General Psychology,* 1937, *16,* 272–279.

Wolf, I. S., & Kellogg, W. N. Changes in general behavior during flexion conditioning and their importance for the learning process. *The American Journal of Psychology,* 1940, *53,* 392.

Woodworth, R. S. *Experimental psychology.* New York. Henry Holt, 1938.

Individual Learning and 'Racial Experience' in the Rat, with Special Reference to Vocalization

Although many species of living organisms "vocalize" and by this and other means "communicate" in at least a rudimentary way, Homo sapiens alone has developed "language." There are probably multiple reasons for this unique accomplishment, but one factor of major importance in the situation appears to be the extent to which different species have voluntary control over their vocalizing responses, in the same sense that they have voluntary control over their skeletal musculature (as in locomotion, manipulation, head movement, etc.).

Any of a great variety of conditioned responses can be learned by rats and other laboratory animals as a means of avoiding noxious stimuli, but exploratory attempts to obtain vocalization in the rat as an avoidance response have given completely negative results. Although these subjects would squeal readily enough when an electric shock impinged upon them, they remained absolutely mute in response to signals which were premonitory of shock. This finding was very puzzling, especially since an examination of the pertinent literature revealed that several other investigators had reported successful vocal conditioning in rats.

Reexamination of the experimental conditions under which we had tried to obtain vocal conditioning in the rat and failed, and of the conditions under which other investigators had made the same attempt and succeeded, revealed a difference which can best be interpreted in terms of phylogenetic considerations, which will be left for the reader to explore in the chapter itself.

This paper was originally published (in collaboration with Florence Palmer and Marjorie D. Sanger) in the Journal of Genetic

Psychology, *1948, 73, 29–48. Incidentally, in one area this paper builds upon the work reported in Chapter 1 of this book.*

⟶

Background and Purpose

This paper is the outgrowth of a paradox which was suggested by earlier laboratory work and which has led to new experimentation and to speculations concerning the emergence and biological meaning of human language. It is offered as background material for the further development and analysis of language theory, particularly as it relates to the principles of learning.

In 1932 Warner reported an incidental observation of conditioned vocalization in laboratory rats; and two years later, Schlosberg, using a different experiment procedure, observed the same phenomenon. Subsequently the senior author attempted to obtain such conditioning, but was unable to do so. In 1943 Cowles and Pennington reported results which indicated that vocal conditioning in rats is not only easy to obtain, but that it is also peculiarly resistant to extinction. Returning to this problem, the first of the present writers again obtained negative results, identical with the original ones. Then, in 1946, appeared Herbert's paper confirming, in general terms, the findings of Schlosberg and those of Cowles and Pennington.

The purpose of the present paper is threefold: (a) to present systematic data showing the virtual impossibility of conditioning the vocal response in rats, under conditions which lead to excellent conditioning of other responses; (b) to analyze the reasons why our conditioning procedure gives negative results while that of the authors cited gives positive results; and (c) to sketch certain broader implications which are suggested by these superficially contradictory findings.

Apparatus and Subjects

The apparatus used in this study has been fully described elsewhere (Mowrer & Miller, 1942). In essence, it consists of an elongated box, the internal dimensions of which are 36 in. (length) by 6 in. (width) by 18 in. (height). The floor consists of a metal grill which can be electrically energized. The front of the apparatus is made of glass, thus permitting convenient observation of the subject.

In the present study, the unconditioned stimulus consisted of an electric shock produced by 120 V, A.C. (60 cycle), with a limiting resistance of 200,000 Ω. The order of presentation and duration of this stimulus will be described later.

The conditioned stimulus was produced in the following manner. Two 15-W electric lamps, located near the top of the rear inside wall of the apparatus, supplied normal illumination between trials. Directly beneath the floor-grill, about equally distant from the two ends, was a third lamp of similar wattage. By a single switching arrangement, the overhead lamps could be turned off and the single lamp beneath the grill turned on, and vice versa. The conditioned stimulus consisted of such an alternation in the source and pattern of illumination, at the rate of four "cycles" per second. The conditioned stimulus, or signal, consisted, in short, of a relatively slow flickering, or "warbling," of the illumination within the apparatus. The rate of the flicker was controlled by a constant-speed motor, and there were no auditory cues accompanying either the onset or the termination of the flicker.

The subjects were 16 Lashley-strain black rats, between 100 and 130 days of age. They were all females.

Procedure and Results

The same general conditioning procedure was used with all animals in this study, but for half of the animals the to-be-conditioned response was a run to the opposite end of the apparatus, and for the other half it was any vocalization, such as a whine, squeak, or "chirp."

Each animal was allowed one minute of habituation when first placed in the apparatus, at the end of which time the conditioned stimulus (flicker) was applied. If, within five seconds, the animal did not make the designated response, that is, vocalization in the one case, running in the other, the electric shock was applied and left on (together with the signal) until the response did occur. Signal and shock were then turned off simultaneously. If, on the other hand, the desired response occurred within the first five seconds after the signal was applied, the signal was immediately terminated and the shock omitted. Trials came at regular, minute intervals. There were 10 trials per day, and the training was continued for 10 days.

Figure 1 shows the very dramatic difference in the ease with which the running response and, the vocalization can be conditioned, under the particular circumstances here described. The animals for which run-

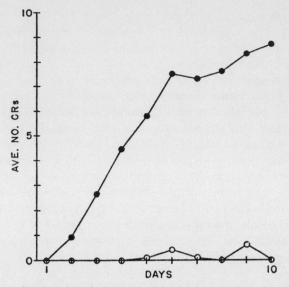

Figure 1. Curves showing the relative ease with which two types of response—a simple running reaction and vocalization—can be elicited in laboratory rats on the basis of avoidance conditioning. The curve with the solid circles shows the high proficiency of one group of subjects in learning to run in response to a conditioned stimulus, whereas the curve with the open circles shows the very low proficiency of a group of comparable subjects in learning to vocalize to the same CS.

ning was the correct response had learned, by the 10th day, to make this response on nearly 90% of the trials to signal alone, thereby avoiding the shock. By contrast, the animals for which the correct response was vocalization never reached an incidence of conditioning greater than about 6%.[1]

It is evident from Figure 1 that in the case of the running and the vocalization we are dealing with two responses which are in some way basically different. In the hope of elucidating the nature of this difference, we have analyzed our data in such a way as to bring out the trial-and-error learning that occurred in response to the unconditioned stimulus. When the signal and shock were initially presented, our animals "didn't know what to do." As a consequence of response variation

[1] On the assumption that our failure to obtain vocal conditioning might be due to an insufficient intensity of the unconditioned stimulus, half of the animals in each of the two groups were subjected to five days of continued training, beyond the original 10, with an increased intensity of shock (150 V, same limiting resistance). The results, however, were not significantly different from those obtained with the original shock intensity.

("random behavior"), half our animals found that running to the opposite end of the apparatus would terminate the signal and shock; the other half found that vocalization would achieve this effect. Presumably, therefore, the first learning that occurred in both groups was on a trial-and-error basis and might be expected to manifest itself as a reduction in the time required to make the correct response to the signal-shock combination.[2] We have accordingly computed, for each of the 10 days of experimentation, the average time elapsing between the onset of the CS and the occurrence of the appropriate response (either as a CR or as an UnCR) for both groups.

These data are presented graphically in Figure 2. Here a striking difference is at once evident: whereas the latency for the running response quickly drops and crosses over the 5-sec line (thus indicating, on the average, a transition from response to signal and shock combined to response to signal alone, i.e., conditioning), the average latency of the vocalization drops very little from its initial latency, and never crosses the 5-sec line.

These results have a clear implication: they suggest that in the case of running we are dealing with a response which can be readily modified through both trial-and-error learning and conditioning, whereas in the case of vocalization, we have a response which is less modifiable, and far more "reflexive." This interpretation is supported by a number of considerations. It will be noted, first of all, that the average latency for vocalization on the first day was lower than that for the running response, thus suggesting an initial prepotency for vocalization.[3] On the first day, vocalization occurred, on the average, 1.38 sec after the onset of the shock (i.e., 6.38 sec after the onset of the CS), and by the 3rd day this latency had dropped to 0.61 sec, near which value it remained for the duration of the experiment. Although this figure is still

[2] In the light of considerations advanced elsewhere (Mowrer & Lamoreaux, 1946; Mowrer, 1947), this statement should be elaborated. While the subject, on the basis of trial and error, or problem solving, is learning (well or poorly) to make the correct *behavioral* response to the shock, the subject is presumably also learning, on the basis of conditioning, to make the *emotional* response of fear to the stimulus which immediately precedes and accompanies the shock. It is presumably this derived drive which then serves to motivate the skeletal response of running or vocalizing when the CS is alone presented. Cf. footnote 7.

[3] Part of this discrepancy was undoubtedly owing to the fact that in the case of vocalization, the response was recorded as occurring at the moment of its onset, whereas running was recorded as occurring, not at the moment the animal started to run, but when it crossed the midline separating the two ends of the apparatus. It should be added that all timing in this experiment was done by means of a stopwatch operated by the experimenter.

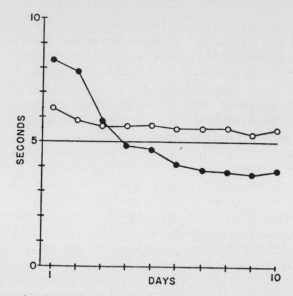

Figure 2. Curves showing the learning by laboratory rats of two responses, vocalization and a simple running reaction. The curve with open circles indicates that, on the average, the vocalization occurred throughout the experiment only *after* the onset of the UnCS (which was presented five seconds after the onset of the CS), and that there was very little improvement in the promptness with which this response could be elicited by the UnCS, that is, little trial-and-error learning. The curve with solid circles indicates that, on the average, the running response, though slow to occur to the UnCS in the beginning, occurred to that stimulus with increasing promptness as the training progressed, and subsequently occurred as a conditioned response, that is, to the CS alone.

considerably above genuine reflex reaction time, its consistency shows that we are here dealing with a highly stable response.

That vocalization can, however, be somewhat modified by experience is indicated, not only by the reduction in average latency between the first and third days, but also by the fact that on the first trial on the first day, the average latency of this response was 4.60 sec, on the second trial, 2.00 sec, and on the third trial, 0.87 sec. We thus see that at the very beginning there was some trial-and-error learning with respect to vocalization. *The problem is to discover why this response so stubbornly resisted conditioning.*

Discussion

With conditioning of the vocal response of the rat so conspicuously successful in the Cowles and Pennington experiment and so conspicuously unsuccessful in our own, it seems probable that the difference in results was owing to some one or more significant differences in the conditions of the two experiments. What may these have been?

In comparing the two experiments, one is immediately struck by two differences: (a) in the Cowles-Pennington experiment the rats were immobilized in a kind of sling,[4] whereas in our own experiment they were completely free, within the confines of the cage-like apparatus; and (b) in the Cowles-Pennington experiment the danger signal and shock were invariably paried ("classical" conditioning), whereas in our experiment the CS and the UnCS were paired only if the CR failed to occur ("instrumental" conditioning).[5] Both of these differences seem to have much the same implication: in the Cowles-Pennington experiment, the subjects were caught, trapped, helpless, unable to "get away"; whereas in our experiment, they were, by contrast, relatively free and "on their own." They were not confined to any one area of the experimental apparatus; by making the appropriate response they could always *escape* from the electric shock; and by making the appropriate response to the danger signal alone, they could even *avoid* the shock altogether. In the Cowles-Pennington experiment, on the other hand, the subjects were "doomed," with all effort at either escape or avoidance to no avail.[6]

Previous work (Mowrer & Lamoreaux, 1942, Mowrer, 1947) has suggested that, in general, the more nearly free an animal is in an experimental situation, the better the conditioning; "natural" situations result in fewer artifacts and better learning than do "unnatural" situations, such as those involving physical restraint or a classical conditioning procedure. Why, then, should this general tendency be reversed in the case of *vocal* conditioning? The solution to this paradox seems to demand that we leave the realm of individual learning and turn to what may be broadly termed "racial experience."

There is a common folk belief to the effect that if one catches a rat in a steel trap and leaves the rat where its squealing can be heard by other rats, they will leave the vicinity; and incidental observations of laboratory rats seem to confirm this belief. Here one is apparently deal-

[4] The same was true of the Schlosberg and Herbert experiments.

[5] In the Schlosberg experiment, a classical conditioning procedure was used with half the subjects, an instrumental procedure with the other half. See footnote 6 for a description of Herbert's procedure.

[6] From the standpoint of methodology, Herbert's experiment falls somewhere between that of Cowles and Pennington and our own in that Herbert, like Cowles and Pennington, immobilized his animals (in a metal cylinder), but, like the present authors, he used an instrumental conditioning procedure rather than the classical one. Appropriately enough, his results fall about midway between those of Cowles and Pennington and our own.

ing with *instinctive* reaction tendencies which go back, obviously, much further than do man-made traps. The jaws of an enemy form a kind of trap with which rats have had encounters for hundreds of thousands of years; and the principle of natural selection clearly intimates why those strains of rats which tended both to squeal when in the claws or fangs of a predator and to flee at the sound of such squealing on the part of other rats survived better than did those rats with no such tendencies.

But what of rats which tended to squeal, not only when actually caught, but also when *in danger* of being caught, that is, when afraid? Would not such behavior be a certain invitation to disaster? The rat which merely sees, hears, or smells an enemy will do well, no matter how terrified, to remain silent, either as it crouches in hiding or slinks away to safety. Here we seem, finally, to have a clue to the difference in the experimental results obtained by the authors cited and by the present writers. If an animal is "caught," it does not much matter if it squeals both to actual pain (shock) and to the mere threat of pain (the danger signal); but if an animal is "free," it makes a great deal of difference whether it squeals to the mere prospect of pain (thus calling, "Here I am," to the hungry pursuer), or squeals only in response to pain itself (thus urging other members of its species to bolt from a possibly similar fate).

If it seems that this interpretation of the difference in experimental results obtained by Cowles and Pennington and by the present writers is rather finely spun, other examples of equally wonderful adaptive behavior are easily cited. (See also the following section.)

If, after weaning, a rat is put into an individual cage, it can be counted on, if not disturbed, to live the rest of its life, and to die, without a single vocalization. It may develop tumors, have presumably painful diseases, be severely deprived of food and water, and experience other forms of more or less intense *internal* discomfort, and yet never utter a sound. The biological utility of such silence in a state of nature is, of course, apparent: a sick or suffering animal does well not to advertise its disadvantaged condition!

Newly born rats vocalize readily in response to almost any discomfort: hunger, cold, pain, etc. But at this stage they are in a protected environment (the nest), and are in a relationship with the mother which means that cries of discomfort are likely to bring relief, not destruction. But as this special social situation ends and the young rats venture beyond the safety of the nest, the situation changes radically. So important is this change that survival of the species seems to demand that a corresponding behavioral change (inhibition of vocalization) be promptly insured by instinctive processes rather than by perhaps fatally tardy individual learning.

At the adult level the one situation other than externally imposed pain which can be counted on to elicit vocalization is a particularly interesting one. We repeatedly noted that after our animals had undergone a daily training session, they would almost invariably squeak when we picked them up in order to take them out of the apparatus. We discovered, in fact, that they would squeak almost equally readily if we merely touched them, and some of our animals would even squeak quite loudly at the mere sight of the experimenter's approaching hand. This latter observation was particularly arresting in view of the virtual impossibility of eliciting an anticipatory, or conditioned, squeal in the experimental procedure proper.

The only way we see of accounting for this paradox is to assume that in a situation in which a rat may attack, he may squeal *as a warning*; but in a situation in which his only disposition is to flee, vocalization is almost completely suppressed, that is, the rat vocalizes readily to anger but not to fear. The plausibility of this hypothesis is increased by the fact that the rat is normally not much afraid of the experimenter's hand, and may actually attack and bite it if the experimenter is hasty or unskillful in his approach to the animal. Similar warnings may also be observed in a group of rats living in a common cage.

Thus far we have assumed that the rather beautifully adaptive control of vocalization in the rat is determined by instinctive mechanisms; it may be, of course, that social experience, i.e., individual learning, is also significant in this connection. We have not as yet systematically checked on this possibility, but our casual observations, imperfectly controlled as they are, suggest that instinctive factors play the dominant rôle.[7]

[7] That vocalization in the rat is mediated more by instinctive mechanisms than by learned connections is further indicated by the fact, reported by Cowles and Pennington, that, under the experimental conditions used by them, the vocal response to a danger signal is peculiarly resistant to extinction. Although it is known that even reflexes can be depressed by repeated elicitation under suitable conditions, one does not expect reflexive or instinctual responses to be subject to extinction in the same degree as individually acquired reactions. Or perhaps another way (suggested to the authors by Mr. H. W. Coppock) of putting the same thing would be to say that in the rat vocalization is largely "involuntary" and under the control of the autonomic nervous system. A number of writers (Kroeber, 1928; Stewart, 1946) have noted the connection between the "cries" of animals and emotional reactions. In fact, de Laguna (1927) has suggested that one of the most important distinctions between animals and human beings is that only in the latter does vocalization become dissociated from emotion and capable of being used for purposes of "analysis" (cf. also Kellogg & Kellogg, 1933). One is also reminded in this connection of the distinction Skinner (1938) has made between responses which are *operants* and those which are *respondants*. In many animals, including the rat, vocalization would appear to be largely in the nature of a respondant, whereas in man and certain other mammals and birds, it is clearly an operant.

It would be interesting to see if the instinctive factors which we are here assuming can be altered by selective breeding. If, for example, we were to take the rats which gave the most conditioned vocal responses in our experiment and selectively bred their offspring for a few generations on the same basis, might we not eventually develop a strain of rats which would display conditioning of this kind fairly readily? Laboratory rats have been selectively bred from wild stock for docility, intelligence, and other traits (Tryon, 1930). It should be equally possible to breed them for the capacity to vocalize in response to fear instead of remaining so grimly silent.[8]

Collateral Evidence

That conditioned responses which would tend to have maladaptive consequences in a state of nature may be instinctively inhibited is a hypothesis for which there is support not only from the field of vocalization, but from at least one other source. James (1937) reports that the leg-flexion response in the opossum cannot be elicited by a danger signal, presumably because an opossum which—as a tree-dweller— flexed its legs to fear would be likely to lose its hold and fall at precisely those times when it could least afford such a mishap. By the same logic it might be predicted that the sloth, when presented with a CS which was premonitory of shock on the foot, would tend to grip with the foot rather than to lift it.

Support for the thesis that animals do well in a state of nature to "suffer in silence" and not to cry out when frightened, except when "caught," is indicated by Darwin (1873) in the following passage:

> We have seen . . . that when the sensorium is strongly excited, the muscles of the body are generally thrown into violent action; and as a consequence, loud sounds are uttered, however silent the animal may generally be, and although the sounds may be of no use. Hares and rabbits for instance, never, I believe, use their vocal organs except in the extremity of suffering; as, when a wounded hare is killed by the sportsman, or when a young rabbit is caught by a stoat. Cattle and horses suffer great pain in silence, but when this is excessive, and especially when associated with terror, they utter fearful sounds. I have often recognized, from a distance on the Pampas, the agonized death-bellow of the cattle, when caught by the

---

[8] Since the above was written, a young male rat has been accidentally discovered in our colony which vocalizes relatively freely to a CS of the kind used in the present study. By selective inbreeding of this male and his female offspring it should be possible to develop a strain of rats in which vocalization in response to fear occurs quite readily. The researches of Keeler (1945) and Keeler and King (1942) review what is known of the genetics of voice quality in rats; but so far as the present writers are aware, no genetic study has yet been made of the factor of vocal inhibition in this species.

lasso and hamstrung. It is said that horses, when attacked by wolves, utter loud and peculiar screams of distress. (pp. 83–84)

But perhaps the most dramatic support for the thesis that vocalization, particularly at times of danger, tends to be inhibited in a state of nature comes from Leopold (1944). In an attempt to increase the supply of game turkeys in North Carolina, a large number of domestic turkey hens were released in the woods. These mated with wild toms, and hundreds of "half-breed" young turkeys were hatched. But few of these survived: they did not have the instinctive intelligence to keep from vocalizing, and were easy marks for foxes, wolves, owls, hawks, and other predators. Since nearly all the young hybrids were lost, and since many of the wild toms had mated with the domestic hens rather than with wild hens, the net result of this enterprise was a lowering rather than an increment in the wild turkey population.

Why turkeys, chickens, guineas, and other domestic fowl have lost their natural caution with respect to vocalization is an interesting problem for speculation. One possibility is that wild fowl have certain habits (or "culture") which are transmitted from parent to offspring by appropriate training. Another possibility is that at an early stage the first domesticated fowl of all species were selectively bred, consciously or unconsciously, for vocalization—so that their nests could be located, and the fowl themselves more readily found when they had strayed or were attacked by natural enemies. Thus, under domestication free vocalization may have become a condition of survival and perpetuation, whereas in a state of nature it seems to have the reverse consequences.

Broader Implications

The writers were led into the present investigation in part by the results of a study previously reported by Mowrer and Viek (1945). In the latter study the authors taught rats to leap into the air as a means of indicating that they wanted food, by a technique which is comparable to the method whereby human beings teach their young to indicate their wants vocally. This procedure, it is thought, plays an important role in laying the basic habits involved in adult human language (cf. Chapter 1).

In the study cited, Mowrer and Viek considered the possibility of trying to use the same technique as a means of teaching rats to "speak" (squeak), rather than leap into the air, as a means of indicating their wish for food; but this technique requires that the response in question be first conditioned to a neutral, or "intermediate," stimulus, and since it was known that the vocal response of the rat would not readily condition under the given experimental circumstances, another response was used instead. However, the present writers were struck by the implication which the apparent impossibility of conditioning the vocal response of the rat in a free situation has for the origin and development of human speech, considered phylogenetically. Since rats and men presumably have the same common primordial ancestors (the "primitive mammal"), the question arises as to why the natural conditions which depress vocalization in the face of danger did not operate equally in the case of rats and of man. Or, said differently, what were the circumstances which freed early man, or protoman, sufficiently from the perils of vocalizing to allow him to develop the great vocal facility and flexibility which he now has and has long had?[9]

The circumstances under which terrestrial mammals vocalize can be quickly enumerated. As adults, animals which are preyed upon are likely to be silent save (a) when, as we have seen, they are caught, (b) when a mother is separated from her young, (c) when seeking a mate, and occasionally (d) when fighting.[10] Predatory animals seem to have slightly greater vocal freedom in that they may vocalize, not only under the four circumstances just mentioned, but also (e) when attacking an intended victim.

Thus, says Darwin:

> Rage leads to the violent exertion of all the muscles, including those of the voice; and some animals, when enraged, endeavour to strike terror into their enemies by its power and harshness; as the lion does by roaring, and the dog by growling. I infer that their object is to strike terror; because the lion at the same time erects the hair of its mane, and the dog the hair along its back, and thus they make themselves appear as large and terrible as possible. Rival males try to excel and challenge each other by their voices, and this leads to deadly contests. (p. 85)

Elsewhere Darwin (1885) continues:

> Although the sounds emitted by animals of all kinds serve many purposes, a strong case can be made out, that the vocal organs were primarily used and perfected in relation to the propagation of the species. . . . The chief and, in some cases, exclusive purpose appears to be either to call or charm the opposite sex. (p. 290)

In support of this latter argument Darwin (1885) points out that "the sounds produced by fishes are said in some cases to be made only by the

---

[9] It is conservatively estimated that human beings have been using speech for at least 80,000 to 100,000 years (Bodmer, 1944; Stewart, 1946), that is, during and since the Stone Age. Writing, in comparison, is a relatively modern invention.

[10] Howard's (1920) highly original study of the use of song by birds to establish "territoriality" warrants perhaps another category.

males during the breeding-season" (p. 291), and that "the voice of the common rook is known to alter during the breeding-season" (p. 196). Beach (1944) reports that the alligator "breeds during the early summer, and it is at this time that roaring is most frequently heard" (p. 481). Others have remarked on this correlation in other species, but reference is seldom made to the fact that even in human beings there is no "change of voice" in the male until the advent of puberty. Presumably it is only at this time that vocal differentiation of the sexes becomes functional.

Whatever its other social utilities, vocalization seems to have evolved primarily as a means of insuring procreation; and, presumably, any lesser necessity would not have been able to offset the hazards to an organism in thus advertising its presence and position, not only to potential mates, but also to enemies.[11] Even the predator cannot afford to vocalize idly, for such activity would serve to keep possible food at a safe distance. Only under domestication, with a relatively adequate supply of food insured without hunting, are dogs, for example, able to indulge in the luxury of indiscriminate social barking.

Darwin (1873) says:

> We know that some animals, after being domesticated, have acquired the habit of uttering sounds which were not natural to them. Thus domesticated dogs, and even tamed jackals, have learnt to bark, which is a noise not proper to any species of the genus, with the exception of the *Canis latrans* of North America, which is said to bark. Some breeds, also, of the domestic pigeon have learnt to coo in a new and quite peculiar manner. (pp. 85–86)[12]

---

[11] The dilemma involved in vocalizing in a state of nature is well illustrated by a recent New Yorker cartoon, in which two bull moose are shown listening to moose-calls in the distance. In the legend below, one moose says to the other, "Hunters or no hunters, I'm going to answer that one."

[12] One of the writers (O.H.M.) has recently visited Hamilton Station of the Jackson Memorial Laboratory at Bar Harbor, Maine, where a pair of African dogs, known as basenjis, were observed. These dogs were "barkless," as is the Eskimo dog and "a dog which Columbus discovered," if popular accounts can be relied upon. More recently, *Time* magazine (March 17, 1947) carried a story on the basenji in which Darwin's comments are borne out: "Barking, like kissing and sending Christmas cards, is a social habit fostered—for better or worse—by civilization. Wild dogs never bark, and among primitive peoples even house pets and hunting dogs seldom speak above a dignified growl. Africa's underslung, *café-au-lait* Basenjis ('bush things') are no exception. For generations they have tracked game for chiefs in the Belgian Congo, emitting only an occasional soft 'groo,' plaintively yodeling during the mating season, but never barking" (p. 28). This point of view, however, is brought into question by Murie's recent observations on that most "primitive" of dogs, the wolf (1944). In his monograph, *The Wolves of Mount McKinley,* he remarks: "Down river I heard a

The problem, then, is this: What are the special circumstances that allowed man, as "the first domestic animal," to develop the phenomenal degree of vocal freedom which is prerequisite for human speech? In human beings voice is under exquisite voluntary control. How, we may ask, did protoman ever secure the safety from predators needed to allow this function to pass from instinctive control over into the realm of responses which are controlled by individual learning?

Without proposing in any sense to exhaust the possible answers to this question, we wish to suggest one line of thought and briefly indicate some of the relevant evidence. We know that birds and arboreal primates are the most vocal of living creatures. Only birds and monkeys are said to "chatter." What do they have in common? In the one case by flight and in the other case by specialized climbing skills, they have both escaped the dangers that beset terrestrial mammals.[13] They alone

---

wolf howl, and a little later from the slope where I was screened by willows I saw a black wolf running. A half mile away it stopped to bark so I was sure the pups were near me. . . . Later another black adult joined the first one. Both barked, sometimes a series of barks, terminating in a long howl" (p. 20). Numerous other references are made by Murie to the "barking" of wolves, so the language used in the quotation can hardly be an inadvertence. Incidentally, the point of the story in *Time* magazine was that one of the basenjis entered in a recent London dog show had disgraced both its exhibitor and itself by barking. "Club Secretary Norman Cutler read the verdict: 'There is only one thing to do,' he said. 'Chanza must never be allowed to breed.'" This is an interesting reversal of the general trend, noted in the text above, for domesticated animals to survive better under domestication because of their vocalization.

[13] Certain insects and amphibia (notably frogs and toads) have also achieved considerable vocal freedom by other means, amphibia by leaping from land into water or from water onto land when attacked by nonamphibious enemies, insects by remaining well hidden or near holes into which they can quickly retreat, by flight, etc. Beach (1944), for example, reports: "Roaring occurs most frequently when the alligator is swimming or floating in the water. Occasionally an animal may roar when it is half in the water and half on the bank; but McIlhenny states that this call is never given when the reptile's body is entirely on land" (pp. 482–483). However, these phyla are severely handicapped in various other ways, and it is no accident that they have not given rise to speaking species. It is instructive to note also that of the common rodents (rabbits, hares, moles, shrews, rats, mice, etc.), tree-dwelling squirrels are easily the most vocal. The bat, or flying rodent, is also highly vocal, albeit at supersonic frequencies. One variety of marmot, the "whistler," utters a loud alarm and then retreats into impregnable rocks. And other rodents seem most likely to vocalize when near a retreat. Thus, Seton (1909) says that the chipmunk is likely to make "a trilled whistle of several different notes that it utters when alarmed. This usually accompanies the final rush it makes into a place of safety . . ." (p. 347).

seem to have attained enough security so that it does not matter if they are "noisy," and only with such security does it seem possible for the enormous experimentation to occur which must have been the precursor of articulate speech.[14]

By this route we are led to the conclusion that man, as a speaking terrestrial mammal, could have evolved as such only as a result of having spent a protracted period of time "in the trees."[15] Whether we wish to call the first creature with articulate speech "man" is perhaps a debatable question, but there appears to be good grounds for suspecting that man, or his immediate ancestor, was already "talking," or at least capable of it, when he descended from the trees and became an earth-dweller. Man seems to have survived on the ground by virtue of peculiar vocal, intellectual, and manipulative skills which developed in connection with aboreal life and which made possible the development of a considerable degree of social integration and perhaps an impressive "culture" before he could hazard existence on the ground. Some anthropologists believe that human culture, in the complexity which we find in even the most primitive contemporary peoples, could never have developed in a tree-dwelling species; but this is not to say that man may not have had an excellent start as a talking and culture-bearing organism before becoming able to exploit the advantages, as well as cope with the disadvantages, of a terrestrial habitat.

These, of course, are highly speculative thoughts, but thoughts to which our initial laboratory observations seem not unreasonably to lead.

Acknowledgment

Drs. Nicholas E. Collias, Frank A. Beach, and John P. Scott have read this paper in preliminary draft and made many valuable suggestions which have been incorporated in the present version. The authors gratefully acknowledge this assistance and generous interest.

[14] The amazing vocal versatility of the mocking bird, the parrot, and certain species of raven bespeaks the specially favored circumstances which birds have enjoyed in this connection, but the fact that their forelimbs became specialized as wings rather than as hands seems to have prevented them from developing true speech (cf. Paget, 1930).

[15] See Collins's delightful little book, *Arboreal Life and the Evolution of the Human Eye* (1922). See also Nissen's (1931) observation that in a state of nature chimpanzees are more likely to make noises (vocalizing, drumming, etc.) when on the ground if they are in "heavily wooded regions than in open country" (p. 95).

References

Beach, F. A. Responses of captive alligators to auditory stimulation. *American Naturalist*, 1944, *78*, 481–505.

Bodmer, F. *The loom of language*. New York: Norton, 1944.

Collins, F. T. *Arboreal life and the evolution of the human eye*. Philadelphia: Lea & Ferbiger, 1922.

Cowles, J. T., & Pennington, L. A. An improved conditioning technique for determining auditory acuity of the rat. *Journal of Psychology*, 1943, *15*, 41–47.

Darwin, C. *The expression of the emotions in man and animals*. New York: Appleton, 1873.

Darwin, C. *The descent of man*. New York: Humboldt, 1885.

De Laguna, G. A. *Speech: Its functions and development*. New Haven: Yale University Press, 1927.

Herbert, M. J. An improved technique for studying the conditioned squeak reaction in hooded rats. *Journal of General Psychology*, 1946, *34*, 67–77.

Howard, H. E. *Territory in bird life*. London: Murray, 1920.

James, W. T. An experimental study of the defense mechanism in the opossum, with emphasis on natural behavior and its relation to mode of life. *Journal of Genetic Psychology*, 1937, *51*, 95–100.

Keeler, C. E. Gene determined physical modifications affecting the sociometry of rats. *Sociometry*, 1945, *8*, 30–41.

Keller, C. E., & King, H. D. Multiple effects of coat color genes in the Norway rat, with special reference to temperament and domestication. *Journal of Comparative Psychology*, 1942, *34*, 241–250.

Kellogg, W. N., & Kellogg, L. *The ape and the child*. New York: McGraw-Hill, 1933.

Kroeber, A. L. Sub-human culture beginnings. *Quarterly Review of Biology*, 1928, *3*, 325–342.

Leopold, A. S. The nature of hereditable wildness in turkeys. *The Condor*, 1944, *46*, 133–197.

Mowrer, O. H. On the dual nature of learning—A reinterpretation of "conditioning" and "problem-solving." *Harvard Educational Review*, 1947, *17*, 102–148.

Mowrer, O. H., & Lamoreaux, R. R. *Avoidance conditioning and signal duration—A study of secondary motivation and reward. Psychological Monographs*, 1942, *54*, No. 247.

Mowrer, O. H., & Lamoreaux, R. R. Fear as an intervening variable in avoidance conditioning. *Journal of Comparative Psychology*, 1946, *39*, 29–50.

Mowrer, O. H., & Miller, N. E. A multiple-purpose learning-demonstration apparatus. *Journal of Experimental Psychology*, 1942, *31*, 163–170.

Mowrer, O. H., & Viek, P. Language and learning: An experimental paradigm. *Harvard Educational Review*, 1945, *15*, 35–48.

Murie, A. *The wolves of Mount McKinley*. Fauna Series No. 5. Washington: U. S. Government Printing Office, 1944.

Nissen, H. W. A field study of the chimpanzee. *Comparative Psychology Monographs*, 1931, *8*, No. 1.

Paget, Sir Richard. *Human speech*. New York: Harcourt, Brace, 1930.

Schlosberg, H. Conditioned responses in the white rat. *Journal of Genetic Psychology*, 1934, *45*, 303–335.

Seton, E. T. *Life histories of northern animals*. (2 Vols.) New York: Scribner, 1909.

Skinner, B. F. *The behavior of organisms.* New York: Appleton-Century, 1938.

Stewart, G. R. *Man, an autobiography.* New York: Random House, 1946.

Tryon, R. C. Studies in individual differences in maze ability. V. Luminosity and visual acuity as symptomatic causes of individual differences and an hypothesis of maze ability. *Journal of Comparative Psychology,* 1931, *4,* 401–420.

Warner, L. H. An experimental search for the "conditloned response." *Journal of Genetic Psychology,* 1932, *41,* 91–115.

The Autism Theory of Speech Development and Some Clinical Applications

The following chapter (published) in the Journal of Speech and Hearing Disorder, *(1952, 17, 263–268) was prepared for and presented at the 1951 Convention of the American Speech and Hearing Association, in Chicago, as part of a symposium on "Speech Development in the Young Child," under the chairmanship of Professor George J. Wischer. There I ventured to suggest certain clinical applications of the autism theory of imitation delineated and documented in the preceding chapter. But before perusing the paper as it is reproduced here, the reader is asked to consider the following maximally simple and, hopefully, clear description of the basic principles involved in the autism theory of language learning. This passage is from an unpublished (Mowrer, 1969) manuscript:*

> *Shortly after I left Yale and arrived at Harvard [Mowrer, 1971], I therefore acquired a collection of parrots, myna birds, parakeets, magpies, and crows, and set about learning how to teach them to "talk." Fortunately, there was already extant a sizable popular literature on this subject, which I acquired and read avidly. Although procedural details varied, there was almost universal agreement in principle: The way to get a bird to "talk" (i.e., to utter some desired word or phrase) is for the trainer to make the specified sound and then follow it by some reward: a morsel of food, gentle stroking of the back of the bird's head, making one's appearance from concealment, or uncovering a hitherto covered cage. In short, it was clear that the articulate sound made by the trainer became and functioned as a conditioned stimulus for, or signal of, something good that was about to happen. And since the subjects in this type of experiment themselves have the "equipment" needed to reproduce such promising, good sounds themselves, it is not in the least surprising that they soon begin to do so.*
>
> *Let me put the matter a little differently. Imagine a Pavlovian conditioning experiment involving dogs in which the sound of a buzzer is*

51

*regularly followed by a morsel of meat. Obviously the buzzer will soon
become a "good" sound, one which the dog is "glad" to hear—and would,
if he could, himself reproduce. The difficulty, of course, is that only the
experimenter has control of the equipment needed for making this type of
sound—the dog does not. Therefore, "imitation" is quite out of the question, that is, the dog, much as he might wish to do so, cannot make or
"reproduce" the buzzer sound (conditioned stimulus). If, however, a bar or
button were made available to the dog, depression of which would produce
the buzzer sound, there can be not the slightest doubt that the dog, as soon
as he discovered what the lever or button accomplished, would immediately
be fascinated by it and would start making the buzzer sound repeatedly,
that is, "imitating the experimenter." The dog's own operation of the buzzer would stabilize more quickly if each occurrence of the buzzer were
followed by primary reinforcement (a piece of meat); but one can depend
upon it that the dog would sound the buzzer at least a few times on the
basis of secondary reinforcement alone, that is, the reinforcement acquired
as a result of the buzzer and the meat having been previously associated by
the experimenter. Thus, in order for any living organism to "imitate"
another organism (trainer), all that is necessary is to make it possible for
the first organism (subject) to reproduce the conditioned stimulus originally
made and reinforced by the trainer. The case of birds learning to utter
wordlike sounds is thus only a special instance of this general principle,
based upon the fact that the birds have, as part of their native vocal equipment, substantially the same apparatus as used by the human trainer in
producing the conditioned stimulus, a circumstance which makes "imitation" much easier than when there is a discrepancy in this response. (If
distinctively marked keys or foot pedals were made available to dogs or
rats, depression of which would electronically reproduce words uttered by
the trainer in connection with a positive unconditioned stimulus, such as
food, they too could learn to "talk," quite as well as a myna bird or a parrot!) [Cf. Gardner & Gardner, 1969].*

*Interestingly enough, B. F. Skinner (1938), in order to facilitate the
teaching of rats to push a "Skinner bar" as a means of obtaining a pellet of
food, has long followed the practice of activating the food delivery
mechanism 60 times himself, thus letting the subject "get the connection"
between the sound thus produced and the appearance of a pellet in the food
trough; the reason being that, as soon as the rat himself happens to push
the bar which activates the delivery mechanism, he is immediately "in
business," that is, the resulting sound now has a well defined "meaning,"—secondary reinforcing value; and the rat is immediately rewarded
for having pushed the bar instead of having to wander around until he
eventually finds the food pellet and thus receives a delayed (and now relatively weak) primary reinforcement. I doubt if Professor Skinner ever
thought of this procedure as involving an attempt on the part of his subjects
to "imitate" him (i.e., make the same sound he had been making); but,
viewed in the proper perspective, the rat's immediate predisposition to
push the bar, once the associated sound of the food delivery mechanism has
been "baited" with secondary reinforcement, makes it obvious that the rat
is very much interested in making precisely the same sound that Professor
Skinner has previously made. And that's imitation! If attention is directed,*

not to who gets the pellet of food (always the rat), but rather to the question of whether the sound associated with the action of the food delivery mechanism is made by the experimenter or by the subject, the whole matter can be seen from a very different perspective—not that of "instrumental learning," but that of "imitation."

The power of the secondary reinforcement acquired by the sound of the food-delivery mechanism in a Skinner box, as a result of having been associated 60 times with food, is illustrated in Skinner's 1938 book where he shows in graphic form the number of times four rats pushed the bar that activated the food-delivery mechanism (although no food was now forthcoming) (see also Mowrer, 1960, p. 107). The number of responses thus made ranged, in the four rats, from approximately 30 to 60, before they stopped responding, extinguished. In other words, this very significant number of bar-pressing responses occurred on the basis of the secondary reinforcement alone, provided by the mere sound of the food-delivery mechanism, without any primary reinforcement (food) whatever.

If, by the principles just described, rats will work this hard to reproduce ("imitate") mechanical sounds made and reinforced by a trainer, why should we not use the same simple concepts to explain the efforts made by birds and human infants to make ("imitate"), with their own vocal apparatus, the sounds which others have presented to them in temporal contiquity with primary reinforcements?

A few preliminary attempts have been made, during the past 20 years, to test the autistic theory of word learning by birds under various laboratory conditions; but the only systematic and extensive investigation of this problem thus far reported, in so far as I am aware, is that of Grosslight and Zaynor (1967). The results were dramatically and decisively negative! How could a theory which has both logical elegance and much collateral empirical support fall so far short of confirmation? Perhaps the theory is simply wrong! But there are certain features of the Grosslight–Zaynor research which will bear reconsideration, and may suggest a possible explanation of these paradoxical findings.

In this research, the myna birds which were used as experimental subjects were put into soundproof boxes, and there periodically heard a tape-recorded word or phrase which was then followed by a pellet of food. According to the autism theory of word acquisition set forth above, these subjects should have learned to reproduce the "conditioned stimulus" (word), that is, to imitate. They did not. By contrast, Skinner's rats performed in precisely the way the autism theory would demand. Why this striking difference? Perhaps we get a clue from the fact that there were two or three mynas around Grosslight's laboratory which his assistants had converted into "pets," and they were all fluent talkers. The experimental subjects were kept in total isolation between experimental sessions, with minimal human contact. During experimentation they were put into soundproof boxes where the only sound they heard was the word which preceded food presentation. By contrast, the "pet" mynas received a great deal of human attention, and developed great interest in and liking for their human companions.

Perhaps in an organism as social as the myna bird, the conditions for "learning to talk" must approximate those implied by the concept of identification (see Chapter 3) rather than by the more rudimentary phenomenon of "imitation." Being less "social," it seems not to have made any difference to Skinner's rats whether they had any sort of "relationship" or "contact" with the human beings who experimented with them or not. With the mynas, however, such a relationship, for reasons about which one can only vaguely conjecture, seems to have been crucial. Thus, the best warranted conclusion is that the autism theory of imitation is basically sound, but that this kind of learning will occur in talking birds (and presumably also human infants) only if there is a relationship with other living organisms, and not simply an impersonal, mechanical arrangement which presents no obstacle to the much less socially oriented laboratory rat—and which would probably also work with dogs.

In any case, there is as yet no conclusive evidence that the autism theory of language learning is wrong—and there is much logical and empirical evidence that it is sound. In fact, the assumptions involved in this theory are so ramified and powerful that it later led to a special conception of learning in general which has been extensively elaborated elsewhere (Mowrer, 1960a,b). Thus, despite the negative results obtained in the work carried out with myna birds by Grosslight and associates (and which seemed to offer an entirely fair test of the autism theory as previously stated most simply), it is not necessary to apologize for the paper which follows, wherein certain "clinical applications" of the autism theory of speech development are suggested.

Recently there has emerged, as a deduction from modern learning theory and psychoanalysis, a hypothesis concerning normal speech acquisition which promises to have interesting applications in the field of speech pathology.

More particularly, this hypothesis comes from an investigation which the author started some five years ago in an attempt to see what could be learned about language and its development in human beings from a study of the so-called talking birds. From an analysis of such anecdotal literature as is available, and our own observations with a small number of birds (including two parrots, a myna bird, two common crows, two Western magpies, and a number of Australian parakeets), it is apparent that birds learn to talk when and only when the human teacher becomes a *love object* for them. This interpretation is consistent with expectations generated by the principle of secondary reinforcement (learning theory) and the principle of identification (psychoanalysis).

Operationally, the first step in teaching a bird to talk is to make a "pet" of it, which is to say, tame, care for, and "baby" it in such a way as to deflect the interests and emotional attachments of the bird away from members of its own species to another species, namely *Homo sapiens*. This is commonly done by isolating the bird from its own kind and making it dependent for food, water, and social attention and diversion upon its human caretakers.

But there is another step involved which only a few species of birds—and apparently no mammal save man—can make. As one cares for and plays with these creatures, one makes certain characteristic noises. These may or may not be parts of conventional speech: any kind of noise will do—be it a word or phrase, a whistled or sung fragment of a tune, a nonsense vocalization, or even a mechanical sound like the creaking of a door or the opening of a food box—anything so long as it is intimately and consistently associated with the trainer and his caretaking activities. As a result of the association of these sounds with basic satisfactions for the bird, they become positively conditioned, that is, they become *good sounds*; and in the course of its own, at first largely random, vocalizations, the bird will eventually make somewhat *similar* sounds. By the principle of generalization, some of the derived satisfaction of pleasure which has become attached to the trainer's sounds will now be experienced when the bird itself makes and hears like sounds; and when this begins to happen, the stage is set for the bird's learning to "talk."

In terms of learning theory, what has happened is that initially neutral sounds, by virtue of their occurrence in temporal contiguity with primary reinforcements, have acquired secondary reinforcing properties. When the bird itself happens to make somewhat similar sounds it is now secondarily rewarded for having done so, and tries to perfect these sounds so as to make them match as exactly as possible the original sounds, and thus derive from them the maximum of pleasure and comfort.

In terms of psychoanalytic theory, the bird, as a result of developing "positive cathexis" (love) for its human trainer, or "foster parent," identifies with and tries to *be like* that person. Birds cannot do much by way of making themselves *look like* human beings, and even if they could they would not ordinarily be able to see themselves and enjoy this resemblance; but they can make themselves *sound like* human beings, and this they do, under the conditions indicated, with evident satisfaction.

Once words, phrases, whistles, snatches of song, or other distinctively human sounds have been perfected on the autistic or self-satisfaction basis just described, these same responses can, of course, be employed socially or communicatively. Birds that have learned human sounds on an autistic basis can later use these sounds instrumentally, as a means of indicating some desire or need, or perhaps just as a device for assembling and holding an admiring and reassurring audience. But the essential first step in this developmental sequence is, in the author's belief, one in which the reproduction and perfection of human sounds occurs, not because of their objective utility, but because of the *subjective* comfort and satisfaction they provide.

In so far as can be determined at present, essentially the same account holds, at least up to a point, for acquisition of speech by human infants. Words or other human sounds are first made by infants, it seems, because the sounds have been associated with relief and other satisfactions, and, as a result, have themselves come to sound good. Human infants, like birds, are vocally versatile creatures, and in the course of random activities in this area they will eventually make sounds somewhat similar to those which have already acquired pleasant connotations; and they will also, for reasons already indicated, have a special incentive for trying to repeat and refine these sounds.[1]

Soon, however, the infant discovers that the making of these sounds can be used not only to comfort, reassure, and satisfy himself directly,

---

[1] It is remarkable that those organisms which are structurally most similar to man in most respects, namely the anthropoid apes, have so little flair for speech. The work of Hayes and Hayes (1951) with an infant chimpanzee has recently confirmed what was already suggested by earlier studies, namely that voluntary control of the vocal cords is so poorly developed in these creatures (probably because of specific cortical deficiencies) as to incapacitate them for even so rudimentary a type of speech development as can be obtained in the talking birds. With an amount of attention and effort equal to—and in respect to speech training a good deal greater than—that which a human infant ordinarily receives, Hayes and Hayes have succeeded in teaching their baby chimpanzee, now three years old, to say only three words—mama, papa, and cup— and even these words are merely whispered instead of being fully phonated.

but also to interest, satisfy, and control mother, father, and others.[2] Up to this point, the speech learning of birds and babies seems to be virtually identical; but before long, somewhere around 18 months or two years of age, human infants begin to do something of which birds, even the most talented of them, are incapable. It is always a big event for the rest of the family (and probably for the baby, too!) when a baby begins to "put words together," that is, to make original, functional sentences. Birds may learn to repeat, "parrot fashion," phrases, sentences, or even longer sequences of human speech; but the indications are that these are never understood and used by birds with their full import and meaning. As De Laguna (1927) has remarked, *predication* is the thing that gives language at the human level its most distinctive quality, and it seems that this is never achieved by infrahuman organisms.

An entirely different example of the same type of psychological mechanism is the trick of teaching a dog to "shake hands." The procedure commonly used consists of *passively* moving the dog's leg in the desired manner and then giving a reward of some sort, such as a morsel of food. Like the buzzer in Pavlov's famous salivary conditioning experiments, the proprioceptive stimuli associated with the passive leg movement come to signify that something agreeable will shortly occur and therefore acquire secondary reinforcing properties. But there is this difference: under ordinary circumstances, Pavlov's dogs could not themselves make the food-promising buzzer sound; they had to *wait* for it to occur. In the present example, however, there is a stimulus pattern which the dog itself *can* produce, merely by performing *actively*, or "voluntarily," the same movement that has previously been performed passively by the trainer, in a manner analogous to the way in which a bird or a baby reproduces auditory stimulation which was originally produced by another.

The discovery that lifting the foreleg which has been involved in the passive hand-shaking training *feels good* (is comforting, reassuring, "promising") may be made by the dog when alone; and the satisfaction thus experienced will tend to insure, on a purely autistic basis, the repetition of the response, and eventually the response will probably be

---

[2] One may thus say that words are first reproduced by infants as a means of recapturing some of the pleasures which parents have provided when parents are not immediately available. By the second use of words, just described, the infant actually recovers the parents, literally "gets them back," and in so doing reduces the necessity for relying upon the autistic, self-supplied satisfactions. It is well known that small children who have "responsive" and 'attentive' parents do not rely upon fantasy (also a form of autistic satisfaction) so extensively and protractedly as do neglected children.

made in the master's presence. The response will then almost certainly be powerfully rewarded externally, just as the first words of a bird or baby which are heard by others are rewarded.[3]

In all the examples given, then, there is a procedure for shortcutting the delay which would be involved if one waited for a given response which one wished to teach to a baby, a bird, or a dog to occur spontaneously. By the procedures indicated, the response is, so to speak, *baited* in advance with secondary reinforcement, so that whenever it or a closely related response occurs, a satisfying experience is assured, without our necessarily being present to provide a reward. The autistic satisfaction thus experienced is, of course, likely to be relatively weak and ephemeral, but it is often strong enough to carry the desired response along until it can occur in the presence of another organism and thus elicit a more powerful, external reinforcement. Then its stability can be assured.

Perhaps this psychological mechansim can be given further substance by contrasting it with *punishment*. In the latter case, a painful stimulus is used to get *fear* attached to some other, formerly neutral, stimulus. This stimulus or "danger signal" may be an external event such as a buzzer or a blinking light, or it may be the particular pattern of internal stimuli associated with the execution of a particular movement. Where punishment has followed a movement, in the future this movement is less likely to be made, because it will produce stimuli which in turn will arouse fear. What is here suggested as the mechanism involved in speech acquisition is, in a sense, the reverse of punishment. In punishment an internal mechanism is set up which tends to *discourage* the occurrence of a particular response, whereas in preparing an infant or a bird for speech an internal mechanism is set up which will tend to *encourage* the occurrence of a particular response, so as to increase the probability of its occurrence, over and beyond what it would be on the basis of change alone. When one considers how unlikely it is that a baby or a bird would ever, in the course of purely random behavior, produce wordlike noises which could then be specifically rewarded, it becomes apparent how necessary is some mechanism of the kind just described.

Implications for Speech Pathology

Two years ago a young woman reported that tests had recently confirmed what she and her husband had suspected for some time,

[3] Konorski (1951) has independently made a similar analysis of the mechanism involved in a dog's learning to "shake hands." But see also Konorski (1969).

namely that their two-year-old daughter was very hard of hearing and that as a result her language development was being seriously retarded. In fact, the child had no real words, and she showed no interests in and refused to wear a hearing aid. The mother was convinced that the little girl had some hearing as evidenced by the fact that if she was engaged in some forbidden activity and the mother shouted "No," the child, even though her back was turned to the mother, would respond.

It was apparent from these meager facts that the only sounds that were getting through to this child were "bad" sounds, and one could conjecture that the less often she heard then the better it suited her. There was, in short, no "appetite" for the vocalizations of others and consequently no desire to make similar sounds herself.

When the situation was interpreted to the mother in these terms, she quickly consented to a regime in which vocalizations would not be used for disciplinary purposes at all but would instead be associated as often and as deliberately as possible with *agreeable* experiences. Ordinarily one announces pleasant events in a soft tone of voice, reserving the raised voice for warnings and condemnations. The prescribed plan thus called for a reversal of the usual situation. The mother was able to carry through, however, and very quickly the child became *interested* in words, was soon willing to tolerate a hearing aid so that she would be more clearly aware of them, and within six months was herself effectively making and using quite a number of words.

More recent follow-up data are not available on this case,[4] nor has there been opportunity to test this type of thinking systematically, with a statistically meaningful number of cases. One case can serve as well as many, however, to illustrate a remedial procedure and the rationale behind it. Other investigators, with more numerous cases of a similar kind at their disposal, may be able to validate the procedure. Even though the theory be entirely correct, one cannot, of course, expect success in all instances. The method's effectiveness presupposes, above all else, parents—and in particular a *mother*—who can and will make the indicated changes in vocal habits. Not all parents have the requisite degree of flexibility and motivation to accomplish this end, but it seems likely that the demands which the method places upon parents will usually be acceptable, and in such cases the method, given other favorable circumstances, should work as well as in the case described.

Sanger (1948), in an unpublished study directed by the author, observed the relationships of a number of mothers and their infants over

---

[4] Some ten years later, a report was received from the father of this child that her subsequent linguistic and intellectual development had been quite satisfactory.

a period of many months, with special reference to the role of vocalization by mother and by infant. One of the first things discovered was that most mothers—and particularly those who, by other criteria, seemed to be the *good* mothers—kept their infants "bathed in sound" most of their waking hours. While caring for their infants or just spending leisure time with them, these mothers vocalized almost continuously; and even when other duties took them to adjoining rooms, they would commonly sing or call to the baby intermittently.

This pattern of behavior is well calculated to make the mother's voice a welcome and reassuring sound, and it seems probable that much of the motivation for the babbling and cooing that infants normally engage in stems from the fact that the human voice, by virtue of the circumstances just described, has taken on pleasurable (secondary reinforcing) properties. Although baby's voice does not sound exactly like mother's voice, the similarity will usually be sufficient to cause a carryover of some of the pleasurable qualities of one to the other; and we may surmise that the production of motherlike sounds, in the form of babbling, is a first and highly useful step in the child's progression toward fully articulate speech.[5]

The fact that congenitally deaf babies babble very little, if any, and do not, without highly specialized instruction, learn to talk at all indicates how crucial is the capacity to hear and inwardly enjoy first the pleasant, reassuring voices of others, and then one's own somewhat similar sounds. Although congenitally deaf children usually have completely normal voice organs, and although their parents would only too gladly reward them for using these organs to make wordlike noises, the fact that such responses, because of the deafness, are not autistically satisfying to the child is a crucial handicap.

It is usually only after a normal infant has had many months of experience with the mother's voice as a good sound that he begins to hear it, on occasion, with implications of warning and threat. That this is an unwelcome development is dramatically indicated by the fact that when parents are scolding or admonishing them, small children will sometimes be seen to put their fingers in their ears, thus shutting out the new distinctly unwelcome human voice. But ordinarily, by the time that parents begin to discipline their offspring by means of speech, the speech-learning process will have already gained sufficient momentum to be able to withstand the shock of this negative use of voice; and the

[5] Because a woman's voice is closer to that of an infant or small child than is a man's voice, it is probably more efficient for women to have primary responsibility for the verbal development of children than it would be for men to have this responsibility.

impact of this discipline, however else it may be reflected, almost never has a permanently harmful effect upon language functions.

When, however, the gentle, loving sounds which good mothers make to their infants have been missed, due to hearing defects, and when the first human sounds to get through to the child are shouts of displeasure and proscription, it is almost axiomatic that the child thus handicapped will not *want* to hear, will not *want* to use even that small portion of his hearing equipment which may still be functional. When this abnormal course of events has occurred, the theory here explored would dictate the corrective procedure already described; and, with reasonably favorable attending circumstances, one should expect results comparable to those obtained in the case reported.

References

De Laguna, G. *Speech: Its function and development*. New Haven: Yale University Press, 1927.

Gardner, R. A. & Gardner, B. J. Teaching sign language to a chimpanzee. *Mental Health Digest*, 1969, *1*, 4–8.

Grosslight, J. H., & Zaynor, W. C. Verbal behavior in the mynah bird. In K. Salzinger & S. Salzinger (Eds.), *Research in verbal behavior and some physiological implications*. New York: Academic, 1967, pp. 5–19.

Hayes, K. J., & Hayes, C. The intellectual development of a home-raised chimpanzee. *Proceedings of the American Philosophical Society*, 1951, *95*, 105–109.

Konorski, J. Mechanisms of learning. In J. F. Danielli & R. Brown (Eds.), *Physiological mechanism in animal behavior*. New York: Academic, 1951.

Konorski, J. Postscript to: On a particular form of conditioned reflex. *Behavior Analysis*. 1969, *12*, 187–189.

Mowrer, O. H. *Learning theory and personality dynamics*. New York: Ronald, 1950.

Mowrer, O. H. *Learning theory and behavior*. New York: Wiley, 1960. (a)

Mowrer, O. H. Learning theory and the symbolic processes. New York: Wiley, 1960. (b)

Mowrer, O. H. *Theory and research—A review*. Urbana: University of Illinois, 1969. (Mimeographed.)

Mowrer, O. H. Autobiography. In G. Lindzey, (Ed.), *The history of psychology in autobiography*. New York: Appleton-Century-Crofts, 1971.

Sanger, M. D. *Verbal behavior of mothers in presence of their infants*. Unpublished manuscript. Graduate School of Education, Harvard University, 1948.

Skinner, B. F. *The behavior of organisms*. New York: Appleton-Century-Crofts, 1938.

Hearing and Speaking:
An Analysis of Language Learning

An abridgment of this article was presented at the annual meeting of the American Speech and Hearing Association, November, 1956, in Chicago. An unabridged version was later published in the Journal of Speech and Hearing Disorders, *1958, 23, 143–152.*

If the reader desires a synopsis of this chapter, one is provided at the end, under the heading of "Summary." But it may be said that at an even higher level of abstraction or condensation, this article consists of a series of both hindsights and foresights. It goes back and picks up and refines arguments which in earlier chapters were given, so to say, merely a glancing blow; and it also shows more clearly than any of the preceding chapters how the work on the psychology of language was to lead, if not to a totally new theory of learning, at least to a new and more powerful synthesis of previously existing theories. Since this paper was written while the two 1960 books on the psychology of learning were in preparation, this new way of looking at learning (which prominently involves the concept of the conditioning of hopes and fears to response-produced sensory feedback) is also sketched here more clearly than before.

Naturally enough, those who have been concerned with the practical skills associated with speech and hearing have looked to established theories of learning for understanding and guiding hypotheses. These theories have not, however, been very helpful. In fact, as will presently be shown, stimulation and assistance have, on occasion, moved in the opposite direction: for example, the manifest realities of language learning have recently pointed the way to a new and improved type of general learning theory. But, first, it will be useful to consider what sorts of inferences one has had to make about language learning on the basis of the older points of view.

Traditional Conditioned-Reflex Theory Inadequate

Conditioned-reflex theory, as developed by Pavlov (1927) and espoused by many others, has been both a help and a hindrance as far as the psychology of language is concerned. The theory explains, quite handsomely, how words acquire their meanings; but it does not provide a satisfactory explanation of how infants *acquire words*. If a word is heard and is then shortly followed by the experience of some *thing*, this sequence of events, if repeated a few times, will reliably cause the word to come to *mean* the associated thing. Part of the total reaction elicited by the thing stimulus "gets conditioned" to the word stimulus, and in this way the latter, as one may say, acquires its *meaning*.

But what of word reproduction, as opposed to mere understanding? As just indicated, the responses called meanings can be shifted, through conditioning, from thing to sign. But what about the responses involved in *making* a sign, or word? If there were some stimulus that would reliably elicit a specific word response (unconditionally, reflexly, innately), then this response could presumably be conditioned to a new, formerly natural stimulus. For example, if the *sight* of a ball were paired with the unconditional stimulus (assuming there was one) for the word "ball," one might expect to have a child soon saying "ball" upon *seeing* a ball. But the fact is that there *are* no unconditioned stimuli for conventional word responses; and, even if there were, it would not be very useful if all the child learned to do by means of the conditioning process were merely to *label* things in the manner described, that is, merely to call out their names upon seeing them. Words, it seems, have more subtle and important functions.

As things stand, the best that classical conditioning theory can do by way of explaining word learning is this: Assume (though the assumption itself is questionable) that babies "babble" reflexively, instinctively. In the course of such behavior many different speech units or "phonemes" will be uttered, some of them repetitively, as in "ba, ba, ba." In such a case, each preceding "ba," as made by the baby, becomes a stimulus, supposedly, for the succeeding one. If, now, someone else later says "ba" just as the baby himself has said it, this sound should, if the theory is sound, be an adequate stimulus to the baby for making this sound himself. And since the response is here much like the stimulus, one may speak of it as "imitative." Thus, by *imitating the baby,* the adult "gets inside" the baby's own stimulus-response system and obtains *control* of his vocal responses, so that the adult can then get the baby to *imitate him.* In this way, supposedly, the adult gets the baby so he will not only say "ba" when the adult says "ba" but also many, many other sounds, including "all." The adult now says "ba-all, *ball,*" the child repeats it and, as the word is uttered, the child is *shown* a ball. After a few presentations of the ball, accompanied by the adult's utterance of "ball" and the baby's repetition of it, it is assumed that the sight of the ball will cause the baby to say "ball," without the unconditioned stimulus being provided by the adult's utterance thereof.

One is, of course, immediately struck by the cumbersome, contrived, and altogether unlikely nature of this analysis of word learning. Moreover, research with talking birds (see Chapter 4) indicates that this simply is *not* the way one goes about getting words out of birds—or, should one say, *into* them? Also, the less systematic but enormous amount of evidence derived from word learning by human infants points in the same direction.

Thus, for good and sufficient reasons, one is inclined to dismiss the account of word learning which seems to be demanded by the classical version of conditioned-reflex learning. As will be seen later, a modified conception of conditioning is highly useful in this connection. But, in the meantime, it is necessary to consider the other great traditional way of thinking about learning, which is associated with the name of E. L. Thorndike.

Language Learning and the Law of Effect

When enunciated by Thorndike in 1898, the law of effect, though new in psychology, was old in common sense. It said, simply, that responses are learned ("stamped in") when followed by reward and that they are eliminated ("stamped out") when followed by punishment. What *is* a reward? Eschewing the circular definition that a reward is whatever "stamps in" a response, investigators have been busy ever since trying to establish exact and dependable criteria thereof. But this is a problem which need not be considered here. Accepting, for the moment, a commonsense or intuitive definition of reward, let us look at the implications which logically flow from the law of effect concerning language learning, implications which Thorndike, in his long and creative life, did not fail to point out.

Thorndike (1943) dubbed the theory of language learning which derives from the law of effect the *babble-luck* theory. If, an infant, said

Thorndike, in the course of *babbling* (a sort of vocal trial and error) has the *luck* to make a noise recognizably like some conventional, meaningful word sound, *and* if an adult then rewards this sound, its likelihood of recurrence will, per theory, be increased. Thus, simply enough, do infants come more and more to make the sounds which constitute the language of the social group into which they are born.

Elegant in its simplicity, the babble-luck theory can also be ostensibly supported by the following sort of empirical evidence. By the time the writer's first child, a little girl, was about three months old, she had begun to babble with great versatility, and in the course of her varied utterances she would occasionally say "da," or "da-da," or perhaps a long string of "da's." Noticing this sound, the father made a practice of always picking the baby up when she was heard to utter it, and obtained the cooperation of the mother and others in doing likewise. The result was that in about three weeks, the father could say to his friends, with studied casualness, "Oh, by the way, you know our baby is beginning to talk." To the incredulous rejoinders which this comment reliably evoked, he would then say, "Oh yes, she can say, "Daddy," very nicely. Wait a moment and I will show you." The little girl would then be brought and laid down somewhere, preferably on a not too comfortable surface, like the top of the table; and the father would start a line of patter, in the manner of a magician similarly bent upon deceiving his audience. And, sure enough, after a little squirming, the baby, with gratifying regularity, would say, "Da, da-da, da-da!" She would then, of course, be picked up, in an atmosphere of wonder and delight on the part of all concerned!

But did this demonstration have anything to do with true language learning? Probably not. The little girl did not *really* talk until the usual age, and her parents did not bother to use the same procedure with two later children. The trouble, obviously, was that the little girl's "da-da" did not *mean* "daddy." If we may say that it "meant" anything, it was: "Please pick me up. Change my position. I'm uncomfortable." This objective might have been equally accomplished by crying or toe-wiggling. The utterance of this sound did not, so far as could be observed, pass over into true language, and the word "daddy" apparently had to be relearned, *in a different manner,* before it could function normally. Its original utterance was, however, a clear instance of trial-and-error learning, and, as such, shows all the weakness of that theory as a general paradigm for language learning.

The law-of-effect conception of learning completely bypasses the problem of meaning. Meaning is not, it seems, intelligible without the concept of conditioning, and Thorndike made little use of the latter.

Within the framework of his theory, a word could "mean" only what it accomplishes for the individual. It could have no abstract reference, and without this capacity words have but limited value.

Even more damaging is the fact that there is poor correspondence between the babble-luck theory and the way things get done in practice. Parents manifestly do not wait for their infants to make conventional sounds and then reward them. Instead, parents first *make the sounds, themselves,* and then expect, usually with good justification, that the baby will *imitate* them. This sequence of events the law of effect, in its traditional form, cannot explain. It is committed to the proposition that the subject must himself *make* a response before it can be rewarded and learned, whereas the evidence is quite overwhelming that just *hearing* words is somehow an important and necessary step in learning to produce them. If this were not true, deaf children could presumably be taught to speak as readily as hearing ones, and various other inferences would follow which are equally unsubstantiated.

Imitation Not a Basic Explanatory Concept

In light of these complicated and rather baffling circumstances, there has been an understandable tendency on the part of some to dismiss the whole problem with the resigned comment: "Language must be learned, then, simply through imitation"—or, alternatively, "through an instinct of imitation." But this is no solution. If asked for a definition of imitation, the proponents of this view are likely to say that imitation is the process whereby one organism comes to reproduce a bit of behavior first observed in another organism, as when a baby copies the words which others are heard to utter. The difficulty here is the familiar and fatal one of circularity; for the very thing one is trying to explain is the *fact* of copying, and just using another term for the phenomenon itself provides no explanation. What is needed, obviously, is an adequate *theory* of imitation.

Pavlov, so far as is known, was never much interested in the imitation problem, and the efforts made by others to derive a conditioned-reflex explanation thereof show how poorly adapted the classical version of conditioning theory was to deal with this phenomenon. Thorndike, on the other hand, met the challenge head-on. Mammals, such as dogs, cats, and monkeys, he concluded, on the basis of extensive laboratory studies, simply do not show the kind of learning commonly called imitation (1898). Parrots, he conceded, do; but he then dismissed this capacity on their part as a biological quirk, not representing anything important in the evolution of living organisms in general. As we shall see in the next section, this bias not only prevented Thorndike from learning something quite important about the acquisition of language by human beings; it also prevented him from deriving a whole new conception of habit formation which carries us considerably further than did his notion of the stamping in and stamping out of simple stimulus-response connections or "bonds."

Clark L. Hull (1943) made a brilliant but not fully successful effort to unify Pavlovian and Thorndikian theory, and Miller and Dollard (1941) have applied Hull's views to the problem of imitation in general and language learning in particular. While suggestive, the latter analysis has likewise left certain questions unanswered and crucial problems unsolved.

What, then, of Gestalt psychology and Field Theory? In the main, persons affiliated with these two related schools of thought have let the language problem go by default. Insight is a key concept for them. As commonly perceived, there is nothing particularly insightful, logical, or gestaltlike about word reproduction; so, most workers of this persuasion (see Brown & Dulany, 1965) have simply not studied the problem. Actually, they might have found here rather striking applications of some of their notions if they had only been more persevering, as will be seen in this paper (see p. 70).

Autism Theory

The theory, now to be proposed as accounting more adequately than any other for language learning, and providing the basis for a new and improved conception of "habit" in general, may seem disappointingly simple and obvious. After the preceding discussion, something rather grand might well be expected. The fact is that, while indeed simple, the theory has not been obvious, and it is proving to have unsuspected implications and explanatory power.

As a result of the work with talking birds, already alluded to in this paper and described in more detail elsewhere (Mowrer, 1950, see Chapter 4; 1952), several things became apparent. It was quickly evident that no procedure based upon either the traditional conception of conditioning or upon the trial-and-error theory of learning would work here. Instead, what had to be done to get these creatures to "talk" was, first of all, to make *pets* of them, so that they were always eager and pleased to have the trainer put in his appearance. Then, the more specific procedure, recommended in the practical literature on bird training and quickly confirmed by experiment, was to associate the appearance and presence of the trainer with some specific sound, for example, with the word "hello." Alone, perhaps bored and hungry, the bird, hearing the trainer's utterance of this sound just before and as he enters the experimental room, knows now that "everything is going to be all right"—food, fun, and friendly companionship.

In the jargon of contemporary learning theory, this sound quickly takes on *secondary reinforcing properties.* Or, in commoner parlance, it becomes a *good* sound, one that the bird is relieved and pleased to hear. Given these conditions, the next step is quickly taken. Being vocally versatile, the bird randomly makes (or possibly, just imagines) sounds, one of which turns out to be a bit reminiscent of the trainer's ever welcome "hello." There is, instantly, special interest in the "feedback" from this response, and we may conjecture that further vocalization will be focused, so to say, in the "locality" of this sound. That is, efforts will be made to repeat it and to perfect it. The closer the bird comes to matching the memory image of the trainer's sound, the more satisfaction (secondary reinforcement) the bird will derive. Hence, through a sort of built-in, self-directed and self-rewarded rehearsal, the bird learns to say "hello" himself—but only after having first learned that it "means" something nice: "Things will be better now."

As already pointed out, conditioning theory provides a very satisfactory explanation of how it is that a word uttered by others takes on meaning for the small child; but one cannot make this same theory, as traditionally expressed, provide an adequate accounted of the learning involved in word reproduction. However, conditioning theory, somewhat modified, can be made highly serviceable here, also. If it be assumed, in the talking-bird paradigm, that the food and other attentions provided by the trainer mediate a sort of *comfort reaction,* then any sign or signal which regularly precedes such attentions should become conditioned to the comfort reaction and capable of producing it, at least in miniature form, somewhat in advance of the occurrence of the more basic rewards. Just as a sign that precedes some unpleasant, punishing experience makes the subject *fearful,* so may a sign that precedes some pleasant, rewarding experience make the subject *hopeful,* which condition, in and of itself, if a form of reward—secondary or derived reward—and is capable of reinforcing behavior which produces it, just as primary reward does. If, therefore hearing the trainer say "hello" makes a bird *hopeful* of good things to come, it follows that the bird will also become hopeful, and happy, upon *hearing itself* make this noise, and will, for the reasons given, be secondarily or "autistically" rewarded for having made the response that produced this sound. In essence, this is what is now known as the *autism theory* of word learning.

The autism theory, as presented here, employs a modified conception of conditioning: conditioning, not of overt action, but of a covert, emotional, subjective reaction or feeling of *hope*. Both in terms of common sense and of mounting laboratory evidence, such a notion is entirely legitimate. However, the autism theory of language learning can be formulated equally well in more "holistic," more gestaltlike terms. The bird that is being trained to talk is familiar with two very different *situations*: (1) situation-without-trainer, wherein the bird is lonely, bored, and possibly hungry and thirsty, and (2) situation-*with*-trainer, wherein distress ends and comfort and well-being ensue. The word-noise, "hello," is a part of Situation 2; and if the bird can itself produce this sound, it can make unpleasant Situation 1 somewhat *more like* pleasant Situation 2. In short, by making the word-noise, "hello," the bird *changes the situation,* psychologically, in a favorable direction. Likewise, it is assumed that baby-without-mother, by making mother-like sounds, changes the situation so that it is likewise more like the baby-*with*-mother situation.

It goes without saying that here only the very first stages of word learning are under discussion: words taking on pleasant connotations, as spoken by others, and, as a result, having pleasant connotations for the bird or baby when he himself makes them. Such secondary or derived pleasure is, of course, unstable, and tends to give way under repetition. But in human infants, and in birds as well, there is much social approval when they "begin to talk"; and the sounds they utter, being parts of a conventional communication system, are soon found also to have the power of command and control. Words now have a more dependable (social) source of reinforcement, and become stably fixated.

No attempt will be made here to deal with the further elaboration of speech into the special word patterns called sentences. The exact nature and function of sentences, psychologically speaking, has until recently been largely ignored; but it now appears that sentence structure and use can be successfully analyzed in terms of the same basic learning principles as have been employed in this paper to understand the development of those more rudimentary aspects of language skill (see Mowrer, 1954; also Part II of this volume). Parsimony of assumptions is manifestly an advantage here.

Autism Theory of Language Learning as a Paradigm
for Habit Formation

Mention has already been made of the fact that the autism theory of word learning has suggested a new way of thinking about learning, more broadly considered. According to Pavlov (1927), all behavior consists of primary, innate reflexes and conditioned reflexes, that is, the same movements as those involved in the primary, unconditioned reflexes but now made to substitute stimuli. And for Thorndike (1913), a "habit" was hardly less automatic and reflexive. All behavior, he assumed, consists of stimulus–response bonds which have, innately, some "strength" and which are then made either stronger or weaker, by reward and punishment, respectively.

The autism theory of word learning, as delineated in this paper, implies a general theory of learning which departs significantly from the views of both Pavlov and Thorndike. It assumes, first of all, that Thorndike's law of effect is empirically and descriptively valid, but that learning does not involve a stamping in and stamping out of the same neural bonds as this law posited. This new view also accepts the concept of conditioning, but departs from classical Pavlovian theory in holding that the reactions that most typically get learned in this way are internal meanings and emotions, rather than specific items of overt behavior. The new version of learning theory, which has recently been more or less simultaneously evolved by a considerable number of investigators (see Mowrer, 1956), makes the further assumption that in so-called habit formation learning does not involve the strengthening of a motive–behavior "connection", but, rather, the conditioning of meanings, emotions, expectations to *response-correlated stimuli*. Habit strength, then, is a matter of whether or not an organism is or is not disposed to make a particular reponse in a particular situation; and this, in turn, is a function of whether that response, made in *tentative, token form* (subjectively formulated as an "intention"), produces a predominantly favorable or unfavorable *feedback*. If the stimuli which are produced by the response have more fear than hope conditioned to them, then the feedback is unfavorable, and the response will not be allowed to procede beyond the "formative" (symbolic) stages; but if the response-correlated stimuli have more hope than fear conditioned to them, the feedback is favorable, and the nascent form of the response will go over into overt action.

Here it has been possible to state this theory only in the briefest, most abstract terms; and the only example of it in action offered is that provided by the acquisition, by birds and babies, of those "habits" called *words*. But this is a particularly good illustration, for here the sensory consequences of, or so-called feedback from, such a response are highly conspicuous. It is seen that, if positive emotional connotations can be given to certain sounds, as produced by others, the subject will, himself, have a strong disposition to make the responses which produce these sounds, without as yet ever having made or having ever been rewarded for making them. The notion that organisms learn only by *doing* is so ingrained in our thinking, if not in practice, that it is sometimes difficult to grasp the new theory; but it is very dramatically supported by the now well known work of Lee (1950), Fairbanks (1955), Black (1951) and others on the effects of delaying the airborne return from speech. Most readers will have heard recordings of, or will have perhaps themselves experienced, the remarkable disorganization of speech commonly produced by throwing vocal responses and their auditory feedback out of phase by ¼ sec. There could hardly be a more convincing demonstration than this of the fact that even such a highly practiced, overlearned, "habitual" activity as talking is *not* a matter of fixated S–R bonds which automatically produce certain responses once the "switch" is thrown, but instead involves a constant "monitoring" and control of behavior *as it occurs*, on the basis of the sensory consequences thereof. Obviously and manifestly one *listens*, very closely, to his own speech; and it is conjectured that one attends, with other senses but no less closely, to all so-called voluntary activity.

For decades it has been known that the sad and irreversible disorder of walking known as *tabes dorsalis* represents a pathological disruption of the neural pathways between the spinal column and the various sensory receptors in the legs. Here the motor pathways are fully intact; and if "habit" were a matter of "purely motor" learning, walking should hardly be affected at all. But the facts are otherwise: disrupt the sensory return from this type of performance, and the resulting impairment of control and coordination is immediate and drastic.

There is, of course, a nice congruence between this new conception of habit and a notion that has been around for some time in speech-correction work (see Fairbanks, 1954; Guttman, 1954; Hall, 1938; Hansen, 1944; Johnson, Brown, Curtis, Edney, & Keaster, 1948; Kelly, 1953; Kronvall & Diehl, 1954; Pronovost & Dumbleton, 1953; Robbins, 1942; Spreistersbach & Curtis, 1951; Travis, 1931; Travis & Rasmus, 1931; Zedler, 1956). Here the assumption is that many speech skills involve, not "purely motor" learning, but learning that is mainly *perceptual,* in the sense of involving *sensory discrimination*. There is no denying that purely structural defects can and do interfere with normal speech; but the point is that, given normal structures, speech is still often imperfect, as for example in lisping. Here improvement depends upon the subject's coming to *hear* slight differences between the sounds produced by one vocal response and those produced by a slightly different one. The theory which flows from this way of thinking holds that *habit,* in general, is a matter of getting hopes and fears (positive and negative feedbacks) conditioned to response-correlated stimuli, and that *skill,* as a refinement of habit, involves learning to discriminate, more and more precisely, between the sensory effects of (or feedback from) strictly correct and not-quite-correct versions of the same act.

Thorndike's law of effect directed attention to those more remote "effects" of behavior known as rewards and punishments while largely ignoring the immediate effects which are here termed response-correlated stimuli, that is, stimuli which are *inherently* associated with the occurrence of a particular response. It is now clear that, in reality, recognition of *both* types of effects is necessary for a satisfactory understanding of learned performances and skills and that (1) the *immediate* effects of action (response-correlated stimuli) function as *conditioned* stimuli, that (2) the later effects of action (rewards and punishments) function as *unconditioned* stimuli, and that (3) what gets "associatively shifted" from unconditioned to conditioned stimulus are the emotional components of the total reaction produced by reward and punishment, namely hopes and fears. Thus, by a special application of conditioning, as Pavlov conceived it, we are able to derive an explanation, apparently quite broadly applicable, of the phenomenon of habit as Thorndike conceived it. [For a fuller elaboration of this general conception of learning, see Mowrer (1960a,b).]

Summary

An attempt has been made to show that none of the major traditional theories of learning provides an entirely satisfactory explanation of language learning and that the hypothesis that such learning is dependent upon "imitation" is tautological, because language learning *is* imitative, and that is what is to be explained.

Systematic work with talking birds, which is supported by incidental observations of speech development in human infants, indicates that words are reproduced if and only if they are first made to *sound good* in the context of affectionate care and attention. Once words, as heard, take on positive emotional connotations, the stage is set for their reproduction, on a purely *autistic,* self-rewarding, noncommunicative basis. Then, once imitated, once reproduced, words can therefore function in the interpersonal, social mode that we call language.

This way of perceiving the learning that underlies the reproduction of words has suggested a new model for habit formation in general. Here the emphasis is not upon conditioned reflexes (in the manner of Pavlov), nor upon stimulus–response connections (in the manner of Thorndike), but, rather, upon the conditioning of positive or negative emotions to the stimuli which a given response produces. "Habits" may thus be either facilitated or inhibited, with or without actual *doing* on the part of the subject. If a response is to be facilitated or "formed," the important consideration is to get *hope* (secondary reinforcement, so-called) attached to the stimuli which are inherently associated with that response. If this can be done, the habit exists, forthwith, and will be manifested, given proper motivation, with little or no "practice." If, on the other hand, a response is to be inhibited, what has to be done is to get *fear* attached to the stimuli which are inherently associated with that response. This, too, at least in principle, can be done either with or without the performance of the response in question by the subject. The important thing is simply to get stimuli which ordinarily accompany a given response to be experienced and then be followed by the appropriate type of "effect" (reward or punishment). The reason that practice or repetition of the response itself is often necessary is that, under some circumstances, it is only by its occurrence that the correlated stimuli can be produced and conditioned, to hope or fear, in the manner indicated. The fortunate thing is that the reverse circumstances hold, in an unusually high degree, as far as speech is concerned. Since a word response can be made by one person and its (major) sensory consequences experienced by another, the resulting stimulation can be conditioned to hope, and the basis thus laid for the other person to start making the word sound himself, without having previously *done* much of anything but "listen." Likewise, an individual can be preconditioned or prejudiced *against* making a particular sound by simply hearing another make it and then experiencing something unpleasant.

Thus it will be seen that the study of word learning has proven highly provocative and instructive as far as a more general psychology of learning is concerned; and it is hoped that the resulting theory will, in turn, helpfully contribute to the improvement of practice in the field of speech pathology and remediation.

References

Black, J. W. The effect of delayed side-tone upon vocal rate and intensity. *Journal of Speech and Hearing Disorders*, 1951, *16*, 56–60.

Dulany, D. E. A stimulus-response analysis of language, thought, and culture. Ann Arbor: Ann Arbor Paperbacks, 1965.

Fairbanks, G. Selective vocal effects of delayed auditory feedback. *Journal of Speech and Hearing Disorders*, 1955, *20*, 333–345.

Fairbanks, G. A theory of the speech mechanism as a servo-system. *Journal of Speech and Hearing Disorders*, 1954, *19*, 133–139.

Guttman, N. Experimental studies of the speech control system. Ph.D. dissertation, University of Illinois, 1954.

Hall, M. Auditory factors in functional articulatory speech defects. *Journal of Experimental Education*, 1938, *7*, 110–132.

Hansen, B. F. The application of sound discrimination tests to functional articulatory defectives with normal hearing. *Journal of Speech Disorders*, 1944, *9*, 347.

Hull, C. L. *Principles of behavior.* New York: Appleton-Century, 1943.

Johnson, W., Brown, S. T., Curtis, J. J., Edney, C. W., & Keaster, J. *Speech handicapped school children.* New York: Harper, 1948.

Kelly, J. C. *Clinicians handbook for auditory training.* Dubuque: W. O. Brown, 1953.

Kronvall, E., Diehl, C. The relationship of auditory discrimination to articulatory defects of children with no known organic impairment. *Journal of Speech and Hearing Disorders*, 1954, *19*, 335–338.

Lee, B. S., Effects of delayed speech feedback. *Journal of the Acoustical Society of America*, 1950, *22*, 824–826.

Miller, N. E., & Dollard, J. *Social learning and imitation.* New Haven: Yale University Press, 1941.

Mowrer, O. H. On the psychology of 'talking birds'—A contribution to language and personality theory. *Learning theory and personality dynamics.* New York: Ronald, 1950.

Mowrer, O. H. The autism theory of speech development and some clinical applications. *Journal of Speech and Hearing Disorders*, 1952, *17*, 263–268.

Mowrer, O. H. The psychologist looks at language. *American Psychologist*, 1954, *9*, 660–692.

Mowrer, O. H. Two-Factor Learning Theory reconsidered, with special reference to secondary reinforcement and the concept of habit. *Psychological Review*, 1956, *63*, 114–128.

Mowrer, O. H. *Learning theory and behavior.* New York: Wiley, 1960. (a)

Mowrer, O. H. *Learning theory and the symbolic processes.* New York: Wiley, 1960. (b)

Pavlov, I. P. *Conditioned reflexes.* (G. V. Anrep, Trans.) London: Oxford University Press, 1927.

Pronovost, W., & Dumbleton, C. A picture-type speech sound discrimination test. *Journal of Speech and Hearing Disorders*, 1953, *18*, 258–266.

Robbins, S. D. Importance of sensory training in speech therapy. *Journal of Speech Disorders*, 1942, *7*, 183–88.

Spreistersbach, D., & Curtis, J. Misarticulation and discrimination of speech sounds. *Quarterly Journal of Speech*, 1951, 483–491.

Thorndike, E. L. Animal intelligence. An experimental study of the associative processes in animals. New York: Macmillan, 1898.

Thorndike, E. L. *Educational psychology, Vol. II. The psychology of learning.* New York Teachers College, Columbia University Press, 1913.

Thorndike, E. L. *Man and his works.* Cambridge University: Harvard Press, 1943.

Travis, L. E. *Speech pathology.* New York & London: Appleton, 1931.

Travis, L. E., & Rasmus, B. Speech sound discrimination ability of cases with functional disorders of articulation. *Quarterly Journal of Speech,* 1931, *17,* 217–226.

Zedler, E. Y. Effect of phonic training on speech sound discrimination and spelling performance. *Journal of Speech and Hearing Disorders,* 1956, *21,* 245–249.

Relations between Speech and Psychology: Accomplishment and Aspiration

In the Preface of this book I indicated that I expected Learning Theory and the Symbolic Processes *(1960b) to be my "last will and testament" as far as the psychology of language was concerned. The present paper, written the same year that* Symbolic Processes *appeared, also attempts a kind of "summing up," but in briefer compass, and suggests certain further developments that could be anticipated in the decades immediately ahead. Considerable optimism seemed justified at that time, since there then existed a general theory of learning which accommodated the psychology of language better than prior learning theories had done. And whereas speech and psychology had, up to this point, been relatively independent disciplines, both administratively and conceptually, it now seemed likely that they would draw closer, at least conceptually. In other words, new syntheses and integrations seemed imminent.*

This paper points out that in the foregoing chapters there are two basic contributions: (1) a theory of word acquisition which is consistent with a revised and elaborated conception of learning in general; and (2) an interpretation of the phenomenon of predication (sentence formation) which can also be encompassed within the same general learning framework. Additional support for and criticism of this theory of predication will be considered in Part II of this book. As pointed out in the prologue to the preceding chapter, the so-called autism theory of imitation has been dramatically confirmed with laboratory rats as subjects; but it appears that, in order for myna birds to imitate the speech of human beings, a more intricate, profound, and "personal" process, perhaps best denoted by the word, identification, is necessary.

The paper which follows was read, by invitation, at the 1960 Conference of The Central States Speech Association (Chicago) as part of a symposium on "The Ideal Speech Department in the Twentieth Century," and was published in Central States Speech Journal, *1961, 12, 165–169.*

⟋‾‾‾➤

At first blush it is a trifle odd that, in the first half of this century, speech and psychology departments should have developed separately. There is, surely, no facet of the speech field that is not in some sense psychological. But when one considers how *non*psychological academic psychology has itself been, it is in no way remarkable that speech has flourished as a separate discipline. The strictures which behaviorism forced upon us in defining the nature and scope of psychology were such as to leave great areas of human experience and practical concern quite untouched—which meant that these areas, if they were not to be neglected altogether, had to develop outside of what has been formally identified as psychology.

But even though, during the second half of this century, speech and psychology departments continue to be autonomous—as they may very well wish to do for administrative reasons—it seems most unlikely that there will be the same conceptual hiatus which has existed for the past several decades. Already psychologists have manifested a new and vigorous interest, on many fronts, in the symbolic processes; and the interaction in respect to research and theory construction in the two fields is extensive and constantly growing.

In the past twenty years, my own work, as a psychologist, has been heavily influenced by problems in the borderland between speech and psychology. And the story I wish to tell is one that has many parallels in the work of other persons in my field.

During the late 1930s, while still connected with the Institute of Human Relations at Yale University, I once heard John Dollard remark that academic psychology, as behavioral science, was not going to make much further progress until it came to grips with language and the symbolic processes in general. So convinced was I that Dollard's judgment was sound that soon after I left Yale, in 1940, to go to another Eastern university, I decided to try to forge at least one link between animal and human behavior by investigating the principles according to which certain species of birds learn to utter wordlike sounds.

Almost immediately it was clear that neither of the two major Behavioristic conceptions of learning—notably that of I. P. Pavlov and that of E. L. Thorndike—was adequate in this situation. Manifestly, the acquisition of wordlike responses by birds is not a matter simply shifting such a response from one stimulus to another, as is characteristic of so-called conditioning, for the reason that there is no unconditioned stimulus for these responses in the first place. And it is also apparent that these responses are not acquired on a Thorndikian trial-and-error basis. Despite the fact that, in recent years, B. F. Skinner (1958) has been able to do quite remarkable things in the way of animal training by what he calls behavior shaping (i.e., the technique of rewarding successively closer approximations to the desired behavior), I challenge anyone to teach a myna bird to say "How are you today?" by this method. Yet the learning of such a response is manifestly possible and does occur.

Something known as imitation is obviously involved here. And I soon discovered that the best way to make this method of training work is to *say* the word or phrase which one wishes the bird to learn and then cause something to happen which pleases the bird. For example, you say "Hello" and then give the bird a morsel of preferred food; hello, food; hello, food; etc. And presently it comes about that if you are a little slow in making the noise which seems to "produce" the food, the bird will *make it for you,* as a means of speeding things up a bit. In other words, if the trainer repeatedly makes "Hello" a sign that food will be forthcoming and does not make this sign at some point when the bird is ready for more food, the bird will take matters into his own "hands" and make this sign or signal himself.

Here we are not, of course, concerned with the question of standard, accepted meanings. If a bird learns to say "Hello" under the circumstances described, the noise rather clearly means, when the trainer utters it, "Food is coming." And when the bird makes this sound it means, "Bring on the food," or "I'm ready for more."

In the vernacular of the learning laboratory, what happens in a situation of this kind is that the sound "Hello," as uttered by the trainer, takes on secondary-reinforcement capacity. In other words, it becomes a *good* sound which the bird is glad to hear the trainer make and is likewise rewarded, secondarily or autistically, by hearing himself make. Like promises in general, this one is immediately rewarding, and will be reproduced by the bird itself if it has the necessary neural equipment. (I say *neural* equipment, incidentally, for if birds have what it takes neurologically, they manage to "talk" despite severe disadvantages in the matter of vocal and oral equipment.)

Here I shall make no attempt to elaborate this conception of language learning, since I assume it is already familiar to many of you and is to others perhaps of no special interest. What I do wish to emphasize, rather, is that, quite unexpectedly, this study of the process whereby one organism becomes able to reproduce a stimulus which is at first presented by another organism has pointed the way to a *powerful new conception of habit formation in general.* We no longer believe that habits are mere conditioned reflexes, in the classical Pavlovian sense, or that they are just S–R neural bonds which have been selectively strengthened by reward. Now we suspect that a habit is learned in exactly the same way as is imitative behavior, except that in habits, the pattern of stimulation which the organism learns to like and to reproduce is initially supplied by the organism's *own behavior* rather than by another organism. In other words, in habit an organism is *imitating itself,* which is to say that as a result of a given action having been repeatedly rewarded, the sensory consequences of or feedback from this action take on secondary reinforcing properties, i.e., becomes "promising," so that when the organism wants something it makes the response which produces the stimulation which has the greatest "sign value" in this connection.

Stated in this abbreviated and somewhat abstract manner, this new conception of habit will not, I fear, be very intelligible to anyone who is not already familiar with it. But it has already been described in a preliminary way (Mowrer, 1950, Chapter 24; Mowrer, 1952; Chapter 7 in this volume); and it has been given more systematic treatment in two recent publications (Mowrer, 1960a; 1969b). Incidentally, I should say that the work of Lee (1950), Fairbanks (1955), Black (1951) and others on delayed auditory feedback powerfully supports this new theory of habit, and has been influential in its development.

This conception of habit formation has particularly interesting implications for the understanding of *skill* and ties in directly with work which has been done in the speech field. For a long time there has been a group of speech therapists who maintain that speech remediation is a matter of *discrimination learning.* These students of the problem hold, for example, that a lisping child who says "glath" rather than "glass" does so, not (ordinarily) because of any lack of motor capacity, but because he does not *hear* these two sounds as different; and those holding this view set about improving speech performance by what may be called *ear* training. The child who clearly hears "glass" and "glath" as different sounds will presumably not *say* "glath" in a situation in which "glass" is appropriate. This conception of skill has many important applications and is thoroughly congruent with the general conception of habit which has been delineated (Mowrer, 1958, 1960a, Chapter 12).

After the autistic conception of the mechanism whereby word learning occurs was well articulated, and after it was clear that this is but a special case of a principle which provides a powerful new conception of habit formation in general, my own interests moved on to the question, What is a sentence or proposition, psychologically speaking? The indications, as I have shown elsewhere (Mowrer, 1954, 1960b), are that the sentence is preeminently a conditioning device, whereby a part of the meaning of the predicate of a sentence is shifted to the subject thereof. While defensible as a first approximation, this statement immediately calls for qualification. It is not, we discover, that the meaning of the predicate word is conditioned directly to the subject of the sentence; instead, the meaning of the predicate is conditioned to the *meaning* of the subject of the sentence. The meaning of the subject of the sentence can thus *mediate* the transfer of the meaning of the subject of the sentence from the subject of the sentence to the referent thereof. This phenomenon, known as *sematic generalization*, must be accounted for by a sound theory of the sentence; and the hypothesis just described does so quite satisfactorily (Osgood, 1953).

Again, I realize that I have not described this mechanism in sufficient detail to make it fully intelligible; but I refer to it here as another illustration of the conceptual rapproachment that is today occuring between psychology and speech.

Now, having shown a number of ways in which the fields of psychology and speech are coming together, at least at the level of formal theory, I must also point to a difficulty—whose resolution will, I believe, still further relate these two fields. I have already described the view that a habit is not an S–R bond or connection, but is instead a matter of secondary reinforcement or hope that has been conditioned to the sensory feedback from the response which has previously been followed by reward. And here I may say that parallel to this conception of habit or response facilitation is the view that response inhibition occurs when a response occurs and produces a characteristic pattern of sensory feedback which is followed, not by reward, but by punishment, so that instead of hope, it is fear that is now conditioned to these stimuli, which means that when the response in question starts to recur, it will be inhibited rather than enhanced.

Now this conception of response facilitation and response inhibition works nicely, once a response is in progress and producing its distinctive pattern of sensory feedback. But it leaves quite unanswered the question of how a particular response, rather than any one of thousands of other possible responses, is selected and initiated. For a primitive form of reflexology such a Pavlov's, or a bond theory such as Thorndike advocated, this problem does not arise: when a given stimulus is presented, a given response follows automatically, per theory at least, because the neural connection between this stimulus and this response is stronger than the connection between this stimulus and any other response. There are, however, many other ways in which this conception of habit is extremely unsatisfactory, ways in which the new feedback conception of habit is much more satisfactory. But we are now faced with this troublesome problem of *response selection and initiation*—or, in the simplest terms, the problem of how the individual *finds* the response which is appropriate in any given situation. At once, many of you will think of certain forms of aphasia, wherein a subject can utter a given word readily enough if someone else "finds" it for him in the sense of first pronouncing it, but who cannot make the proper association if, for example, he is merely shown the object for which the word stands.

At the Interdisciplinary Seminar on Aphasia which was held in Boston in the summer of 1958, the view was expressed that clinical studies of abnormal language behavior provide a "foundation for broad conceptions of human symbolic processes" (Osgood, 1958, p. 3). And I am certainly inclined to agree that if we can discover how it is that we find or fail to find the right word as needed, we will be well on our way to knowing how responses in general are selected and executed.

Already inquiry, in both the speech and psychological fields, has moved far enough to suggest that the answer to this problem lies in the long-neglected phenomenon of *imagery*. Learning, we now suspect, normally has both an affective *and* a "cognitive" aspect. The former we have already alluded to in connection with the conditioning of the emotions of hope or fear to stimuli characteristically produced by a given response. But this is not all that is learned. There are, besides, memories, cognitions, images, knowledge. And it now appears that, although particular responses do not become bonded to specific stimuli, it may well be that images and memories *do* operate in this way. In other words, it is entirely possible that the association of ideas obeys connectionistic and associationistic principles, whereas behavioral acts themselves do not, and that an image or memory, once it recurs, then sets the goal or (in cybernetics jargon) the reference level toward which behavior then moves (Mowrer, 1960b, Chapters 5 and 7; also Straus, 1959).

In the notion of Dr. Hildred Schuell (1957) that the rehabilitation of certain types of aphasia calls for a "reauditorization," that is, the

establishment of new auditory imagery, and Bluemel's (1935) suggestion that in aphasia "the image recoils from the stream of consciousness," we seem to have clear intimations of a parallel line of thinking on
the part of certain workers in the field of speech.

I realize, of course, that the types of problems to which I have here
alluded are still somewhat below the level of complexity at which many
persons in the field of speech operate, for example, in the area of debate
and dramatics; but what I have said at least suggests a growing
articulation of the highest levels of contemporary behavior theory with
at least the lowest, simplest levels of the speech field. In the second half
of this century, I expect this articulation to become closer and more
secure. This, I believe, will be an advantage to speech as well as
psychology.

References

Black, J. W. The effect of delayed side-tone upon vocal rate and intensity. *Journal of Speech and Hearing Disorders*, 1954, *16*, 56–60.

Bluemel, C. S. *Stammering and allied disorders*. New York: Macmillan, 1935.

Fairbanks, G. Selective vocal effects of delayed auditory feedback. *Journal of Speech and Hearing Disorders, 1955, 20*, 333–346.

Lee, B. S. Effects of delayed speech feedback. *Journal of the Acoustical Society of America*, 1950, *22*, 824–826.

Mowrer, O. H. *Learning theory and personality dynamics*. New York: Ronald, 1950.

Mowrer, O. H. Speech Development in the young child: I. The autism theory of speech development and some clinical applications. *Journal of Speech and Hearing Disorders*, 1952, *17* 263–268.

Mowrer, O. H. The psychologist looks at language. *American Psychologist*, 1954, *9*, 660–694.

Mowrer, O. H. Hearing and speaking: An analysis of language behavior. *Journal of Speech and Hearing Disorders*, 1958, *23*, 143–152.

Mowrer, O. H. *Learning theory and behavior*. New York: Wiley, 1960. (a)

Mowrer, O. H. *Learning theory and the symbolic processes*. New York: Wiley, 1960. (b)

Osgood, C. E. *Method and theory in experimental psychology*. New York: Oxford University Press, 1953.

Osgood, C. E. (Ed.) *Report of an interdisciplinary seminar and conference held at the Boston Veterans Administration Hospital, June* 15 *to July* 30, 1958. Mimeo-graphed.

Schuell. H. A short examination of aphasia. *Neurology*, 1957, *7*, 627–634.

Skinner, B. F. Reinforcement today. *American psychologist*, 1958, *13*, 94–99.

Straus, E. W. Human action: Response on project? *Confinia Psychiatrica*, 1959, *2*, 148–171.

Addendum

In Chapter 6, as in Chapter 5, it has been pointed out that prior research on the development and function of language provided the basis for a new theoretical approach to learning in general, which has been elaborated upon in *Learning Theory and Behavior* and *Learning Theory and the Symbolic Processes,* simultaneously published in 1960. Both books were reasonably well received; but late in 1979, the author, to his surprise, was notified that the first of these volumes "has been cited over 380 times since 1961" and would be, for the week of February 4, 1980, "This Week's Citation Classic" in *Current Contents* (Institute for Scientific Information, Philadelphia). Accordingly, he was invited to prepare a statement of some 550 words setting forth any unusual or interesting circumstances that attended the inception, writing, or publication of this book.

The submitted material was accepted as satisfactory, except for a request that a sentence or two be added to indicate "why you feel this work has been so widely cited." The following brief paragraph was supplied in response to their request:

> Perhaps the most distinctive, and useful, feature of this book is that it turned out to be congruent with what is now called General Systems Theory, as indicated by the 24 references in the subject index to "feedback," three to "cybernetics," but none to "systems" (cf. "integration").

The term, General Systems Theory, seems to have been coined by Ludwig von Bertalanffy, who in 1968 published a volume with that title (New York: George Braziller). Also pertinent is a book, *Living Systems,* published in 1979 by James G. Miller (New York: McGraw-Hill). The present author's two 1960 books thus articulate with the principles of self-regulation (adaptation) found in both mechanical and electronic servomechanisms and in the phenomenon of physiological homeostasis (Walter B. Cannon, *Bodily Changes in Pain, Fear and Rage* [New York: Appleton, 1915]; *The Wisdom of the Body* [New York: Norton, 1932]). These books are also basically congruent with the "purposive behaviorism" of Alfred Adler. (For an excellent summary of the work of both Adler and Rudolf Dreikurs, see *Adlerian Counseling and Psychotherapy,* by Don C. Dinkmeyer, W. L. Pew, and Don C. Dinkmeyer, Jr. [Monterey, California: Brooks/Cole, 1979].)

The conception of learning and language propounded by the 1960 books, as well as in the present volume, may thus be said to have unusual "power," scope, and sophistication, not exceeded perhaps by any other theoretical formulation. Both of the 1960 books, regrettably, were allowed to go out of print in the early 1970's, but a reprint edition of *Learning Theory and Behavior* has been provided by Robert E. Krieger Publishing Company (Huntington, N. Y., 1973).

Psycholinguistics Revisited

As the chapters comprising Part III of this book will indicate, my interest in the psychology of language has, for the past decade, been restricted almost exclusively to the type of language abuse and perversion we call *deception*—and to the personal and social disintegration produced thereby. From these same chapters, it will also be apparent that the principles of learning which serve us well in Part I are also congruent with the phenomena considered in Part III. It was therefore not merely surprising but almost incredible to find that during this same decade (1960–1970), an approach to the field of psycholinguistics developed and gained wide currency, under the advocacy of Professor Noam Chomsky, which preemptorily dismissed the whole psychology of learning and purported to show that language is best dealt with in an entirely different frame of reference.

In the Preface, I have already explained how the manuscript comprising Part II of this volume came into existence and need not repeat that explanation here. However, I should perhaps add that although I personally believe that Chomsky is a Pied Piper who simply bedazzled a number of otherwise sensible scholars into a fantastic and retrogressive way of dealing with the whole field of psycholinguistics, I do not categorically deny that there may be something of substance in what he has said. I nevertheless do my best to show that this, in point of fact, is *not* the case; but at the same time I have to admit that the psychology of learning is itself neither a finished nor an entirely unified science and that we may have something to learn from what Chomsky (however obscurely) has propounded.

For some time, my old friend and colleague, Professor Charles E. Osgood, kept telling me of the "outrageous" attacks which Chomsky and associates were making on the attempts which he, myself, and many others made in the 1940s and 1950s to construct a psychology of language or psycholinguistics on a solid foundation of learning theory and urged me to join in the defense of our bastion. But I did not find either the time or the incentive to do this until 1969, when I received the invitation to prepare the New York Academy of Science address. I am not at all sure that Professor Osgood will approve of the particular *way* in which I have now joined in this counteroffensive, but I trust he will take some satisfaction in the fact that I have at last joined. Although I here inveigh lustily against the Chomsky position, I hope there will still be a certain tentativeness about what I have to say in this connection, and a recognition that Chomsky may, however unlikely, after all be right.

Since this section does not consist of separate articles or chapters but is, in effect, a monograph, there seems to be no need for a prologue of the kind that has introduced the preceding chapters. The foregoing will thus serve both as the Introduction to Part II and the prologue to the single, though subdivided, chapter which follows.

Why All the Chafing over Chomsky?[1]

The course in introductory psychology which I took as a freshman at the University of Missouri, in 1925, was taught by Max F. Meyer, who, in 1911, had written the first psychology textbook with the word "behavior" in the title. Meyer had been originally trained (in Germany) as a physicist, with only a tangential interest in psychology; and when he emigrated to the United States and entered the latter field, it was with an intransigent objectivism which pervaded his writings and which he would not allow his students to violate, even in the slightest degree, in the classroom. As a behaviorist, Meyer thus antedated John B. Watson, whom I also read avidly; and A. P. Weiss had been one of Meyer's early students. So if I lay claim to having once been a "primitive behaviorist" myself, I submit that my credentials are of the highest order.

Then, in 1929, I entered graduate school at The Johns Hopkins University, where Watson, only a few years before, had been Head of the Department of Psychology, which Knight Dunlap now chaired. Although stressing the importance of a scientific and objective point of view, Dunlap, under whom, in 1932, I took my doctorate in Experimental Psychology, was not as implacable on this score as Meyer and Watson had been. Then, between 1934 and 1940, I had considerable contact with another behaviorist, Clark L. Hull, at the Yale Institute of Human Relations. But his interests were far-ranging and flexible, and it was during this period that I became convinced that absolute objectivism in psychology, although an understandable rebellion against the amorphous and flaccid mentalism which had previously dominated psychology, was itself not an adequate or viable discipline, and that it often

[1] Presented Tuesday, October 14, 1969, in abridged form, under the title "Perception and the Learning and Uses of Language," at a conference sponsored by the New York Academy of Sciences (Section of Psychology) on "Various Approaches to the Study of Perception."

precipitated dilemmas where, from the standpoint of even the most rudimentary common sense, none needed to exist.

I was therefore eventually persuaded that Tolman (1932), who also called himself a behaviorist of sorts, was right in his inclusion, as the legitimate data of psychology, not only observable stimulation (S) and response (R), but also unobservable "intervening variables" within the organism itself (O). And one of the first of these which I introduced into my own research on avoidance learning in the late 1930s was *fear,* a concept which would have horrified Max Meyer and released in him verbal behavior toward anyone who used it that would almost certainly have inhibited any future repetition of it. But the explanatory power of this concept, in the field in which I was now working, was simply enormous; and, little by little, I cautiously introduced a few other "intervening variables," and by imperceptible degrees ceased to be a primitive or "pure" behaviorist and became a neobehaviorist (see Mowrer, 1950a).

Probably sometime in 1939, shortly before I left Yale to join the faculty of the Harvard Graduate School of Education, I had heard John Dollard express the opinion that before we could make much further progress in our interdisciplinary study of the varied problems of "human relations," we were going to have to pause and take up the problem of *language.* Although I had not independently had this idea, I felt it was absolutely correct as soon as Dollard voiced it; and, in the fall of 1940, when I moved on to my new academic post, I carried with me a resolve to do whatever I could to build a psychology of language on the basis of the learning theory which had by this time been firmly founded, we thought, on the work carried out during the preceding decade or so at Yale and elsewhere.

The Present State of Confusion in "Psycholinguistics"

The two problems to which I eventually addressed myself were: (a) the original process of word learning by small children, and (b) the basic structure and psychosocial function of the sentence. But before I review the ensuing developments, I should speak briefly about some rather astonishing recent developments in the field of psycholinguistics. Up to the time I published, in 1960, my two books, *Learning Theory and Behavior* and *Learning Theory and the Symbolic Processes,* it seemed to me and a good many other psychologists that the attempt to develop learning theory so that it would give us a sound psychology of language was proceeding very nicely. In 1962 I published a paper designed to show, in at least a preliminary way, that learning theory could also be extended over into the field of elementary mathematics (or "number behavior"); and I even had some thoughts about the development of a comparable psychology of music.

But then something happened. We began to hear the ominous rumble of criticism and condemnation of this whole approach, led by Professor Noam Chomsky, a linguist by trade and training, who, it soon appeared, had many devoted and vociferous followers. When Chomsky (1959a) had himself written a long and blistering review of B. F. Skinner's 1957 book, *Verbal Behavior,* this was fine; for this book, predicated as it was on radical, primitive, naive (choose your own adjective) behaviorism, was, in my own estimation, very far from adequate to the task it had set itself; and I did not in the least mind seeing it criticized. But when, in 1965, in an article entitled, "Could Meaning Be an r_m?", one of Chomsky's followers, J. A. Fodor, severely criticized some of my own work, the situation suddenly took on a different coloration. However, as it happened, I was then more interested in other matters, and did not feel constrained to respond. But my colleague, Professor C. E. Osgood, whose work in this field and my own have always had a good deal in common (Osgood, 1953, 1963), was by now also catching much the same sort of criticism, and, being both more courageous and technically better qualified than I am in linguistics proper, has replied salvo for salvo (see Osgood, 1966, 1968; also Berlyne, 1965, 1966; and Fodor, 1966). In any case, Chomsky and his associates were not only badly "rocking our boat"; one somehow got the impression that they wouldn't mind in the least if they succeeded in *sinking* it!

The prevailing state of affairs was thus very confused, not to say chaotic. When I originally accepted the invitation to take part in The New York Academy of Sciences Conference, it was with the hope that the participating experts in the Psychology of Perception might bring clarity and peace into this murky and turbulent situation. However, I have had second thoughts about all this and must confess to some skepticism and a certain uneasiness. In the first place, I don't find "perception" a very useful term and hardly ever use it either in ordinary speech or in professional writing or lecturing. I hoped I would at least be open-minded on this score and prepared to be pleasantly surprised if "phenomenology" proved more potent and resourceful in this area than I previously believed it to be. But then it occurred to me that the perceptionists, with their mentalistic emphasis which is so congenial to Chomsky and his associates, might actually side with them and simply give the coup de grace to our enfeebled neobehavioristic approach to the field of psycholinguistics. However, now that I was committed to this enterprise, I might as well stake out my position and take my chances, although I could well imagine that I would end up with a well-founded wish that I had stayed home.

The Seminal and Still Largely Valid Early Observations of Bertrand Russell on Language: Acquisition of Word Meanings

Although I did not publish my first paper on the psychology of language (in collaboration with Peter Viek) until 1945 (see Chapter 1) I had read, as an undergraduate, probably sometime in 1928 or 1929, what I now regard as far and away the most penetrating analysis of language then extant—and one which, on the whole, still makes excellent sense. This was at a time when Bertrand Russell was publishing a series of popular books on a wide range of subjects; and I read most of them, including one simply entitled *Philosophy* (1927), in which there is a 15-page chapter again with a single-word title, "Language."

At the outset, Russell makes his general position clear. He is not going to follow the rationalistic approach of "traditional philosophy" which assumed that "words exist to express 'thoughts.'" Instead, Russell says that his approach is going to be "behavioristic" and adds: "The only satisfactory way to treat language, to my mind, is to treat it . . . as Dr. Watson does" (p. 43). This is not quite accurate; Russell does a far better job with the problem of language than Watson ever did; but it did no harm for Russell to indicate, explicitly, what his point of departure was.

Russell quite correctly I believe, begins his discussion of the psychology of language with an analysis of the process whereby individual words originally, in the small child, acquire their *meanings*. He says:

> The two questions we have to answer, apart from the problems raised by sentences as opposed to words, are: First, what sort of behavior is stimulated by hearing a word? And secondly, what sort of occasion stimulates us to the behaviour that consists in pronouncing a word? I put the questions in this order because children learn to react to the words of others before they learn to use words themselves. It might be objected that, in the history of the race, the first spoken word must have preceded the first heard word, at least by a fraction of a second. But this is not very relevant, nor is it certainly true. A noise may have meaning to the hearer, but not to the utterer; in that case it is a heard word but not a spoken word. (I shall explain what I mean by "meaning" shortly.) Friday's footprint had "meaning" for Robinson Crusoe but not for Friday. However that may be, we shall do better to avoid the very hypothetical parts of anthropology that would be involved, and take up the learning of language as it can be

observed in the human infant of the present day. And in the human infant
as we know him, definite reactions to the words of others come much
earlier than the power of uttering words himself.

A child learns to understand words exactly as he learns any other
process of bodily association. If you always say "bottle" when you give a
child his bottle, he presently reacts to the word "bottle", within limits, as
he formerly reacted to the bottle. This is merely an example of the law of
association which we considered in the preceding chapter. When the
association has been established, parents say that the child "understands"
the word "bottle", or knows what the word "means". Of course the word
does not have all the effects that the actual bottle has. It does not exert
gravitation, it does not nourish, it cannot bump on to the child's head. The
effects which are shared by the word and the thing are those which depend
upon the law of association or "conditional reflexes" or "learned reactions". These may be called "associative" effects or "mnemic" effects—the
latter name being derived from Semon's book *Mneme* (1921), in which he
traces all phenomena analogous to memory to a law which is, in effect not
very different from the law of association or "conditioned reflexes." . . .
The law of conditioned reflexes is subject to ascertainable limitations, but
within its limits it supplies what is wanted to explain the understanding of
words. The child becomes excited when he sees the bottle; this is already a
conditioned reflex, due to experience that this sight precedes a meal. One
further stage in conditioning makes the child grow excited when he hears
the word "bottle." He is then said to "understand" the word. (pp. 48-49)

We may say, then, that a person understands a word which he hears
if, so far as the law of conditioned reflexes is applicable, the effects of the
word are the same as those of what it is said to "mean." This of course
only applies to words like "bottle," which denote some concrete object or
some class of concrete objects. To understand a word such as "reciprocity"
or "republicanism" is a more complicated matter, and cannot be
considered until we have dealt with sentences. But before considering
sentences we have to examine the circumstances which make us use a
word, as opposed to the consequences of hearing it used (pp. 49-50)

There was not, in 1927, and there is not today, I venture to say,
any better way of explaining the process whereby words acquire meanings in a particular lexicon or "language" than the one just quoted from
Russell. In 1954, when I published a paper entitled "The Psychologist
Looks at Language," I used the diagram shown in Figure 1 as a means
of graphically representing the process delineated by Russell. To my
knowledge, no other hypothesis even approximates this one, either in
terms of simplicity or power.

In the extended passage which has just been quoted, Russell says:

If you always say "bottle" when you give a child his bottle, he
presently reacts to the word "bottle," *within limits,* as he formerly reacted
to the bottle [itself]. . . . Of course the word does not have *all* the effects
that the actual bottle has. . . . The law of conditioned reflexes is subject to
ascertainable limitations, but within its limits it supplies what is wanted to
explain the understanding of words. (pp. 48-49, italics added)

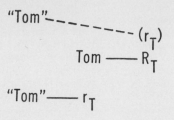

Figure 1. Schematic indication of the way in which the word, "Tom," through the process of conditioning, comes to denote, mean, or imply a certain person, Tom.

It is a well established observation that the conditioned or anticipatory reaction made to a stimulus signifying an approaching opportunity for the occurrence of a consummatory reaction of some sort is never precisely the same as the consummatory response itself. Thus, Pavlov's dogs, when given food as a so-called unconditioned stimulus, salivated, lowered their heads to the food trough, "gobbled up" and swallowed the food. The response made to the conditioned stimulus or "signal" alone consisted, typically, of salivation, which can be precisely measured, and what Pavlov called the "orientation reflex," that is, a fixing of "attention" upon the food trough, in readiness for the appearance of the food. Clark Hull (1930, 1943) called the conditionable portion of a total consummatory response a "fractional anticipatory goal reaction, r_g," which may involve observable reactions of the kind just described or, in human beings at least, such intervening (but unobservable) variables as images, felt but unexpressed emotions, etc. When Russell says, "Of course the word does not have *all* the effects that the bottle has," he is clearly denoting what Hull was later to term "fractional anticipatory goal reactions," which, as we shall see later, provide the basis for the explanation of another phenomenon which is centrally important in language theory, namely, *mediation*.[2] But the point is that, in 1927, Russell knew precisely what he was talking about in this connection, and it took us psychologists a while to catch up with him.

But in his discussion of whether human beings first uttered (used) or heard (understood) words, Russell is considerably less felicitous. On this score he says:

> It might be objected that, in the history of the race, the first spoken word must have preceded the first heard word, at least by a fraction of a second. But this is not very relevant, nor is it certainly true. A noise may

---

[2] An alternative to Hull's "fractional anticipatory goal response" is *the conditionable component(s) of the total response to the unconditioned stimulus.*

have meaning to the hearer, but not to the utterer; in that case it is a heard
word but not a spoken word. . . . Friday's footprint had "meaning" to
Robinson Crusoe but not for Friday. However that may be, we shall do
better to avoid the very hypothetical parts of anthropology that would be
involved, and take up the learning of language as it can be observed in the
human infant of the present. And in the human infant as we know him,
definite reactions to the words of others come much earlier than the power
of uttering words himself. (p. 48)

One certainly cannot fault Russell for deciding, in his analysis of
the understanding or meaning aspect of language learning, to stick to
observations which can be endlessly verified in contemporaneous
families where there is a small child, instead of falling back upon what
he termed the "very hypothetical parts of anthropology." As I have previously indicated, debates on the historical origin of language have often
proven quite unproductive.

The question of where and how man got his words, especially those
whose origins lie far back in racial experience, has occasioned more interest
and speculation, probably, than any other single aspect of the whole language problem. In fact, so much attention was being paid to this matter in
Europe during the eighteenth and nineteenth centuries that the French
Academy of Science passed a rule formally excluding any more communications on this topic in its transactions. (Mowrer, 1954, p. 676)

There is, however, one theory of language origination which would
have served Russell's purposes very nicely and would have extricated
him rather neatly from the dilemma in which he found himself inad-
vertently involved. There is now extensive evidence, some of which will
be reviewed presently, that the so-called "bow-wow" or onomatopoietic
theory as to how language developed in the historical sense has much to
recommend it. It holds, quite simply, that many of protoman's first
words were merely imitations of *natural sounds* which already *had*
meaning for him and his fellows, so that we may say, in keeping with
Russell's general thesis, that word meaning and understanding
(remember that, after all, "words" are just particular sounds or noises)
did indeed "come first," even historically speaking, and word reproduction later. This process of word derivation can *still* occasionally be seen
operating in already well-developed language systems. A few years ago,
for example, a Turkish student told me the following story. Early in
World War II, certain Turkish cities were occasionally bombed by
squadrons of German airplanes. At that time, Turkish peasants had no
word for "airplane," but they coined the term "gurgur," onomato-
poetically, from the sound which a formation of propeller planes make
at high altitudes. As will be indicated later in this chapter, it is possible
to reproduce an experimental analogue of this process in laboratory ani-

mals, and it is also congruent with what I believe to be the correct
theory of the process whereby small children learn to reproduce and *use*
words which are already well established in their "mother tongue." (cf.
Chapters 4 and 5). We turn now to Russell's discussion of this latter
phenomenon.

Amplification of Russell's Analysis of the Reproduction of Words, as Distinct from Their Understanding, by Small Children

Immediately after the passage last quoted from Russell, this author
goes on to assert:

> Saying a word is more difficult than [understanding it], except in the
> case of a few simple sounds which infants make before they know that they
> are words, such as "ma-ma" and "da-da." These two are among the many
> random sounds that all babies make. When a child says "ma-ma" in the
> presence of his mother by chance, she thinks he knows what this noise
> means, and she shows pleasure in ways that are agreeable to the infant.
> Gradually, in accordance with Thorndike's law of effect, he acquires the
> habit of making this noise in the presence of his mother, because in these
> circumstances the consequences are pleasant. But it is only a very small
> number of words that are acquired in this way. *The great majority of
> words are acquired by imitation, combined with the association between
> thing and word which the parents deliberately establish in the early stages
> (after the very first stage).* It is obvious that using words oneself involves
> something over and above the association between the sound of the word
> and its meaning. Dogs understand many words, and infants understand far
> more than they can say. The infant has to discover that it is possible and
> profitable to make noises like those which he hears. (This statement must
> not be taken quite literally, or it would be too intellectualistic.) He would
> never discover this if he did not make noises at random, without the inten-
> tion of talking. He then gradually finds that he can make noises like those
> which he hears, and in general the consequences of doing so are pleasant.
> Parents are pleased, desired objects can be obtained, and—perhaps most
> important of all—there is a sense of power in making intended instead of
> accidental noises. But in this whole process there is nothing essentially dif-
> ferent from the learning of mazes by rats. It resembles this form of learn-
> ing, rather than that of Köhler's apes, because no amount of intelligence
> could enable the child to find out the names of things—as in the case of the
> mazes, experience is the only possible guide. [Italics added.]
>
> When a person knows how to speak, the conditioning proceeds in the
> opposite direction to that which operates in understanding what others say.
> The reaction of a person who knows how to speak, when he notices a cat,
> is naturally to utter the word "cat"; he may not actually do so, but he will
> have a reaction leading towards this act, even if for some reason the overt
> act does not take place. It is true that he may utter the word "cat" because

he is "thinking" about a cat, not actually seeing one. This, however, as we shall see in a moment, is merely one further stage in the process of conditioning. The use of single words, as opposed to sentences, is wholly explicable, so far as I can see, by the principles which apply to animals in mazes.

Certain philosophers who have a prejudice against analysis contend that the sentence comes first and single words later. In this connection they always allude to the language of the Patagonians, which their opponents, of course, do not know. We are given to understand that a Patagonian can understand you if you say "I am going to fish in the lake behind the western hill", but that he cannot understand the word "fish" by itself. (This instance is imaginary, but it represents the sort of thing that is asserted.) Now it may be that Patagonians are peculiar—indeed they must be, or they would not choose to live in Patagonia. But certainly infants in civilized countries do not behave in this way, with the exception of Thomas Carlyle and Lord Macaulay. The former never spoke before the age of three, when hearing his younger brother cry, he said, "What ails wee Jock?" Lord Macaulay "learned in suffering what he taught in song," for, having spilt a cup of hot tea over himself at a party, he began his career as a talker by saying to his hostess, after a time, "Thank you, Madam, the agony is abated." These, however, are facts about biographers, not about the beginnings of speech in infancy. In all children that have been carefully observed, sentences come much later than single words.

Children, at first, are limited as to their power of producing sounds, and also by the paucity of their learned associations. I am sure the reason why "ma-ma" and "da-da" have the meaning they have is that they are sounds which infants make spontaneously at an early age, and are therefore convenient as sounds to which the elders can attach meaning. In the very beginning of speech there is no imitation of grownups, but the discovery that sounds made spontaneously have agreeable results. Imitation comes later, after the child has discovered that sounds can have this quality of "meaning." The type of skill involved is throughout exactly similar to that involved in learning to play a game or ride a bicycle. (pp. 50–52)

I am persuaded that the foregoing quotation from Russell is right in almost every particular. Let us begin with the assertion that "it is only a very small number of words that are acquired . . . in accordance with Thorndike's law of effect." My wife and I soon discovered that our own first child, when she was two or three months old, was a great little babbler; and in the course of her verbal play, she would often say: "da, da, da, da, da." So my wife and I, both being psychologists, decided to carry out a little "experiment." We resolved that whenever our little girl was lying down and, in the course of her random verbalization, made the da-da sound, we would pick her up and play with her for a while. As might have been predicted, it was not long until we could say, casually, to our friends: "Oh, by the way, Linda is learning to talk." They would say: "But you're kidding, she isn't more than three or four months old, is she?" We would reply, "That's right! She's just three

and a half months old, but she's nevertheless learning to talk." At
which point we would go get the child or, if we were already holding
her, we would lay her down on a flat surface (preferably a hard one,
like the surface of a table); and, sure enough, she would presently begin
to wriggle and out would come, clear as could be, "Oh, da, da." We
don't know how she happened to pick up the "Oh," but the occurrence
of the utterance was, to us, otherwise no mystery. It did not in the least
mean "father," but rather: "Won't someone please pick me up?"—a
request that could quite as well have been made, if the "reinforcement
contingencies" had been different, by touching her left eye or wiggling
her little finger (cf. Chapter 5).

Thorndike, on the basis of his very extensive work on trial-and-
error learning (problem solving) with laboratory animals, in a book
entitled *Man and His Work* (1943), tried to found a general theory of
language acquisition on this type of learning. In a chapter entitled "The
Origin of Language," Thorndike wrote:

> It is perhaps time to attach a name to the theory which I am expound-
> ing. Let us save everybody trouble by giving it an opprobrious name from
> the start! Since it relies on the miscellaneous vocal play of man instead of
> his alleged mimetic or emotional utterances, it could be called the "babble-
> babble" theory. Since it starts with languages private to single persons, and
> progresses gradually toward speech in the full speaker–hearer relation
> (which, indeed, my expositin has not yet reached) it could be called the
> "onety-twoty" theory. Since it depends on successive selections of chance
> variations in sound–reality connections, it could be called the "chancy-
> chance" or "luck-luck" theory. Or we may combine its two main dynamic
> features and call it the "babble-luck" theory. (p. 97)

In other words, what Thorndike is saying here is that, in the
process of *babbling,* children have the *luck* to make sounds which are
enough like standard words in the society (or speech community) into
which they have been born so that they are rewarded and thus learn, on
the basis of Thorndike's general theory of learning by trial and error
(or, more precisely, trial, error, and success), eventually to acquire as
many specific word responses as the individual's communicative needs
demand.

It is astonishing how widely Thorndike's trial-and-error conception
of language learning has been accepted, particularly in the field of
speech and speech correction; but I fully agree with Russell in rejecting
this as adequate to account either for the original development of language in protoman or by the offspring of present-day *Homo sapiens.*
Thorndike had no theory of imitation—in fact, didn't even "believe" in
it, except as a very peculiar "instinct" limited to parrots and a few other

avian species. On page 12 of the opus cited, Thorndike sums up his positions in this matter by saying:

> Very little of it [human behavior in general] is (in my opinion) learned by a faculty of imitation in the sense of a tendency to make sounds as a result of hearing them made by man, and to make movements as a result of seeing them made by man.

Russell is, it seems, far closer to the facts when he takes the diametrically opposite position and maintains that, at least as far as verbal behavior is concerned, *most* of it is learned by imitation, and comparatively little by trial and error. However, in 1927, Russell himself had no really adequate theory of imitation; and since imitation had commonly been supposed to be an "instinct," and instincts were going out of fashion, there was a greater tendency to go along with Thorndike (who stressed individual learning) than with Russell, who, tacitly at least, seemed to be invoking the then generally unacceptable concept of instinct. Fortunately, we now have a way of accounting for imitative behavior strictly in terms of learning principles; so there is no longer any need to shy away from Russell's general position on this account.

A Learning-Theory Derivation of Imitation

In a chapter entitled "On the Psychology of 'Talking Birds'—A Contribution to Language and Personality Theory" which appeared in my *Learning Theory and Personality Dynamics* (Mowrer, 1950), I have outlined what is known as the *autistic* conception of imitation (see also Chapter 4) as follows:

> Of the numerous problems which seem feasible of attack with talking birds, both at the observational and at the experimental level, the following may be cited as illustrative. Although the children in every well-ordered household learn language as a matter of course, it is little short of miraculous that they should do so; for language learning involves a remarkable feat, the feat of learning to reproduce, as responses, certain of the noises which impinge upon them as stimuli. Because language learning is such a commonplace, we are likely not be be properly impressed with the magnitude of the accomplishment which it represents. We say, of course, that this accomplishment is "due to imitation," but to name a process is not to explain it.
> Darwin stressed the expressive function of the infant's early sounds and believed that from this emotionally toned behavior articulate speech somehow evolved [see above quotation from Russell, on pp. 96–97]. Others have sought to solve the problem—but have succeeded only in glossing it over—by positing an "instinct of imitation." E. B. Holt attacked the prob-

lem more squarely, but his reflex-circle principle falls far short of providing a really satisfactory solution. That language is learned on a strictly trial-and-error basis has been suggested, but this theory, too, has important weaknesses. Still other hypotheses have been put forward, but they are even less complete, and give us no really integrative principle.

On the basis of many converging lines of evidence, it now appears that the most plausible explanation of the first stage of language learning [in the sense of word reproduction and use] lies along lines quite different from those usually suggested—lines which can be clearly traced only against the background of modern behavior theory and clinical theory. The essence of the hypothesis here proposed is that babies and birds alike first learn to reproduce the conventionalized noises which we call words, not because they can either understand or use those words in any ordinary sense, but because of what is, at first, a purely autistic function. Both birds and babies, according to this hypothesis, make their first efforts at reproducing words because these words *sound good* to them.

It is very generally agreed, in all human societies, that a good mother is one who is loving and attentive to the needs of her child, and it is also a common expectation that mothers will coo and make other gentle noises when caring for their young. These two practices—loving care combined with vocalization—presumably create in the infant a predisposition to react with emotional satisfaction, first to the vocalizations of others and later to his own vocalizations. Since the sound of the mother's voice has often been accompanied by comfort-giving measures, it is to be expected that when the child, alone and uncomfortable, hears his own voice, it will likewise have a consoling, comforting effect. In this way it may be supposed that the infant will be rewarded for his own first babbling and jabbering, without any necessary reference to the effects they produce on others.

Gradually, from what the infant probably perceives as an inarticulate murmuring or warbling on the part of the mother, certain specific, recognizable words emerge which are especially welcome and reassuring, so that when, in the course of random vocalization, the child hits upon a sound that is recognizably like a sound which the mother (or possibly the father) makes, the child is motivated to reproduce that noise over and over and to try to perfect it, since a perfect reproduction of it is more satisfying than is an imperfect one. If one wishes to call this a kind of self-contained trial-and-error learning, there can be no objection, provided we remember that it has been preceded by important emotional conditioning [i.e., acquisition of secondary-reinforcing properties, in the terminology of contemporary learning theory] and that the success of the infant's efforts at vocalization is not necessarily dependent upon the reactions of others. It is the child's own reactions to the sounds he makes which seem all-important at this stage.

In suggesting that the utterance of word-like noises occurs first on a purely autistic basis, I mean, specifically, that when a child or a bird is lonely, frightened, hungry, cold, or merely bored, it can comfort and divert itself by making noises which have previously been associated with comfort and diversion. These sounds have become "sweet music"; and they are reproduced, not because of their social effectiveness, but because of the intrapsychic satisfaction they provide. Later, once particular sounds have been learned on this autistic basis, the stage is set for them to *function instrumentally,* in connection with the child's (or bird's) interactions with the external world; but this appears to be a second stage in language learning, not the first one. (pp. 698–700)

The only two adumbrations of this way of conceptualizing the language learning of infants of which I am aware are the following:

> Since the mother talks to the child while administering primary rewards such as food, the sound of the human voice should acquire secondary reward value. Because the child's voice produces sounds similar to that of his mother's, some of this acquired reward value generalizes to it. . . . From this hypothesis it may be deduced that children talked to while being fed and otherwise cared for should exhibit more iterative and imitative babbling than children not talked to while being rewarded. (Miller & Dollard, 1941, p. 247)
>
> The infant pattern gradually becomes more like that of the speech he hears about him, elements foreign to the culture into which he is born dropping out and those indigenous to it becoming more prominent. Since a large part of this 'acculturation' occurs before the child can actually be said to speak, it appears that the infant in its babbling is differentially reinforced for making parentlike sounds—and much of this reinforcement is probably self-administered, i.e., the child obtains greater pleasure from produced sounds that facsimilate those heard about him. (Osgood, 1950)[3]

Here Osgood is referring, he says, to events (consisting largely of babbling) that occur at the age of about five months, before "true language" (presumably meaning the use of words and sentences) has appeared.

Interestingly enough, in the 1927 book already cited, Russell at least skirts the conception of imitation as a learning process of the kind just described. As already indicated, we are in full agreement with his description of the process whereby infants learn to *understand* the meanings of words; and we also concur with his conclusion that Thorndike's "babble-luck" theory does not provide an adequate explanation of how infants learn to reproduce and *use* conventional word sounds. And repeatedly Russell notes that the process of *imitation* must be invoked to explain the process by which young children learn to *speak.* Although Russell did not understand the phenomenon of secondary reinforcement and was unaware of certain other refinements which were shortly to be forthcoming in the psychology of learning which are essential to an adequate theory of imitation, it should nevertheless be

---

[3] This quotation, which appears in footnote 26 on p. 709 of "On the Psychology of 'Talking Birds'" (1950), was taken from an early draft of Osgood's *Method and Theory in Experimental Psychology,* which was not published until 1953. The published version of the foregoing statement (pp. 686–687) is slightly but not significantly different.

noted that he made statements (albeit somewhat inexplicit and ambiguous ones) such as these:

> The infant has to discover that it is possible and profitable to make noises like those which he hears. (This statement must not be taken quite literally, or it would be too intellectualistic.) He would never discover this if he did not make noises at random, without the intention of talking. He then gradually finds that *he can make noises like those which he hears, and in general the consequences of doing so are pleasant* [i.e., are autistically or secondarily reinforcing]. (p. 15, italics added)

Russell then goes on to say:

> Parents are pleased, desired objects can be obtained, and—perhaps most important of all—there is a sense of power in making intended instead of accidental noises. But in this whole process there is nothing essentially different from the learning of mazes by rats. (p. 15)

It is clear that Russell is here failing to make an important distinction, namely, that between *autistic* satisfaction and *instrumental* power or gratification. But the introduction of this distinction, far from weakening his argument, materially strengthens and clarifies it. And when he says that "this whole process [of language learning in at least its rudimentary aspects] is nothing essentially different from the learning of mazes by rats," he is again on sound grounds, although he perhaps could not then have cited much empirical evidence for his position. As I have argued elsewhere (Mowrer, 1960a,b), habits in general importantly involve secondary reinforcement or autistic processes ("hope"); and an experimental analogue will presently be cited, wherein a rat learns to press a bar on an exlusively autistic (secondary reinforcement) basis, without any extrinsic (primary) reinforcement whatever. The process of "putting through," such as is commonly involved in teaching a dog to "shake hands," further establishes the communality between a child's learning to reproduce the significant sounds he hears around him and rudimentary animal learning principles (Mowrer, 1954, 1960a).

Evidence for (and against) the Autism Theory of Imitation, with Special Reference to the Problem of Language Acquisition

Although Thorndike's views, as set forth in preceding sections of this chapter were at one time the predominant ones in books on speech and speech correction, and in such scant space as was devoted to language learning in general psychology textbooks, the autism theory has, by and large, been generously received. On the basis of preliminary presentations of this theory, before its full elaboration in 1950, an eminent American psychologist (Professor Percival M. Symonds) had responded, in a personal letter, as follows:

> There is no doubt that your dynamic theory of the origin of spoken language has considerable merit. It fits in well with dynamic theory in general. However, I wonder if you shouldn't push it back a step or two. As I understand your theory, it is that the infant's first language sounds come at a period of frustration and are the infant's attempts to recapture, in this somewhat symbolic fashion at least, satisfactions or reactions that were coincident with previous satisfactions. The sounds are in the nature of a conditioned reaction in the frustrating situation. Isn't it necessary, however, to introduce the further factor that in the frustrating state the infant is afraid of loss or separation and the sounds are an attempt to recapture, at least symbolically, the presence of the mother who is the source of the satisfaction? This sort of dynamic explanation as an attempt to avoid anxiety has been used to explain other similar phenomena.

In the 1950 chapter on language which has already been cited, I responded to these observations as follows:

> Perhaps the most exact way of formulating this notion is as follows. The bird (baby) discovers that when it is alone it may get hungry, thirsty, cold, hurt. On the other hand, when the trainer is present, these discomforts vanish. Therefore the presence of the trainer is an important stimulus element in the total situation, serving to convert it from situation-in-which-I-may-be-uncomfortable (helpless) to situation-in-which-everything-will-be-all-right. In this way the bird will be rewarded by the appearance of the trainer and disturbed by his departure, even though none of the primary drives mentioned is actually operative at the moment. It is fully understandable that, when alone, the bird should try to reduce its apprehensions by reproducing the trainer symbolically, i.e., by making his noises (in somewhat the same manner, perhaps, as human beings are said to "whistle in the dark"). As we have seen, creatures which are less talented vocally must use something more tangible for this purpose, e.g., the coveralls on which little Gua became so dependent [Kellogg & Kellogg, 1933]. Cf. Lair's (1949) remarks concerning the "hallucination wish mechanism used by the child in the first half of the first year to bring back or recall the nurse who had sole charge of her and was a substitute mother" (p. 255). (Mowrer, 1950, p. 726)

And in the September, 1969 issue of the journal, *Developmental Psychology,* there is an article by Vivian Paskal entitled "The Value of Imitative Behavior" which concludes as follows:

> These findings indicate that though children are likely to imitate behaviors which have been directly associated with reinforcing events, they also show some tendency to imitate behaviors which have been indirectly associated with those reinforcing events. The data give some support for the notion that the process which activates this indirect association is a form of mediated generalization.

Support for the second feature of the Mowrerian hypothesis is clearly seen in the significant positive correlation between subjects' difference scores and their particular imitation scores, when those subjects had been exposed to a nurturant model. Those subjects for whom the model's particular stereotyped behaviors had acquired greater secondary reinforcing value were also those subjects who imitated those behaviors more often. This finding was statistically significant among Grade 1 subjects, but there was only a tendency for such a correlation among Grade 2 subjects. The fact that there is a substantial difference between the data of Grade 1 and Grade 2 subjects leads to some interesting notions about developmental changes in imitative processes. (p. 468)

There is addtional evidence which indicates that susceptibility to classical conditioning decreases with age (e.g., Razran, 1933). Moreover, White (1965) has analyzed many of the data concerning learning among young children and has suggested that between 5 and 7 years of age there is a rather clear-cut change in the child's learning processes. White (1965) characterized this change as one in which "the cognitive level of operation depends critically upon the inhibition of associative function, or at least the response, which the association function is capable of determining." (p. 213)

In summary, the data available from the present study permit the conclusion that the behaviors which children imitate are those which have reinforcing value for them. The process by which these behaviors acquire value may change from younger to older children. Among younger children, one mechanism involved appears to be that of classical conditioning. Among older children, the same mechanism may still function, but its effectiveness appears to be somewhat attenuated by other factors. Specifically, it is suggested that the age of the children interacted with the effectiveness of nurturance as an unconditioned stimulus within the classical conditioning paradigm. (p. 469)

Between the Symonds letter (written some 20 years ago) and the very recent article by Vivian Paskal, there has been a succession of evaluations, both theoretical and empirical, too numerous to mention. (For a review, see Patterson, 1968, pp. 345–353.) But one line of inquiry, involving research with myna birds, should be specifically mentioned. Grosslight (personal correspondence, but see also Grosslight & Zaynor, 1967) found that although it was easy enough to teach birds of this kind to "talk" if they were kept as "pets" around the laboratory, they did not learn to repeat, "autistically," words which were presented to them just prior to primary reinforcement in sound-insulated compartments somthing like oversized "Skinner boxes."

Walters (1967) has described some research reported by Foss and adds a commentary:

Foss (1964) tested Mowrer's (1950) secondary-reinforcement hypothesis that talking birds imitate only sounds that have been associated with primary or secondary reinforcement by playing whistles to myna birds

in both the presence of food and its absence. He found that imitative vocalizations occurred equally readily under both conditions and arrived at the
following conclusion: "The result of this experiment is disappointing.
Mowrer's theory was welcome in that it showed that this particular kind of
imitation learning could be explained in terms of accepted principles of
learning. One is left with the unsatisfactory alternative of saying that myna
birds have a tendency to imitate." (p. 88)

There is ample evidence that imitative learning may occur in the
absence of rewards to the observer (Bandura, 1962, 1965; Bandura &
Walters, 1963). In fact, Mowrer (1960b) has himself suggested alternatives
to his secondary-reinforcement theory. The sole alternative to a secondary-
reinforcement theory is certainly not to postulate an innate tendency or
"instinct" to imitate. (pp. 1–2)

A few years ago, I learned that Prof. Robert L. Crossette, of
Hofstra University, was in process of initiating extensive research on the
problem of autistic imitation with myna birds as subjects. In response to
a recent letter of inquiry, Prof. Crossette replied (March 20, 1969), in
part, as follows:

About seven years ago I began a study supported eventually by NSF
that was concerned with determining the conditions under which Mynas
come to imitate human speech phonemes; in addition I desired to test
Mynas' capacity to discriminate various speech phonemes in a manner
similar to, or different from, that of humans. Incidentally, I became
interested in this project after reading one of your excellent and stimulating
papers.

Unfortunately, I have very little data to report. Apparatus problems
immediately arose and since I had just started an animal lab here at
Hofstra, our equipment and other resources were almost non-existent. To
make matters worse, I had volunteered in my proposal to NSF to construct
most of the electronic equipment myself, and thereby construct the Bird
Lab as well. While trying to solve these problems, I began to use Mynas
for a comparative analysis of successive discrimination reversal (SDR)
learning—the success of this latter project was sufficiently rewarding that I
neglected to devote my full time and energy to completing the phonemic
discrimination and imitation study with Mynas. I am currently trying to
resume this project, however, especially since NSF deserves a terminal
report long overdue, and also because I find it intrinsically interesting.

From our abortive study we have learned that Mynas are very good
experimental subjects, though rather messy and sensitive to food depriva-
tions. They are also a very "bright" bird and learn discriminations
rapidly. From the spectrographic analysis of vowel sounds initiated by a
couple of our birds we can conclude that Myna acoustic patterns for at
least one class of phonemes, e.g. "e", cannot be distinguished from that of
humans.

We attempted to train seven or eight subjects to imitate speech
phonemes constructed from a machine in Haskin's Lab, under the supervi-
sion of Dr. Al Libeman from the University of Connecticut, that were
repetitively played into their individual and isolated home cages. Only two

of these birds ever learned to imitate. At that point, this project was set
aside for the time being as I became submerged by the comparative
vertebrate studies I had previously initiated.

I am sorry that it is not possible to provide you with any written
reports of our attempted research with Mynas; but as this project is slowly
resumed I will send you any information that develops, if you wish. If I
can be of any service to you in the matter of Myna research, please let me
know.

Thus, in all of the studies of which I am aware in which an
attempt has thus far been made, under rigorous laboratory conditions,
to verify my inferences (see also the references made earlier to Miller
and Dollard, 1941, and to Osgood, 1953) concerning the process
whereby certain species of birds learn to reproduce (imitate) human
vocalizations, negative results have been obtained. However, two special
considerations need to be taken into account. The first of these is that
myna birds are very sociable creatures and do not like to be placed in
isolation. So it may well be that putting them in soundproof boxes,
where they can neither hear nor see other birds or human beings, may
have a critically inhibiting effect upon all vocalization. I recall, many
years ago, having kept two young myna birds together for some weeks
and then separating them. One of the birds became very apathetic, ate
very little, and gave all the external signs of being "depressed" for
several weeks. So I think it not unlikely that isolation, for experimental
purposes, may have a generally inhibiting and subduing effect upon
these creatures.

Also, the "wolf whistle," which one so often hears pet myna birds
emit, is not I think, a learned response at all but a part of their native
vocal repertoire. At least I have never seen a myna which did not make
this sound spontaneously, if under circumstances which were at all
familiar and congenial; so this fact casts some doubt on the research
which Foss has reported. These interpretations are put forth very tenta-
tively, but I believe they have some plausibility.

Also there are, as I have already indicated by the references to
Symonds and to Walters, many other lines of evidence which support
the autism theory of word learning; and unlimited empirical confirmation of this sort of learning can be obtained from our favorite laboratory
subject, the white rat. As early as 1954, in the paper entitled "The
Psychologist Looks at Language," I described a rather dramatic
example of this type of learning:

As is well known, any sound (or other stimulus) which is associated
with primary satisfaction tends to acquire secondary reinforcing properties.
Therefore, as I have tried to show more fully elsewhere (Mowrer, 1950b,
1952; see also Miller & Dollard, 1941, pp. 81, 139, and 277), if a living

organism can itself reproduce such a sound, or a reasonable approximation thereof, the particular responses involved will get secondarily, or "autistically," reinforced and will tend to become a part of the organism's response repertoire. For other organisms with similar background experiences, such sounds, when thus reproduced, will have much the same meaning as the sources by which they were originally produced and may thus serve for signaling or even symbolic purposes. . . . As I have indicated in the studies cited, such a notion accounts relatively well for what we know about word learning by babies (and also by "talking birds") from adults who already have command of these sounds; and it also provides, as just suggested, a not improbable conception of how prehistoric man may, in turn, have acquired at least certain verbal forms from nature (cf. p. 95). Of the various classical theories of word origination, the one most closely related to this scheme is obviously the "onomatopoetic" or so-called "bow-wow" theory.

This conception of word genesis can be illustrated in a crude but probably valid way as follows: Suppose that just before or as we give a laboratory rat a bit of food, we sound a tone of standard pitch and intensity. This tone, as we know from numerous studies, will take on secondary reinforcing properties. And if the rat could, *with its own vocal cords,* make a noise reasonably like the tone, we would predict, on the basis of principles already cited, that it would soon begin to do so. Unhappily, in view of the severe limitations on vocalization in the rat which have already been mentioned (see Chapter 3), we cannot expect this to happen. However, if we place the electronic oscillator used by the experimenter in producing the tone at the disposal of the rat, on the basis of movements which the rat can easily make, we should not be in the least surprised if the rat, under these circumstances, is disposed to "make" the sound. So let us, after the rat is well trained with respect to tone associated with food, make a Skinner bar available, depression of which will have the same action, with respect to producing the tone, as the telegraph key previously used by the experimenter. *Figure 2* (p. 108) shows the behavior of a hungry rat toward such a bar during a 20-minute period, in the course of which bar pressing produced no food, only the "promise" of it in the form of the tone and the secondary reinforcement it has acquired from prior pairings with food. How energetically a rat, trained in the manner just described, will continue using the tone as a signal to the experimenter, if the experimenter will only cooperate, is suggested in *Figure 3* (p. 109). Here will be seen what happens if, when the rat pushes the bar and produces the tone, another organism reponds to it as a sign that the rat wants food—and obliges. A stimulus which was originally made by the environment to the rat is thus "taken over" by the rat and "made back" to the environment; and if another organism will respond thereto, it becomes a "social act," or true sign. Of course, on the basis of trial-and-error learning alone, without the presence of a signal of any sort, a rat would eventually learn to press the bar if it produced food. But the precipitous nature of the learning shown in Fig. 3 suggests, and experimentation reported elsewhere (Mowrer, 1950, ch. 11) confirms, that the intermediation of a stimulus with previously acquired secondary reinforcing properties produces a performance markedly superior to what can be expected on the basis of trial and error alone. (Mowrer, 1954, pp. 678–679)

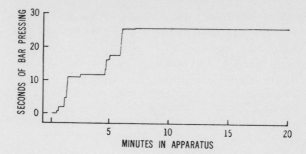

Figure 2. Graphic record of bar pressing by rat, where this performance produced a tone which had been previously associated with food. The bar-pressing "habit" was thus learned solely on the basis of the secondary reinforcement provided by the tone. As the secondary reinforcement extinguished, the animal ceased to press the bar. In this situation the experimenter may be said first to have made the signal to the rat as a means of indicating that it was going to get food. The rat, when given an opportunity to push a bar which turned on the tone, made the signal "back" to the experimenter, but the experimenter did not respond (cf. Figure 3).

In summary, the foregoing analysis suggests that although there is a pervasive tendency for instrumental behavior to degenerate into gestures, such contractions do not seem to have provided a common basis for spoken words. A more likely hypothesis is that sounds naturally associated with gratifying experiences were, by the mechanisms indicated, "copied" by protoman and thus gave rise to at least the beginnings of language as we know it today.[4]

Perhaps it should be added that what is said here is not intended as in any sense providing a completely adequate theory of the origin of articulate speech. But it is a way of thinking about the problem of word origin which meshes comfortably with learning theory and has, apparently, also some plausibility with respect to what we know about language itself.

Here is clear, easily reproduced, and dramatic evidence for the operation of the mechanism assumed to underly autistic, imitative learning. And the theory involved is all the more striking because it not only offers a simple and plausible explanation of how infants learn to reproduce individual elements of their "mother tongue" from their mothers, fathers, and other caretakers, but also how mankind may have first learned to "speak," thousands of years ago, by reproducing sounds provided by "Mother Nature." Once the value of such "words" had become apparent to early man, he undoubtedly set about industriously "manufacturing" more of them, in much the same way that, after he

[4] The mechanism whereby "bad" sounds were copied and used as words is obviously different and, probably, more complex. This problem invites further inquiry. See Stewart's references (see p. 25) to the word "ouch" (Mowrer, 1954, p. 680).

had first become a tool usuer, he invented and made an ever increasing
variety of new tools and material artifacts of various kinds. But man's
first words, our theory would suggest, developed in the more automatic,
less self-conscious manner that has been suggested and documented.

It would have been gratifying if the myna bird research had turned

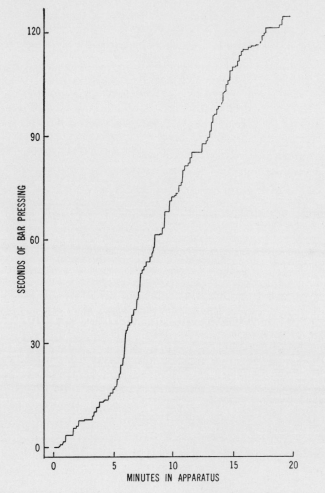

Figure 3. Graphic record of bar pressing by a rat where this performance produced a
tone previously associated with food, and caused the experimenter to provide food. After
several trials, there was something like an "insight" (see upward inflection of curve at
about 5 minutes). As the animal became satiated, toward the end of the recording, the
rate of responding declined. In this record we see what happens if an organism learns
the meaning of a signal, is then permitted to make that signal, and some other organism
responds appropriately thereto. Trial and error learning is much slower.

out more clearly positive; but despite the rather mysterious debacles that have occurred in this connection, the autism theory, as it applies to both the original evolution of language and the far more rapid learning of language by individual children today, still has, I believe, much to commend it, and is not seriously challenged, in scope or explanatory power, by any alternative conception.

Russell's Approach to the Psychology of the Sentence

We return now, once again, to the Russell chapter on Language in his 1927 book, *Philosophy*, for the purpose of examining his discussion of sentences and sentence formation, as distinct from but not unrelated to the understanding and use of individual words. This, in my estimation, is the weakest part of the Russell chapter, which is all the more surprising in light of Russell's interest in propositions and their place in logic and mathematics. Russell's brief, and very far from adequate, treatment of the psychology of sentences follows:

> Hitherto we have spoken of single words, and among these we have considered only those that can naturally be employed singly. A child uses single words of a certain kind before constructing sentences; but some words presuppose sentences. No one would use the word "paternity" until after using such sentences as "the fire makes me warm." Sentences introduce new considerations, and are not quite so easily explained on behaviourist lines. Philosophy, however, imperatively demands an understanding of sentences, and we much therefore consider them.
>
> As we found earlier, all infants outside Patagonia begin with single words, and only achieve sentences later. But they differ enormously in the speed with which they advance from the one to the other. My own two children adopted entirely different methods. My son first practiced single letters, then single words, and only achieved correct sentences of more than three or four words at the age of two [years] and three months. My daughter, on the contrary, advanced very quickly to sentences, in which there was hardly ever an error. At the age of eighteen months, when supposed to be sleeping, she was overheard saying to herself: "Last year I used to dive off the diving-board, I *did*." Of course "last year" was merely a phrase repeated without understanding. And no doubt the first sentences used by children are always repetitions, unchanged, of sentences they have heard used by others. Such cases raise no new principle not involved in the learning of words. What does raise a new principle is the power of putting together known words into a sentence which has never been heard, but which expresses correctly what the infant wishes to convey. This involves the power to manipulate form and structure. It does not of course involve the apprehension of form or structure in the abstract, any more than the use of the word "man" involves apprehension of a universal. But it does not involve a causal connection between the form of the stimulus and the

form of the reaction. An infant very soon learns to be differently affected by
the statement "cats eat mice," from the way he would be affected by the
statement "mice eat cats"; and not much later he learns to make one of
these statements rather than the other. In such a case, the cause (in hearing) or the effect (in speaking) is a whole sentence. It may be that one part
of the environment is sufficient to cause one word, while another is sufficient to cause another, but it is only the two parts in their relation that can
cause the whole sentence. Thus wherever sentences come in we have a
causal relation between two complex facts, namely the fact asserted and the
sentence asserting it; the facts as wholes enter into the cause and effect relation, which cannot be explained wholly as compounded of relations
between their parts. Moreover, as soon as the child has learned to use correctly relational words, such as "eat," he has become capable of being
causally affected by a relational feature of the environment, which involves
a new degree of complexity not required for the use of ordinary nouns.

Thus the correct use of relational words, i.e., of sentences, involves
what may be correctly termed "perception of forms," i.e., it involves a
definite reaction to a stimulus which is a form. Suppose, for example, that
a child has learnt to say that one thing is "above" another when this is in
fact the case. The stimulus to the use of the word "above" is a relational
feature of the environment, and we may say that this feature is "perceived"
since it produces a definite reaction. It may be said that the relation *above*
is not very like the word "above". That is true; but the same is true of
ordinary physical objects. A stone, according to the physicists, is not at all
like what we see when we look at it, and yet we may be correctly said to
"perceive" it. This, however, is to anticipate. The definite point which has
emerged is that, when a person can use sentences correctly, that is a proof
of sensitiveness to formal or relational stimuli.

The structure of a sentence asserting some relational fact, such as
"this is above that," or "Brutus killed Caesar," differs in an important
respect from the structure of the fact which it asserts. *Above* is a relation
which holds between two terms "this" and "that"; but the *word* "above"
is not a relation. In the sentence the relation is the temporal order of the
words (or the spatial order, if they are written), but the word for the relation is itself as substantial as the other words. In inflected languages, such
as Latin, the order of the words is not necessary to show the "sense" of the
relation; but in uninflected languages this is the only way of distinguishing
between "Brutus killed Caesar" and "Caesar killed Brutus." Words are
physical phenomena, having spatial and temporal relations; we make use
of these relations in our verbal symbolisation of other relations, chiefly too
show the "sense" of the relation, i.e., whether it goes from A to B or from
B to A.

A great deal of the confusion about relations which has prevailed in
practically all philosophies comes from the fact, which we noticed just now,
that relations are indicated, not by other relations, but by words which, in
themselves, are just like other words. Consequently, in thinking about relations, we constantly hover between the unsubstantiality of the relation itself
and the substantiality of the word. Take, say, the fact that lightning
precedes thunder. If we were to express this by a language closely reproducing the structure of the fact, we should have to say simply: "lightning,

thunder," where the fact that the first word precedes the second means that
what the first word means precedes what the second word means. But even
if we adopted this method for temporal order, we should still need words
for all other relations, because we could not without intolerable ambiguity
symbolise them also by the order of our words. All this will be important
to remember when we come to consider the structure of the world, since
nothing but a preliminary study of language will preserve us from being
misled by language in our metaphysical speculations.

Throughout this chapter I have said nothing about the narrative and
imaginative uses of words; I have dealt with words in connection with an
immediate sensible stimulus closely connected with what they mean. The
other uses of words are difficult to discuss until we have considered
memory and imagination. In the present chapter I have confined myself to
a behaviouristic explanation of the effects of words heard as stimuli, and
the causes of words spoken when the words apply to something sensibly
present. I think we shall find that other uses of words, such as the narrative and imaginative, involve only new applications of the law of association. But we cannot develop this theme until we have discussed several
further psychological questions. (pp. 54-57)

Although he does not make explicit reference to it in the foregoing
passages, it is clear from the context that Russell is here verging upon
Gestalt psychology. He refers to *form, structure, wholes,* and *perception,* all common Gestalt terms; and what he seems to be saying alternatively, in a quasi-behavioristic language, is that sentences are what Hull
used to refer to as "compound stimuli," which make finer discriminations possible than does a single, "unqualified" (uncomplicated) stimulus or word. This is an approach to the psychology of sentences which
has been followed by a few subsequent writers; but it does not, I think,
serve to bring us to the heart of the matter.

The key to the psychology of the sentence, as I understand it, is the
phenomenon of *prediction.* Russell does not even use the word, and the
nearest he comes to implying it is when he says that the "temporal
order of words" is somehow relevant to the problem and alludes to
"new applications of the law of association." But I have not been able
to find where Russell later pursues these matters, as he here promises
to do.

The Sentence as a Special Conditioning Device

In the 1954 paper entitled "The Psychologist Looks at Language"
to which reference has already been made, the hypothesis was advanced
that a sentence, basically, is simply a conditioning device, in which the
subject serves as the conditioned stimulus and the *predicate* as the

unconditioned stimulus. No attempt will be made here to review that hypothesis in all its ramification. The article as a whole is available in two different publications (Mowrer, 1954; Jakobovitz & Miron, 1967) and in paraphrase in a book published in 1960 (Mowrer, 1960b; see also Chapter 4 in this book). A few paragraphs show here the general tenor or the argument in the original paper:

> The term "language" has been used in varied contexts. We hear of the language of animals, the language of nature, the language of love. Scientifically, what does the term mean, or, more precisely, what can we most usefully make it mean?
>
> Since the actual historical origin of language is lost beyond any hope of recovery, we are left with only more or less plausible surmises, or fictions. My favorite fiction in this connection is one that has the advantage of giving us, by implication, also a good working definition of language. In his book, *Man, An Autobiography,* George Stewart (1946), professor of English at the University of California, goes about the problem in this way. He supposes that a sound like "Ouch" may have developed as a half-reflexive reaction to sudden pain. And then, says Man, speaking auto-biographically:
>
> "After awhile, when a creature had as good a brain as mine, [such] sounds would be more standardized, and their meanings fitted to the situation. Thus, 'Ouch!' might be used playfully, when the individual felt no real pain, or it might warn a child not to pick up a bee." (pp. 31–32)
>
> "Again [says Man], something which could start more for playfulness than for 'use' might soon come to be of value in other ways. When the band was foraging, one of them might signal his position by calling 'Coo!' like a dove, to let the others know where he was.
>
> "Eventually came the union of the noun-idea and the verb-idea. It may be that a woman came back without her companion, and much troubled. All attempts at gesture failed to tell what had happened. In desperation, naturally enough and yet with a stroke of genius, she cried, 'Coo-ouch!' Then they knew that he who was called Coo had been taken with a sudden pain. Such a combination of two ideas was more than mere expression of personal feeling, and more also than mere pointing-out of an individual. *It was the setting of two ideas into a new relation, and thus the beginning of real language.*" (pp. 32–33, italics added)

The foregoing passages are the relevant ones for our immediate purposes, but they are followed by a brief paragraph which I cannot resist also quoting. The author goes on to say:

> "I like to think that the mothers may first have made and practiced language, and that for some generations the fathers still sat around merely grunting while the mothers chattered happily. At least I notice that girl-babies are still quicker to speak than boy-babies, and that they grow up in general to be more fluent talkers. Besides, there has always been in language a great deal of an illogical and emotional quality. I might say, 'Women invented language, but men invented grammar.'" (p. 33)

With the male ego thus saved, let us return to our inquiry. What Professor Stewart has done here, following Grace DeLaguna (1927) and others, is to make the phenomenon of predication, i.e., the combination of two (or more) signs into a so-called sentence, the bedrock of true language development. Certainly anyone who has been present when a child starts, as we say, "putting words together" know what a momentous event it is. I shall never forget when my own first child, a little girl, met me at the door one evening and excitedly exclaimed: "Pammy-kitty! Pammy-kitty"! I knew that our daughter had visited our little neighbor, Pammy, that afternoon. Therefore, "Pammy-kitty" clearly said, "Pammy (has a) kitten," and the enthusiasm which accompanied the statement also implied the qualified phrase, "which is really quite wonderful." (Mowrer, 1954, p. 661)

Against the background of the foregoing observations, we may now ask the question: What is the psychological *function* of sentences. Or, more simply, what do sentences *do*? The answer here offered to this question in the article cited goes as follows:

In the preceding discussion we have asked and in at least a preliminary way answered, the question: What is the *nature* of a sentence? We have tried, that is to say, to determine what sentences, scientifically considered, *are*. In the present section an attempt will be made to discover what sentences *do*, i.e., how they *work,* psychologically speaking.

There is a very widespread assumption, which we will later have occasion to question, that in the process of spoken or written communication we, somehow, transfer meanings from mind to mind. To communicate, it is suggested, is to make something common, shared; and this something is meaning, understanding, thought, knowledge, ideas, information. One writer puts the matter this way. He says that language, broadly speaking, is characterized by a "transfer of meaning." It is the device "by which men have conveyed significant messages to one another since the dawn of history." . . . "Meaning may be transferred by devices that have nothing to do either with the spoken language or with its written counterpart, and this basic proposition few will be so hardy as to deny" (Pei, 1949, p. 10).

Another writer says:

"When the day arrived on which one person could make such movements, gestures, or grimaces as would lead another person to avoid or to accept an object, that is to say, when a meaning could be transferred to one mind from another, language was created" (Griffith, 1924, pp. 207–208).

And yet another says:

"The philosophy of language, we may then say, to begin with, is concerned with the evaluation of language as a bearer of meanings, as a medium of communication and as a sign or symbol of reality (Urban, 1939, p. 37).

And to this the same writer later adds:

"On the question as to what linguistic fact is not, linguists are in general agreed. They are also agreed upon what it is that constitutes positively linguistic fact. The sine qua non of language is precisely the meaning of which the sounds, the motor processes and tactual sensations, are the bearers" (p. 66).

The first of the writers just cited is a linguist, the second a psychologists, and the third a philosopher. We thus see how widely accepted is the notion that the basic function of language is to transfer or bear meanings from person to person, from mind to mind.

It is not hard to understand how this conception of language has arisen; and, as we shall see later, there is a certain limited sense in which it is undoubtedly correct. But in another, perhaps more basic sense, this notion seems to be wide of the mark and to have been a barrier to the development of a psychology of language with real "power."

Let us explore now, instead, the proposition that in communication we are not transferring meanings from person to person so much as we are transferring meanings *from sign to sign* within a given person, within a single mind. Said a little differently, the suggestion is that in order for us to communicate effectively with another person, he must already have the meanings with which we shall be dealing [i.e., *understand* the words we are using] and that in the communicative act we are, for the most part, merely changing the signs to which particular meanings are attached, merely shifting or transferring meanings from one sign to another. One person, by the use of appropriate words or other signs, can arouse, or "call up," particular meanings in the mind of another person; but he does not transfer or implant them there. The communicative act, in its most salient and significant aspect, lies rather in the combination, juxtaposition, or association of the meanings thus aroused in novel, "informative" ways.

A rudimentary sentence will illustrate this notion. Let us assume that John is telling Charles that: Tom is a thief. It is clear, is it not, that for the intended effect to be produced by this sentence, Charles must already know Tom and must know about thieves and thievery. In other words, Charles must already have meanings attached to the words, *Tom* and *thief*. What, then, is the function of the sentence, "Tom is a thief"? Most simply and most basically, it appears to be this. "Thief" is a sort of "unconditioned stimulus"—we shall later want to qualify this term, but for the moment it will suffice—a sort of "unconditioned stimulus" which can be depended upon to call forth an internal reaction which can be translated into, or defined by, the phrase, "a person who cannot be trusted," one who "takes things, steals." When, therefore, we put the word, or sign, "Tom" in front of the sign "thief," as shown in Fig. 4, we create a situation from which we, as psychologists, can predict a fairly definite result. On the basis of the familiar principle of conditioning, we would expect that some of the reaction evoked by the second sign, "thief," would get shifted to the first sign, "Tom," so that Charles, the hearer of the sentence, would thereafter respond to the word, "Tom," somewhat as he had previously responded to the word, "thief." Thus, in the Steward example of the prehistoric woman saying "Coo-ouch," some of the quality of "ouchness" presumably gets attached to the word, "Coo," and in the case of the little girl saying "Pammy-kitty," the hearer likewise comes to make some part of the "kitty" reaction to "Pammy." The notion under examination in the present paper is that the sentence is, preeminently, a conditioning device,

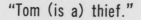

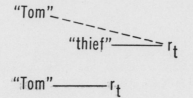

Figure 4. Diagram illustrating how the sentence, "Tom is a thief," can be recast in the vernacular of conditioning theory.

> and that its chief effect is to produce new associations, new learning, just as any other paired presentation of stimuli may do. This position is congruent with the traditional notion that prediction is the essence of language and may indicate, perhaps more precisely than purely linguistic research has done, the basic nature of this phenomenon.
>
> This notion is presented here in a frankly exploratory manner, as a hypothesis which others are invited to consider and test against the prevailing concepts and facts of their particular specialties. The remainder of this paper will be concerned with an examination and elaboration, both theoretical and empirical, of this hypothesis from a psychological point of view, with special reference to learning theory. (Mowrer, 1954, pp. 663–665)

In other for this conception of the psychology of the sentence to be entirely satisfactory, it is necessary to introduce the notion of *mediation* (Figure 5); but in the interests of brevity, no attempt will be made to describe it here. However, there is ample evidence for its reality, as indicated, for example, by the work of Shipley (1933), Osgood (1953), and Staats (1968, 1971) and Staats and Staats (1958).[5]

Although this conception of the way in which a sentence functions, basically, has not been by any means universally accepted by psychologists, it has been received as a reasonable hypothesis and com-

[5] The most extensive recent investigations of mediation have been carried out by Professor James J. Jenkins of the University of Minnesota and co-workers. In the beginning of these researches, some difficulty was encountered in obtaining the phenomenon in question; and for a time the investigators entertained some doubt concerning its reality. But they have since published extensively and positively in this area (Jenkins, 1965a,b; and Jenkins, Foss, & Odom, 1965). In the 1965a reference, Jenkins says: "The proposition [that mediation effects really can be found] has been rather firmly established; any counter contention faces too much evidence to survive" (pp. 210–211). The references here cited are only a few of the many publications on mediation and its relation to the psychology of language (see, for example, Jenkins, 1965a) which have issued from the Minnesota laboratory.

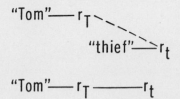

Figure 5. Replication of Figure 4, but with the mediating response, r_T, included rather than omitted (cf. Figure 1).

monly cited and discussed. And it certainly avoids many of the difficulties which more traditional interpretations of the sentence have encountered. I have therefore found it very difficult to understand why Chomsky and his associates have not only dismissed this particular analysis of the sentence (Fodor, 1965), but all the underlying assumptions concerning the way in which human infants learn to understand and use (at first singly and then in combination) the words that constitute their mother tongue. The next section will attempt to throw some light upon this paradox.

The Linguists' Attack on the Application of Learning Theory to the Domain of Language

Near the beginning of this paper, I alluded to Chomsky's (1959a) highly critical review of B. F. Skinner's radically behavioristic book, *Verbal Behavior* (1957), a review with which I found myself in essential agreement. But when Fodor (1965) later criticized my own neobehavioristic paper, "The Psychologists Looks at Language" (1954), the justification seemed much less clear to me. However, I was preoccupied with other matters at the time and read the Fodor paper only hastily and made no attempt to reply to it. Here I wish to comment in some detail (although by no means exhaustively) on this paper, in the belief that it will put us on the trail which will lead to an understanding of the otherwise mysterious state of affairs which presently exists in the fields of linguistics, psycholinguistics, and the psychology of language.

Fodor begins his paper by reviewing Chomsky's criticisms of the Skinner book, and then proceeds to give an extended, accurate, and fair synopsis of my own paper, which he concludes as follows:

It thus appears to be Mowrer's view that precisely the same process that explains the shifting of r_t [the meaning response to the word "Tom"] from occasions typified by the presence of Tom to occasions typified by the utterance of "Tom" may be invoked to account for the association of the semantic content of the predicate with that of the subject in such assertive sentences as "Tom is a thief." In either case, we are supposed to be dealing with the conditioning of a mediating response to a new stimulus. The mechanism of predication differs from the mechanism of reference [acquisition of the meaning of words] only in that in the former case the mediating response is conditioned from a word to a word and in the latter case from an object to a word.

Thus, a view of meaning according to which it is identified with a mediating response has several persuasive arguments in its favor. First, it yields a theory that avoids a number of the major objections that can be brought against single-stage S-R theories. Second, it appears to provide an account not only of the meaning of individual words, but also of the nature of such essential semantic relation as predication. Third, like single-stage S-R theories, it yields a conception of meaning that is generally consonant with concepts employed in other ares of learning theory. It thus suggests the possibility that the development of an adequate psycholinguistics will only require the employment of principles already invoked in explaining non-verbal behavior. Finally, these benefits are to be purchased at no higher prices than a slight increase in the abstractness permitted in psychological explanations. We are allowed to interpose S-R chains of any desired length between the S's and R's that form the observation base of our theory. Though this constitutes a proliferation of unobservables, it must be said that the unobservables postulated are not different in kind from the S's and R's in terms of which single-stage theories are articulated. It follows that, though we are barred from direct, observational verification of statements about mediating responses, it should prove possible to infer many of their characteristics from those that S's and R's are observed to have. (p. 77)

But Fodor then suddenly takes the position that, despite all the advantages indicated, the theory is essentially worthless. Specifically, he says:

Nevertheless, the theory of meaning implicit in the quotations from Mowrer cited above is thoroughly unsatisfactory. Nor is it obvious that this inadequacy is specific to the version of the mediation theory that Mowrer espouses. Rather, I shall try to show that there are chronic weaknesses which infect theories that rely upon mediating responses to explicate such notions as reference, denotation, or meaning. If this is correct, then the introduction of such mediators in learning-theoretic accounts of language cannot serve to provide a satisfactory answer to the charges that have been brought against single-stage theories. (p. 77)

There then follow several more specific criticisms, some of a purely logical character about which one could argue endlessly but to no avail, and some of a more empirical nature which can be easily refuted by appropriate reference to the literature on the psychology of learning. But what is most striking is that, after making such extended criticism of the approach to the psychology of language set forth in my 1954 paper, Fodor himself then offers no alternative paradigm or theoretical model for handling the same phenomena. Conant has often been quoted as saying that theories are never overthrown by argument or even by contravailing evidence, but only by a *better theory*; and Fodor not only fails to offer a *better* theory—he offers no theory at all!

Under these circumstances it was perhaps natural to assume that Fodor was simply presupposing the general approach of Chomsky to such matters, so I made a serious attempt to read the latter's main works, but found that to me, as a psychologist, they were simply incomprehensible. I therefore sought counsel from a colleague who is trained both as a psychologist and as a linguist, and he recommended that I read the three following things: (1) Chapter 7 in Lenneberg's book, *Biological Foundations of Language* (1967); (2) Chapter 1, "Methodological Preliminaries," in Chomsky's 1965 book, *Aspects of the Theory of Syntax*; and (3) a paper by Jakobovitz (1968) entitled: "Implications of Recent Psycholinguistic Developments for the Teaching of a Second Language."

Since Lenneberg, although a follower of Chomsky, is a psychologist by training, it was thought that his writings might be more intelligible to me than those of Chomsky himself. Unfortunately this did not prove to be the case. Jakobovitz, I may say, is trained both as a psychologist and as a linguist (or at least as a "psycholinguist"); I found his paper more illuminating and helpful than the Lenneberg chapter. The Jakobovitz article begins as follows:

> This paper attempts to summarize some recently developed notions about the language acquisition process and makes some preliminary suggestions about the implications of these ideas for the problem of teaching a second language. The original impetus in demonstrating the shortcomings of traditional psychological and linguistic theories in the understanding of the processes of language structure and language acquisition must be credited to Chomsky (1957; 1959a) who also developed new theories to cope with the problem. Subsequent writers have elaborated upon this new outlook pointing out the various specific inadequacies of the earlier notions and making concrete suggestions for new approaches (see Miller, 1965; Katz, 1966; McNeill, 1966; Lenneberg, 1967; Slobin, 1966; and several others; see also the contributions of Bellugi and Brown, 1964). To appreciate fully these new developments it is necessary to consider briefly the nature of the inadequacy of the earlier notions on the language acquisition process. (pp. 89–90)

And by way of summary, Jakobovitz says:

> Traditional psychological theories about language acquisition em-
> phasize the role of reinforcement provided by environmental agencies and
> view language as a set of vocal habits that are conditioned to stimuli in the
> environment. Imitation and practice of new forms are conditioned to
> stimuli in the environment. Imitation and practice of new forms are the
> processes by which language behavior develops and generalization of
> learned forms are the processes by which language behavior develops and
> generalization of learned forms is supposed to account for the novel uses of
> language. Recent developments in linguistics have influenced our concep-
> tion of the structure of language, hence the nature of the knowledge that
> the child has to acquire. *A radically new psycholinguistic theory of lan-*
> *guage acquisition has been proposed which emphasizes the developmental*
> *nature of the language acquisition process and attributes to the child*
> *specific innate competencies which guide his discovery of the rules of the*
> *natural language to which he is exposed. Imitation, practice, reinforce-*
> *ment, and generalization are no longer considered theoretically productive*
> *conceptions in language acquisition.* The implications of these new ideas
> for the teaching of a second language lie in the need for controlled exposure
> of the student to linguistic materials in a manner that will facilitate his
> discovery of the significant features of the language. "Shaping" of
> phonological skills, discrimination training on sound "units" and pattern
> drills are rejected in favor of "transformation exercises" at the phono-
> logical, syntactic and semantic levels. (p. 89, italics added)

The picture was now beginning to become somewhat clearer, albeit
in a most extraordinary way: it was beginning to look as if Chomsky
and his school were set upon disavowing and discrediting contemporary
learning theory both generally and, particularly, as it has been
developed and applied to the problem of language during the past three
or four decades. With this dawning possibility in mind, I then resolved
to go back and read the recommended Chomsky chapter (cf. p. 30),
despite my discouraging experiences with his other writings. And
eventually this resolution "paid off": toward the end of the chapter,
Chomsky explicitly aligns himself with a type of rationalistic and subjective psychology, which has long been abandoned by most contemporary psychologists as quite sterile and useless. But first it will be in
order to present some of the material from earlier parts of this chapter.
The following more or less randomly selected passages will convey the
general nature of Chomsky's style of discourse and the content—to the
extent that this can really be ascertained. I realize that it is often an
injustice to quote an author "out of context"; but in this instance the
injustice seems minimal, since, even *in* context, these passages are still
extremely obscure and abstruse. And in the end, as I shall show, the
author himself concedes that others have also had great difficulty understanding him, and that what he is saying falls far short of giving really

definitive answers to the problems with which he is purportedly struggling. Here are some samplings from *Aspects of the Theory of Syntax* (Chomsky, 1965):

> This study will touch on a variety of topics in syntactic theory and English syntax, a few in some detail, several quite superficially, none exhaustively. It will be concerned with the syntactic component of a generative grammar, that is, with the rules that specify the well-formed strings of minimal syntactically functioning units (formatives) and assign structural information of various kinds both to these strings and to strings that deviate from well-formedness in certain respects. (p. 3)

> Linguistic theory is concerned primarily with an ideal speaker–listener, in a completely homogeneous speech-community, who knows its language perfectly and is unaffected by such grammatically irrelevant conditions as memory limitations, distractions, shifts of attention and interest, and errors (random or characteristic) in applying his knowledge of the language in actual performance. This seems to me to have been the position of the founders of modern general linguistics, and no cogent reason for modifying it has been offered. To study actual linguistic performance, we must consider the interaction of a variety of factors, of which the underlying competence of the speaker–hearer is only one. In this respect, study of language is no different from empirical investigation of other complex phenomena. (pp. 3–4)

> Hence, in the technical sense, linguistic theory is mentalistic, since it is concerned with discovering a mental reality underlying actual behavior. Observed use of language or hypothesized dispositions to respond, habits, and so on, may provide evidence as to the nature of this mental reality, but surely cannot constitute the actual subject matter of linguistics, if this is to be a serious discipline. The distinction I am noting here is related to the langue–parole distinction of Saussure; but it is necessary to reject his concept of langue as merely a systematic inventory of items and to return rather to the Humboldtian conception of underlying competence as a system of generative processes. For discussion, see Chomsky (1964). (p. 4)

> Within traditional linguistic theory, furthermore, it was clearly understood that one of the qualities that all languages have in common is their "creative" aspect. Thus an essential property of language is that it provides the means for expressing indefinitely many thoughts and for reacting appropriately in an indefinite range of new situations (for references, cf, Chomsky, 1964).[6] The grammar of a particular language, then, is to be

---

[6] Any informed and unbiased consideration of the neobehavioristic, mediational approach to the psychology of language (as described and then rejected by Fodor) will show that this model imposes no "creative" limitations whatever upon linguistics; and, unlike the Chomskian model, it has to presuppose *only one* "innate idea" or native mental capacity (see also the following section): namely, the capacity of the human nervous system to mediate the phenomenon of *conditioning*, in a free and intricate way not found in other mammals.

supplemented by a universal grammar that accommodates the creative aspect of language use and expresses the deep-seated regularities which, being universal, are omitted from the grammar itself. Therefore it is quite proper for a grammar to discuss only exceptions and irregularities in any detail. It is only when supplemented by a universal grammar that the grammar of a language provides a full account of the speaker–hearer's competence. (p. 6)

Returning to the main theme, by a generative grammar I mean simply a system of rules that in some explicit and well-defined way assigns structural descriptions to sentences. Obviously, every speaker of a language has mastered and internalized a generative grammar that expresses his knowledge of his language. This is not to say that he is aware of the rules of the grammar or even that he can become aware of them, or that his statements about his intuitive knowledge of the language are necessarily accurate. Any interesting generative grammar will be dealing, for the most part, with mental processes that are far beyond the level of actual or even potential consciousness; furthermore, it is quite apparent that a speaker's reports and viewpoints about his behavior and his competence may be in error. Thus a generative grammar attempts to specify what the speaker actually knows, not what he may report about his knowledge. Similarly, a theory of visual perception would attempt to account for what a person actually sees and the mechanisms that determine this rather than his statements about what he sees and why, though these statements may provide useful, in fact, compelling evidence for such a theory. (p. 8–9)

If (4^{ii}) is correct, then we have evidence for a conclusion about organization of memory that goes beyond the triviality that it must be finite in size. An optimal finite perceptual device of the type discussed in Chomsky (1959b) need have no more difficulty with self-embedding than with other kinds of nesting (see Bar-Hillel, Kasher, and Shamir, 1963, for a discussion of this point). To account for the greater unacceptability of self-embedding (assuming this to be a fact), we must add other conditions on the perceptual device beyond mere limitation of memory. We might assume, for example, that the perceptual device has a stock of analytic procedures available to it, one corresponding to each kind of phrase, and that it is organized in such a way that it is unable (or finds it difficult) to utilize a procedure while it is in the course of executing. This is not a necessary feature of a perceptual model, but it is a rather plausible one, and it would account for (4^{ii}). See, in this connection, Millar and Isard (1964). (p. 14)

One might ask whether attention to less superficial aspects of grammatical structure than those of (3) could lead to somewhat deeper conclusions about performance models. This seems entirely possible. For example, in Miller and Chomsky (1963) some syntactic and perceptual considerations are adduced in support of a suggestion (which is, to be sure, highly speculative) as to the somewhat more detailed organization of a perceptual device. In general, it seems that the study of performance models incorporating generative grammars may be a fruitful study; furthermore, it is difficult to imagine any other basis on which a theory of performance might develop. (p. 15)

> Since transformations will not be considered here in detail, no careful distinction will be made, in the case of a sentence with a single element in its basis, between the basic string underlying this sentence and the sentence itself. In other words, at many points in the exposition I shall make the tacit simplifying (and contrary-to-fact) assumption that the underlying basic string is the sentence, in this case, and that the base Phrase-marker is the surface structure as well as the deep structure. I shall try to select examples in such a way as to minimize possible confusion, but the simplifying assumption should be borne in mind through-out. (p. 18)[7]

One could continue indefinitely citing such incomprehensible and enigmatic passages, but I have decided not to proceed, for this purpose, beyond the section entitled "justification of grammars" (p. 18). There is, however, one further exhibit, taken from a few pages later, which shows not only the abstruseness of the theory itself which Chomsky is attempting to expound, but also the ineptness and the ambiguity which often characterize Chomsky's own use of language. One might expect a sentence now and then like the following one from a psychologist, but hardly from a linguist:

> However, many questions that can realistically and significantly be formulated today do not demand evidence of a kind that is unavailable or unattainable without significant improvements in objectivity of experimental technique. (p. 21)

No, on second thought, there are two other later passages that should also be quoted to show the remarkable tenor of Chomsky's thought:

> Incidentally, it is often not realized how strong a claim this is about the innate concept-forming abilities of the child and the system of linguistic universals that these abilities imply. Thus what is maintained, presumably, is that the child has an innate theory of potential structural descriptions that is sufficiently rich and fully developed so that he is able to determine, from a real situation in which a signal occurs, which structural descriptions may be appropriate to this signal, and also that he is able to do this in part in advance of any assumption as to the linguistic structure of this signal. To say that the assumption about innate capacity is extremely strong is, of course, not to say that it is incorrect. Let us, in any event, assume tentatively that the primary linguistic data consist of signals classified as

---

[7] Earlier in this paper, I have admitted to a certain distaste for or at least indifference to the concept of "perception," in both ordinary and psychological discourse. The foregoing passages are replete with the terms "perception," "perceptual device," "perceptual model," etc. So far as I can see, these terms only compound the obscurity which is already quite abundant in Chomsky's disquisition.

sentences and nonsentences, and a partial and tentative pairing of signals
with structural descriptions. (p. 32)

> The child who acquires a language in this way of course knows a
> great deal more than he has "learned." His knowledge of the language, as
> this is determined by his internalized grammar, goes far beyond the
> presented primary linguistic data and is in no sense an "inductive
> generalization" from these data. (pp. 32–33)

Chomsky acknowledges the difficulties others have had in compre-
hending his writings when he says, on page 38: "All of this has been
said before. I repeat it at such length because it has been so grossly
misunderstood." And then Chomsky also cautions the reader how
tenuous all this is and how much the whole field of linguistics, as he
conceives it, is still dominated by ignorance. Here are two pertinent
passages:

> The illustrative examples of the preceding paragraph must be
> regarded with some caution. It is the full set of notational conventions that
> constitute an evaluation procedure, in the manner outlined earlier. The
> factual content of an explanatory theory lies in its claim that the most
> highly valued grammar of the permitted from will be selected, on the basis
> of given data. Hence, descriptions of particular subsystems of the grammar
> must be evaluated in terms of their effect on the entire system of rules. The
> extent to which particular parts of the grammar can be selected inde-
> pendently of others is an empirical matter about which very little is known,
> at present. (p. 44)

> In brief, it is clear that no present-day theory of language can hope to
> attain explanatory adequacy beyond very restricted domains. In other
> words, we are very far from being able to present a system of formal and
> substantive linguistic universals that will be sufficiently rich and detailed to
> account for the facts of language learning. To advance linguistic theory in
> the direction of explanatory adequacy, we can attempt to refine the evalua-
> tion measure for grammars or to tighten the formal constraints on gram-
> mars so that it becomes more difficult to find a highly valued hypothesis
> compatible with primary linguistic data. There can be no doubt that
> present theories of grammar require modification in both of these ways, the
> latter, in general, being the more promising. (p. 46)

It is not surprising that an author should display some modesty in
what he feels he has been able to do by way of providing an adequate
conceptual model (or theory) in any field as intricate as human language. And certainly those of us who have approached this area in
terms of learning theory have regarded our accomplishments as the
merest beginnings, which require extensive elaboration. But it *is*
surprising that authors who adopt the Chomsky position as basic to
their thinking should be so confident and categorical in their rejection of

other approaches, especially in light of Chomsky's own disclaimers in this connection!

Chomsky's Antiquated Philosophical, Antipsychological Bias

Earlier reference has been made to the fact that near the end of the Chomsky chapter which is here under scrutiny one discovers a sort of "key" which at least partially unlocks the more mysterious aspects of the whole Chomskian approach—and particularly the boldness with which many of his followers attack almost everything that is contemporary in the psychology of learning. In a section entitled "Linguistics Theory and Language Learning" (pp. 47–60), Chomsky, so to say, "lets the cat out of the bag" by admitting that his sympathies lie more with the antiquated notion of *innate ideas*—and for this reason he very much dislikes the *tabula rasa* conception of Locke on which the learning emphasis in modern psychology is based. Chomsky describes his position and that of some of his precursers as follows:

> A rather different approach to the problem of acquisition of knowledge has been characteristic of rationalist speculation about mental processes. The rationalist approach holds that beyond the peripheral processing mechanisms, there are innate ideas and principles of various kinds that determine the form of the acquired knowledge in what may be a rather restricted and highly organized way. A condition for innate mechanisms to become activated is that appropriate stimulation be presented. Thus for Descartes (1647), the innate ideas are those arising from the faculty of thinking rather than from external objects. (p. 48)

> Still earlier, Lord Herbert (1624) maintains that innate ideas and principles "remain latent when their corresponding objects are not present, and even disappear and give no sign of their existence"; they "must be deemed not so much the outcome of experience as principles without which we should have no experience at all . . . [p. 132]." Without these principles, "we could have no experience at all nor be capable of observations"; "we should never come to distinguish between things, or to grasp any general nature . . . [p. 105]." These notions are extensively developed throughout seventeenth-century [sic] rationalist philosophy. To mention just one example, Cudworth (1731) gives an extensive argument in support of his view that "there are many ideas of the mind, which though the cogitations of them be often occasionally invited from the motion or a pulse of sensible objects without made upon our bodies; yet notwithstanding the ideas themselves could not possibly be stamped or impressed upon the soul from them, because sense takes no cognizance at all of any such things in those corporeal objects, and therefore they must needs arise from the innate vigour and activity of the mind itself . . . [Book IV]." Even in Locke one

finds essentially the same conception, as was pointed out by Leibniz and
many commentators since. (p. 49)

Chomsky continues for a number of additional pages to cite similar
views from other early writers, which are certainly very much
at variance with the conceptual stance of contemporary learning
theorists—and, incidentally, also quite antithetical to the philosophical
position taken by Russell at the outset of the chapter on language
already cited. There Russell says:

> The subject of language is one which has not been studied with suffi-
> cient care in traditional philosophy. It was taken for granted that words
> exist to express "thoughts," and generally also that "thoughts" have
> "objects" which are what the words "mean." It was thought that, by
> means of language, we could deal directly with what it "means," and that
> we need not analyse with any care either of the two supposed properties of
> words, namely that of "expressing" thoughts and that of "meaning"
> things. Often when philosophers intended to be considering the objects
> meant by words they were in fact considering only the words, and when
> they were considering words they made the mistake of supposing, more or
> less unconsciously, that a word is a single entity, not, as it really is, a set of
> more or less similar events. The failure to consider language explicitly has
> been a cause of much that was bad in traditional philosophy. I think myself
> that "meaning" can only be understood if we treat language as a bodily
> habit, which is learnt just as we learn football or bicycling. The only satis-
> factory way to treat language, to my mind, is to treat it in this way, as Dr.
> Watson does. Indeed, I should regard the theory of language as one of the
> strongest points in favour of behaviourism. (p. 43)

Now it is by no means inconceivable that both Russell and the
whole contemporary psychology of learning are wrong, particularly in
their approach to the problem of language, and that Chomsky and his
followers are correct. But in view of certain historical facts as well as
extensive empirical evidence, one cannot escape the suspicion that the
Chomsky School has an "ax to grind," and that with it they mean to
separate psychology and linguistics. Linguists have an antipsychological
bias of long standing; and, as will be shown in the next and concluding
sections of this paper, "psycholinguistics" has represented a sort of
forced marriage, which was congenial enough to the psychologists, but
apparently not to the linguists. In other words, it looks as if Chomsky
and his collaborators are trying to effect a divorce of these two erstwhile
partners, quite possibly because it is felt by some linguists that
"psycholinguistics" is more psychological than linguistic, and that disa-
vowal of the relationship is the only way to preserve the identity
(prevent the emasculation and possible extinction) of what has traditionally been known as linguistics. This, of course, is a somewhat
figurative and loose way of speaking about the situation; but, as we

shall shortly see, there are some other rather substantial grounds for believing that this description of the situation is a reasonably close approximation to reality.

Observations on the History of "Psycholinguistics" and an Evaluation of the Extent and Durability of Chomsky's Impact

Having arrived at the tentative interpretation of the present situation prevailing in the field of "psycholinguistics" which has been set forth immediately above, I again consulted my psychologist–linguist friend and asked for guidance in pursuing the history of the term "psycholinguistics" and the "wedding" of psychology and linguistics it implies. My friend told me that although the term had occasionally been used previously, it was, so to say, officially established by the publication of two volumes, both of which were entitled *Psycholinguistics,* the one by Osgood and Sebeok (1954), and the other by Saporta (1961). The first of these volumes was reissued in 1965, with a supplement by A. R. Diebold entitled *A Survey of Psycholinguistic Research, 1954–1964.* Sebeok's Preface to the 1965 edition of this volume proves particularly enlightening for our purposes. With one insignificant omission, it follows:

> "Mixing memories and desires," in Eliot's haunting phrase, this edition of *Psycholinguistics* recalls a period of ferment, records a decade of solid accomplishment, and forecasts an exciting future. The idea of reuniting linguistics and psychology in the middle of the twentieth century was conceived and sparked by the Carnegie Corporation's John W. Gardner, a psychologist deeply concerned with the possible implications of such a rapprochement for education problems at all levels, and was first articulated by John B. Carroll, a psychologist attuned to linguistics from boyhood under the tutelage of Benjamin Lee Whorf. In a seminar on psycholinguistics, held at Cornell University in the summer of 1951 under the sponsorship of the Social Science Research Council, six of us attempted to clarify, in a preliminary way, the relations between the two disciplines. Three of the participants—Carroll, Osgood, and I—continued the search, with three other senior workers and five graduate students, in a second seminar, held at Indiana University two summers afterwards and under the same auspices, resulting in the monograph published in 1954.
>
> *Psycholinguistics* was aimed at an unusually large potential readership and was therefore published in two simultaneously issued but essentially identical formats: one for linguists, through the network reached by the *International Journal of American Linguistics,* and another for psychologists, through that of *The Journal of Abnormal and Social Psychology.* Both editions were rapidly exhausted. Their effects, however, continued to reverberate in many directions, punctuated by further concentrated group efforts, notably the Southwest Project in Comparative

Psycholinguistics, and a series of more or less productive work conferences
on selected research topics inspired by the book. . . . Several of these
conferences resulted in major collective works enmeshing an ever widening
circle of scholars from a variety of disciplines beside[s] linguistics and
psychology; these foci of diffusion include books edited by I. de Sola Pool,
Trends in Content Analysis (1959), Thomas A. Sebeok, *Style in Language*
(1960, 1964), Charles E. Osgood and Murray S. Miron, *Approaches to
the Study of Aphasia* (1963), and Joseph H. Greenberg, *Universals of Language* (1963).

Sol Saporta's reader was, of course, yet another summative "attempt
at shaping a large body of available information about language" in what
its editor sensed was, in 1961, still an inchoate academic pursuit. His readings, in turn, provided Diebold with a frame of reference for an admirably
erudite history of ideas, stimulating him to trace the many, but only seemingly separate, threads woven through the conglomeration of solitary
efforts and highly organized research attacks of the past ten years, which
seem at last to have crystallized into the discipline that he—as many
others—prefers to continue to identify under the unifying label of psycholinguistics.

The practitioners of this discipline—which is apparently destined to
continue to function under this descriptive title—are the new breed of
young men and women whom Miller, in his disarming and elegant article
appended to this 1965 edition, dignifies, and gives fresh character to, as
"The Psycholinguists." If the 1954 monograph stirs memories, and
Diebold's account links the past with the present, Miller's essay envisions
the frontiers of a new science facing a range of fundamental human problems the solutions to some of which are already palpable; others—of
understanding and belief—may never be tractable, at least within its scope.
I envy those who will have the opportunity to review the progress of
psycholinguistics from the vantage point of 1975. (pp. v–vi)

Our surmise that "psycholinguistics" was not originally the outcome of a natural "love affair" but something of a tour de force is thus
confirmed; and the considerations reviewed earlier in this paper suggest
that it has not been, during its relatively brief existence, a very harmo-
nious union. In fact, one can hardly escape the conclusion that Chomsky
and his associates are today determined to disengage linguistics and
psychology, that is, to obliterate psycholinguistics, as such, once and for
all, unless one is willing to assume that the Chomskian thrust is aimed
at creating a *new* psycholinguistics by espousing a psychology very different from that presently popular in academic, professional, and lay
circles. If it does not force the marriage analogy too far, one might even
say that linguistics is divorcing contemporary empirical psychology to
marry the philosophical psychology of the seventeenth and eighteenth
centuries!

But this fact, if such it be, does not seem to have much reduced the
interaction between contemporary psychology and the phenomenon of

language itself. In other words, psycholinguistics, in the sense of a "linguistics" as defined by psychologists themselves (language "behavior") rather than as defined by linguists, seems to be a thriving and burgeoning enterprise. I shall not attempt to establish this thesis with any finality. But here are a few samplings of attitude and practice drawn from a number of more or less related sources.

The greatest concern with language on the part of general psychologists is to be found in the area of child development. Here is what Johnson and Medinnus, in the second (1969) edition of their popular and successful book, *Child Psychology: Behavior and Development,* have to say on this score. Although these writers give both direct and indirect evidence of having read Chomsky, they obviously have not been greatly impressed or influenced by him. Consider the following vigorous paragraph:

> Word making and sentence making are, in a way, innately determined human propensities, since we humans are unique in this respect; yet these activities also require practice. The use of words and sentences is so rewarding, in the sense that one can make his needs and ideas known to and responded to by others, that this general reinforcing quality of speech itself appears to be a much stronger motivational force than specific parental rewards for such things as imitation of adult sentences. Learning to speak sentences probably requires more than learning the rules of sentence construction; it also requires, probably before any specific rule learning, awareness on the part of the child that communication pays off in terms of obtaining desired ends. Once provided with speech models, but in a process different from direct imitation and reward for direct imitation, the child—still really an infant—expends a great deal of time on drilling himself in speech in order to gain these desired ends. Despite high motivation toward learning to speak, the child has certain handicaps that interfere with learning; adequate speech models may not be available; a short memory span limits learning and performances. But within these limits, Weir's data suggest that the child's learning of a first language is motivated by the same kinds of force that any of us, as adults, would feel if thrown into a group whose language we did not understand. To understand and to be understood leads to rewards; we would work hard, if need be, to get these rewards. Weir's data (1962) suggest that children learn in much the same way as do adults, for highly similar reason. Their lack of prior knowledge may slow down learning in situations when prior learning could facilitate the new learning, but may cause learning to be more rapid in situations when prior learning would produce negative transfer of training, as often is the case in learning a second language. (p. 156)

Although, as already noted, not a few psychologists with an interest in language have been at least temporarily beguiled over into the Chomskian camp (see also Dixon & Horton, 1968), two of the "founding fathers" of modern psycholinguistics, although they may have been swayed, have by no means been persuaded—as the following excerpts, the first from Staats (1968), indicate:

> In 1959 the linguist Chomsky wrote a critique of Skinner's account of verbal behavior (1957), which has never been answered. Following this successful challenge of Skinner's operant conditioning interpretation of certain aspects of language, there has been a tendency to disqualify all learning approaches to language, as if they had been tarred with the same brush. It is apparently felt by psycholinguists at any rate that criticizing one learning theory is criticizing them all (see also Bever *et al.*, 1965, for an example).
>
> As has been indicated, however, the various learning approaches to language have been separatistic and by themselves have been incapable of dealing comprehensively with language. Furthermore, the major learning interpretations of aspects of language (such as Skinner's) have not included supporting experimental evidence.
>
> It is suggested, however, that an integrated learning theory of language provides a more comprehensive interpretation of language learning and function, including experimental evidence, than is otherwise available. (This is thus the major answer to criticisms of the importance of learning to language development.) Although it is not possible herein to completely discuss the linguistic and psycholinguistic challenge to learning theory (see Staats, 1971, for a more complete discussion), the following discussions will deal with topics that are relevant to this topic. (pp. 154–155)

Although we cannot here pursue, even in synoptic form, Staats' full argument as he subsequently develops it, the following two paragraphs make a salient point which will suffice for present purposes:

> This limitation of linguistic theory has not always been clear to the individuals interested in this approach such as Bever *et al.* (1965), McNeil (1966b), as well as Chomsky. That is, various psycholinguistic theorists have assumed, following Chomsky, that the linguistic rules which describe in a formal manner the utterances of people are explanatory concepts. They assume that there are cognitive structures or processes that correspond to these rules. Thus, the utterance, the verbal behavior, is thought to be caused by the cognitive structure (linguistic rule). Remember, however, that the linguistic rule was derived from observations of language behavior. The linguistic rule is the representation of the language behavior, albeit in very abstract, symbolic, form. This being the case, no matter how abstract the linguistic rule appears to be, it is a description of the language behavior, and cannot be thought to explain the language behavior. As stated, for explanation one must have contact with the events that "cause" the language behavior.
>
> Furthermore, it is not possible for the cognitive structure (psycholinguistic) theory of language to be proven by showing that learning theories are inadequate. Such criticisms may indicate the limitations of the learning theory involved. But in no way does this support the conception of a cognitive structure interpretation of language. The individual who wishes to develop a cognitive structure explanation of language must have observations of such cognitive structures or processes; which means observations in

the biological realm. There are no such observations available. Thus, this type of psycholinguistic theory is at present a weak hypothesis—not an explanatory theory. (p. 156)

In the rather extended quotations from Osgood (1968) which now follow, it is apparent that this writer, despite the many categorical rejections of contemporary learning theory and all its works by members of the Chomskian school, is, in the paper under examination, taking a conciliatory position and still hoping that something good may yet come from trying to *integrate* (as was the pristine objective of "psycholinguistics") certain of the complex phenomena in which linguists are uniquely interested and informed and the rudimentary foundations which have been laid by the learning-theory approach. Although this guardedly optimistic point of view needs to be represented at some length, my own reluctant conclusion is that the Chomskians have committed themselves to such an outmoded and mystical position in general that the prospects for a theoretical integration or reconciliation are, at this point, exceedingly dim, and that learning theorists (including many workers in the field of speech and hearing, to which reference will shortly be made) may instead have to struggle along *alone* to extend and elaborate their own type of logical analysis and research, *unless* there shortly occurs a *counterrevolution* in the field of linguistics (see next section). Osgood's position, as presented in the 1968 paper, must nevertheless be delineated, for the reasons already given—and also because it brings further clarity to certain aspects of the psychological developments which are already moving in the direction of the more complicated types of linguistic phenomena.

In the first of the two extended excerpts, Osgood says:

> The thrust of my commentary on the papers of Garrett and Fodor [1968], McNeill [1968], and Johnson [1968] will be that neither the models of the language user proposed by contemporary behavior theory nor, by inference, from contemporary linguistic theory are sufficient. Each needs supplementation from the other. Although these papers differ in substance, they are similar in other respects which concern me as a psycholinguist. First, they provide evidence for the psychological relevance of transformational grammers (i.e., such grammers are not mere logical exercises, as some psychologists would like to believe); second, they stress the "competence" of native speakers as the primary criterion toward which psycholinguistic explanations must aspire ("competence" remaining a concept to be conjured with); and third, McNeill and Garrett and Fodor, at least, repeatedly state that S–R theory (as they call it) is incapable of incorporating the phenomena described by a transformational grammar—in principle.
>
> I agree completely with the concluding remarks of Garrett and Fodor: "The problem for general S–R theory is thus clear. Either it must be

demonstrated how an appeal to the sorts of learning mechanisms S–R theory allows can account for the assimilation and application of the kinds of linguistic information incorporated in the more powerful competence models, or associationistic accounts of language learning and of speech must be abandoned." But this particular shoe fits on their feet as well as mine. The implication given in the Garrett–Fodor paper, as well as in the McNeill paper, is that any kind of S–R theory has already been ruled out of the running, as far as incorporating language behavior is concerned. It is their responsibility to demonstrate, rigorously and conclusively, that this is the case. I will try to show that this has not been done and, further, that a sophisticated behavior theory, utilizing S and R constructs along with principles of association, is becoming increasingly compatible with theories of linguistic competence, as both mature. Since I want my comments on theory to apply to my discussion of experiments, I shall take up theory first and experiments second.

None of the papers under discussion makes a clear distinction among the varieties of behavior theory, so I must do so. In the first and simplest case, there is single-stage S–R theory; it has two versions, (Pavlovian) conditioning and (Skinnerian) operant learning. Second, there is the type of nonrepresentational mediation theory, represented by Bousfield, Jenkins, and others, and somewhat more complexly by Braine. Third, there are several varieties of representational mediation theory, represented by Mowrer and myself among many others. Finally, there is a three-stage behavior theory, utilizing S and R constructs but including S–S and R–R association as well as S–R association (both single and two-staged), which—as far as I know—is uniquely my own. These varieties have been described in the literature in considerable detail. I shall refer to their totality as "behavior theory," but obviously I shall rely primarily upon my three-stage version, since it includes the major assumptions of the others.

It would seem to me that, just as psychologists interested in language have an obligation to master as best they can the intricacies of generative grammars, linguists interested in models of the language-user have an obligation to master as best they can the parallel intricacies of behavior theory—particularly if they are going to make statements about its inadequacy. What pains me, frankly, is not that Garrett and Fodor believe my version of behavior theory to be inadequate, but rather that they fail to support this conclusion by references to my own papers. They list, for example, both my Nebraska Symposium paper of 1957 and my APA address of 1963 among their references yet never refer to my notions of sensory and motor integration or of semantic and grammatic coding—even to refute them.

To make the distinction between nonrepresentational (e.g., Jenkins *et al.* and Braine) and representational (e.g., Mowrer and Osgood) mediation theories is crucial for my evaluation of Fodor's (1965) recent critique of mediation theory of the Mowrer–Osgood type. (pp. 495–496)

The other excerpt from Osgood's 1968 paper follows:

To the distinctions already made, I must add the fact that my own variety of behavior theory is not, strictly speaking, an S–R theory. In order to account for symbolic processes (within which I will include both semantic and grammatic features) I utilize a two-stage, mediational S–R theory. But it has been obvious to me from my first contact with linguistics (see *Psycholinquistics: A Survey of Theory and Research Problems,* 1954, particularly section 3.1.1.2) that even an extended S–R theory is insufficient—*in principle*. In order to incorporate the essential characteristics of gestalt theories of perceptual organization (which are obviously involved in the development of linguistic perceptual units) and the essential characteristics of motor skill, as so well described by Lashley in 1951 (which are obviously involved in the development of linguistic response units, like the syllable), I found it necessary to add what I call *an integration level* (or stage) to both decoding and encoding processes.

The integration level includes both S–S and R–R learning, based upon frequency, redundancy, and contiguity principles, but not reinforcement (sheer exposure is assumed to be sufficient). The underlying principle is this: the greater the frequency (redundancy and contiguity) with which sensory signals at the termini of sensory projection systems, or motor signals at the initiation of motor projection systems, are simultaneously active, the greater will be the tendency for their more central (integrative) correlates to activate each other. This may be a simple assumption, but it has rather broad implications. As well as being an attempt within associationistic theory to incorporate the well-documented gestalt data on perception—including the basic notions of closure, good figure, "thing"-perception and the like—it provides a natural basis for the stable relation between frequency-of-usage of word-form units and their perceptual thresholds, both visual and auditory. It also provides psycholinguistics with what I believe is a crucial distinction—between words as meaningless forms (sensory and motor integrations) and words as psychological units of meaning (by virtue of their semantic and grammatic coding). Evidence for integration mechanisms in language is presented in both the 1957 and 1963 papers of mine which Garrett and Fodor cite. (pp. 497–498)

As I conclude this section, I have before me a mimeographed draft of Professor Osgood's most recent paper, entitled "Where Do Sentences Come From?" (1970). Although interesting in its entirety, the two passages of this paper which bear most pointedly upon our present concerns are reproduced below. Here it will be seen that, as compared with his attitude expressed in the 1968 paper last cited, Osgood's mood with respect to the whole Chomskian enterprise is today much less hopeful and conciliatory than it formerly was.

Most linguists and many psycholinguists, convinced by Chomsky's review (1959) of Skinner's *Verbal Behavior* (1957) and Fodor's critique of neo-behaviorism's mediation models (1965, 1966) that contemporary learning theories are incapable "in principle" of handling language behavior, have been looking elsewhere for a "more powerful" theory of performance. Not finding anything else of interest in psychology, it was natural to turn to generative grammer itself as not only a theory of language competence but also as a model for a performance theory as well. This approach has proven quite sterile, as Chomsky himself (1961) predicted it would: "The

attempt to develop a reasonable account of the speaker has, I believe, been
hampered by the prevalent and utterly mistaken view that a generative
grammer itself provides or is related in some obvious way to a model for
the speaker (1961, footnote #16)." Not only can it be easily shown that
any contemporary generative grammar is itself incapable "in principle" of
handling language performance, but I have tried to demonstrate elsewhere
(Osgood, 1966, 1970) that Fodor's critique of representational mediation
theory is untenable. (pp. 51–52)

And then, a few pages later, we find a reiteration of what Osgood's
position in this area has been essentially for nearly two decades:

Representational mediation theory is the only learning approach that
has seriously attempted to incorporate the *symbolic processes* in general
and *meaning* in particular within an S–R associationistic model. It is
traceable directly to the germinal work of Clark L. Hull (1930, 1943),
although he utilized it primarily in drive and reinforcement connections
(the fractional anticipatory goal reaction, r_g). It was extended as a general
rather than occasional explanatory device in the writings of people like
Miller and Dollard (1941), Mowrer (1960b), Goss (1961), The Kendlers
(1962) and many others, including the writer (Osgood, 1953 and subsequently). In its present form it has come to be known as two-stage learning theory or *neo-behaviorism* (and r_g has become r_m, or representational
mediation process). Actually, my own version of neo-behaviorism is a three
stage (or level) theory, including a level of sensory (s–s) and motor (r–r)
integration designed to account for gestalt-like phenomena of perceptual
organization (e.g., closure) and motor skill or programming phenomena.
(See Osgood, "A Behavioristic Analysis of Perception and Language as
Cognitive Phenomena," 1957a).

The learning-theory approach to the psychology of learning is certainly by no means perfect, as it presently stands. And how much more
as yet unexploited potential it still has remains to be seen. It would, of
course, be unrealistic to suppose that it, or any other model, will ever be
completely satisfactory. (This is probably a scientific and logical
impossibility.) But the evidence to date indicates, rather clearly, that
this is the best thing we presently have, and that no other radically different model (such as the one proposed by Chomsky) is likely to
provide, either immediately or at some foreseeable point in the future, a
better one.

The Contemporary Situation in the Field of
"Speech and Hearing" ("Communication") as Regards the
Chomskian Controversy

There was a time, a dozen or so years ago, when I occasionally
attended meetings of the American Speech and Hearing Association and

had at least a cursory knowledge of the pertinent literature. But in the interim, as a result of other preoccupations, I had all but lost contact with this field; so it was with more than idle curiosity that I recently renewed contact with it, in order to see to what extent it had been influenced by the "revolution" which Chomsky seems to have produced in linguistics proper—and the disruption he has brought about in psycholinguistics. I had contributed two short chapters (for one of which, see Chapter 12 in this book) to the book published in 1968 under the editorship of Professor Hugo H. Gregory, of Northwestern University, entitled *Learning Theory and Stuttering Therapy*, and found that there was no reference whatever in this volume to the work of Chomsky. As the title itself implies, this book is an attempt to approach the problem os stuttering, and the field of speech generally, almost exclusively in terms of the psychology of learning, an approach which the editor, in the Preface to this volume, characterizes as follows.

> There has been a steadily developing interest in the interpretation of stuttering behavior using a psychological learning theory frame of reference, with particular emphasis on the contributions of Hull, Miller, Mowrer, and Skinner. Thus, it has become increasingly essential for the speech pathologist working with stutterers to have a rather extensive comprehension of learning theory.
>
> This book grew out of lectures presented at a symposium, "Principles of Learning and the Management of Stuttering," held at Northwestern University in the summer of 1965. The participants revised their own chapters, and the concluding chapter was written [by the editor] during the first six months of 1967.
>
> Interest in this topic has been intensified by the recent emphasis within psychology on behavior therapy—and application of learning theory to the treatment of psychological disorders. Behavior therapists and speech pathologists have found the problem of stuttering a disorder which—due to the nature of its development, observability, and susceptibility to modification—is of mutual interest. The purposes of this series of lectures were to focus attention upon basic principles of learning which have been related to the onset and development of stuttering and to appraise the application of these learning theory concepts, alone or in conjunction with other approaches, to the treatment of stuttering. (pp. v–vi)

But the Gregory volume is rather highly specialized and written from an admittedly parochial point of view, so it was clear that I needed to look at some *more general* works in this field. On the advice of the director of our University of Illinois Speech and Hearing Clinic, I consulted the following three books: Dixon and Horton's *Verbal Behavior and General Behavior Theory* (1968); Luchsinger & Arnold's *Voice-Speech-Language—Clinical Communicology: Its Physiology and Pathology* (1965), and Gertrude L. Wyatt's *Language Learning and Communication Disorders in Children* (1969). Unfortunately, the first of these volumes turned out to be 24 somewhat disjointed chapters, written by a variety of different individuals (mainly psychologists and a few linguists), which merely reflect, once again, the confusion now prevailing in the field of psycholinguistics, as it has already been amply described, discussed, and documented. Hence there was nothing new or particularly useful here, from the standpoint of our immediate interests. But the second volume, by Luchsinger and Arnold, is something very different: it is highly authorative, comprehensive, integrated, and illuminating.

The Luchsinger–Arnold book first appeared in 1949 under the German title: *Lehrbuch der Stimm- und Sprachheilkunde.* In 1959 this volume was reissued in a revised and much expanded version; and the 1965 edition has not only been translated into English (by Arnold and Dr. Evelyn Robe Finkbeiner) but again updated and further enlarged, to 812 fact-packed pages. In a Foreword, Robert W. West, Ph.D., says:

> This book should serve as a principal source of information for professionals in the fields of speech pathology and audiology, voice training, special education, reading disability, pediatrics, otorhinolaryngology, prosthodontia, orthodontia, plastic surgery, neurology, psychiatry, clinical psychology, and physical medicine and rehabilitation. (p. vi)

And in a second Foreword, Harry P. Schenck, M.D., says:

> The wide scope of this volume is not to be found in any other publication dealing with these subjects. Moreover, as in the previous German edition, there is a coalition of American and European thought, research and practice, and a union of authors and scholarship not achieved by any other work devoted to these related problems. (p. vi)

The first noteworthy fact about the Luchsinger–Arnold volume is that in an eight-page Name Index, there is not a single reference to Noam Chomsky. Here is fairly conclusive proof that as of 1965 the speculative and pseudologicomathematical writings of this linguist had had little or no impact in the field of speech and hearing. And the second fact to be noted is that the chapter "The Development of Language" (pp. 344–356), written by Arnold, while recognizing innate individual difference in what may be called language "talent," (inherited musical and athletic abilities), puts a heavy stress upon the role of individual learning in language acquisition. The following key excerpts establish the general tenor of this chapter:

> Inheritance and environment, or nature and nurture as Sheldon (1940) puts it, represent the two pillars of life between which the individual features of linguistic expression are formed. Even the first speech attempts are tied to certain preconditions of normal maturation of the senses and the entire development of the body. (p. 345)

While biogenetic explanations are valid for many details of somatic development, they cannot be so strictly applied to the psychological factors of specifically human brain function. A certain reminder of phylogenetic language evolution does exist, in that the human infant must himself acquire the single functions and structural degrees of language in the course of his speech development. Kainz (1941–1956) stressed that the biogenetic principle should not be extended to an assumed recapitulation of generic developmental tendencies in the individual. Since the learning child accepts the finished language of his environment, he is in a situation totally different from the generations of early man who, without precedents, invented primordial language.

When Pithecanthropus slowly acquired speech, he had to learn "what means what," a significance which goes beyond simple neuromotor responses, for it represents "meanings rather than a chain of habit," to use Simon's (1957) words. The same author also compares the language acquisition of early man to the learning of modern children before their mastery of language. It is the mode of language learning by early man that Simon believes to be similar to the preverbal learning of primates and human infants. In other words, infantile speech is not produced by language invention on the part of the child, since he grows up in the environment of a specific mother tongue. When a child does invent his own language, as has been observed in some cases of isolated identical twins, or in certain instances of grave environmental neglect, the outcome is a pathological condition known as genuine idioglossia (or idiolalia). Several cases have been described in the literature, such as those by L. and W. Winnen (1958). (p. 345)

Although, in the foregoing passages, Arnold certainly does not cite Chomsky by name nor give any other evidence of having ever read him, the position he here takes concerning the process of language acquistion could hardly be more antithetical to the one (that is, if I understand it even approximately) which Chomsky himself espouses. The position outlined by Arnold is, however, quite concordant with the presuppositions of most non-Chomskian psychologists who have worked in the language area.

Arnold's position regarding the order in which various language functions typically develop is also consistent with the one espoused by Russell, in this paper, and by students of language behavior generally, namely, that children learn to understand the meanings of words before they start uttering or "using" them, and that sentence formation comes third in this sequence. Specifically, with respect to meaning acquisition, Arnold says:

Speech comprehension develops about the third trimester of the first year. The child begins to form elementary associations between the objects of his immediate environment and the correlated speech elements. Auditory and visual impressions now assume increasing importance. Not infrequently, at this time there may occur a stage of complete muteness, which

has therefore been called *physiological audimutism*. With great attentive-
ness the child now observes all that goes on around him and develops his
memory for sounds and word patterns. Meanwhile, the learned elements of
speech comprehension become increasingly secure so that the first attempt
at spontaneous speech can proceed rapidly.

At this stage the child also learns to observe other *prelingual forms*.
To these belong the conscious and unconscious gestures of the speaker,
such as movements of the head, hands, and eyes. The prosodic inflection of
speech initially offers another important aid to speech comprehension. (pp.
348–349)

As do most non-Chomskian writers in the field of language, Arnold
introduces the utterance and use of words (singly or repetitively) as the
second major step in language development, although the comprehension of new word meanings is as yet by no means complete and
continues to expand concurrently with the development of word
utterance and usage. On this score Arnold says:

The development of symbolic language after the 18th month depends
primarily on the mother's teaching efforts. Through constant example and
encouragement, the parents and siblings guide the infant's acquisition of
the mother tongue. From this point on, learning assumes increasing
importance in the interplay of nature and nurture. "If inheritance be
regarded as the potentialities for the development of structures and functions, maturation is the development of these structures and functions
under environmental conditions." This definition by Simon (1957)
establishes a summarizing connection between the conclusions reached in
later chapters on inheritance and cerebral maturation.

Despite a normally developed speech mechanism, the child will not
spontaneously produce articulate speech if deprived of the usual speech
environment. That the phenomenon of "wild boys" has occurred many
times proves that the possession of normal oral structures alone does not
assure the conventional use of vocal symbols. This condition of alalia ex
spearatione, as defined by Kainz (1959) is known best through Jakob
Wassermann's (1963) biographical novel about Kaspar Hauser, the mysterious foundling of Nuremberg. After release from isolation, such children
or adolescents learn normal speech within a very short time, just as normal
children learn additional languages with great ease (cf. p. 515). Simon
(1957) ascribes to environment the differences in the speed of language
learning, not only between early man and the modern child, but also
among modern children of different cultural backgrounds. Nevertheless,
genetic and constitutional factors remain operative throughout the process
of differentiating the reflexive babbling sounds into meaningful symbols.
Like early man, the child must learn what means what, and when. This
process involves relearning of many instinctive babbling sounds and linking
them with the meanings of a conventionalized code. (p. 349)

Arnold's treatment of the development and use of *sentences* once
again follows the same general course as previously described and

followed in this chapter. The two opening paragraphs of his treatment of "Development of Sentences" read thus:

> With increasing abstraction the single word grows into a carrier of concept formation. Prerequisites for this development are progress in experiencing relationships and the audiophysic analysis of sound patterns. Only then does the child learn to identify single words within the speech of adults.
>
> In this way, at about 18 months, the child acquires the first unstructured (paratactic) pluriverbal sentences composed of at least two words. The progress from the sentence function of the single word to the synthetically and syntactically structured sentence proceeds with the rediscovery of the relationship between subjective nouns and predicative verbs. This level is achieved when the child joins its own word symbol for "dog" with that for "disappear" and says something like "Wowo out," in order to express, "The dog is gone." Toward the end of the 2nd year, the first wishing words are followed by declarative and interrogative sentences. Around this time unstructured word sequences originate. Nothing matters in these amorphous word aggregates but the "completeness of semantic elements, without any regard to form and structure" (Kainz). At the end of the third year, main and inverted clauses begin to be used without linking conjunctions. (p. 351)

This author then proceeds to make some observations about *grammar* which have a pertinent bearing upon Chomsky's extraordinary and mysterious views in this connection:

> The egocentric and subjective orientation of the child explains its initial disregard of grammatical rules. During the stage of physiological dysgrammatism, the child uses the imperative and infinitive forms of verbs. Only at a later stage does he comprehend the meaning of past and future tenses. Similarly, for a long time the use of the child's own name precedes the concept of "I." With regard to the French child, Pichon and Borel-Maisonny (1947) assume a delay in language development when the use of the "I" concept has not been achieved at the beginning of the 3rd year. It is obvious that such rules may be established only for the average developmental stages within specific areas. Accordingly, the dysgrammatic substitution of "me" for "I" by a child growing up in New York City indicates a sign of delayed linguistic maturation only if it persists after the 4th year. In that case, however, it belongs to the stereotyped signs of maturational dyslalia or general language disability. (p. 351)

The reader will recall the repetitive insistance of Chomsky and his associates that there is something *innate and universal* about grammar. The empirical facts of individual language development, such as those just cited, and the multitudinous grammatical patterns of *different* languages (see the next section of this paper) would seem to argue quite to the contrary. Moreover, persons who speak what is regarded by "properly educated" persons as an ungrammatical English dialect regard their language patterns as right and proper (otherwise they wouldn't use them); and members of nonliterate societies who never learn to speak anything but "Pidgin English," nevertheless manage to communicate quite effectively, although again very "ungrammatically" from the standpoint of a highly literate person for whom English is the mother tongue.

What is "grammatical" and what is "ungrammatical" therefore seems to be very much a matter of convention (one may almost say "caprice") and in no sense an expression of some universal (unconscious) predisposition implanted ("embedded") in the human nervous system. *Many different* verbal constructions seem to be capable of "doing the job" as far as effective communication is concerned, at least at a rudimentary level, in spite of structural forms which, by *someone's* standards, are glaringly "wrong," "ungrammatical."

So far as I can determine, the only thing that is "universal" (or nearly so) about sentence structure ("grammar") is *the temporal sequence of subject and predicate!* As was shown by Pavlov (1927) experimentally, and commonly recognized by human beings generally for probably thousands of years, conditioning is always *forward in time*. And the reason is obvious: in order to be of any adaptional value, a signal must *precede* a given event (or other stimulus). If it is to function as a *signal*, an indicator of *things to come,* the so-called conditioned stimulus must "come first". There is a research literature on so-called backward conditioning (see, for example, Hilgard & Marquis, 1940), which adds up to the conclusion that backward conditioning either does not actually occur or, if it does seem to occur, the explanation lies in some artifact in the experimental situation. Note that we invariably say that a sentence consists of *a subject and a predicate,* in that order, and that we do not speak "of a predicate and a subject." It is true that, in actual speech, subject and predicate are occasionally *inverted.* I recall having once heard Charles Osgood give the following example: "Garlic, I smell!" But what rather obviously happens in cases of this kind is that the predicate, when it occurs first, is simply "stored" and held until the listener gets (rather quickly) the subject, and the predicate is then "tacked onto" the subject in the conventional subject–predicate (forward-conditioning) temporal order.

A colleague who, earlier in his career made an extensive study of languages (not as a "linguist" but as a Catholic seminary student), tells me that, in comparative language studies, there is an expression, "inversion for emphasis," which means that subject and predicate are sometimes reversed in their temporal order as a means of arresting the reader's *attention*. This seems like a reasonable explanation of the phenomenon in question—and calls to mind an interesting and otherwise rather curious passage in Johnson–Medinnus (1969) who say:

> Children's defects in short-term memory lead to interesting questions regarding the effects of language structure, within a given culture, on the child's language development. Yngve (1960) hypothesized that (at least to the speaker) languages are right-branching; that is, that the first word determines, to a degree, what the second word could be, and so on, through the sentence (for example, with a first word of "A," we could say "cat" but could not properly say "cats").
>
> For us, left-branching structures are difficult and sound ill-constructed (see McNeill, 1966, for examples of left-branchingness developed in rocketry). In English, for the most part a right-branching language, we need only to keep a few words ahead of ourselves in our thoughts. We do not need to know how a sentence is going to end before we begin it, since, so long as syntax is correct, each new word involves many different choices.
>
> Left-branching languages do exist, although they are in the minority. Japanese, most American Indian languages, and Turkish are examples of largely left-branching languages. In these languages the speaker must know the end of a sentence before he can construct the beginning of the sentence correctly. Rather than moving from beginning to end, as in English and other right-branching languages, he must construct each of the preceding portions of the sentence to fit the end word or phrase. Clearly, left-branching sentences demand a great deal more from memory than do right-branching sentences, and are difficult even for adults to handle— especially if they have been raised in a right-branching language group, but even if they have been raised in a left-branching language group (Forster, 1966). (pp. 157–158)

All of which can be taken as at least indirect evidence for the hypothesis, suggested earlier in this paper, that a sentence is basically a *conditioning device,* involving what Osgood calls "representational mediation" and Hull referred to as "fractional anticipatory goal reactions" (r_g). The fact that sentences are, to use the Johnson–Medinnus terminology, normally "right-branching" means that the subject normally comes first, temporally speaking, in a sentence, followed by the predicate, which is the sequence involved in *forward* conditioning; and the instances of left-branching in language (implying backward condition) are probably explicable, ultimately, in terms of forward conditioning, through some system of "holding" or "storage" of the type already referred to.[8]

At this point it may be objected that perhaps the reason there is no reference to the work of Chomsky in so comprehensive and authorative a source as the Luchsinger and Arnold volume is that it appeared *too*

---

[8] The reference to "left-branching" in rocketry computer programming would be an intriguing one to pursue but would carry us too far afield to undertake here.

soon to have been able to incorporate these new "discoveries." Such an objection cannot have much force. *Voice-Speech-Language* was published in 1965, by which time Chomsky had already long since elaborated at least the rudiments of his principal theses. Nevertheless, let us *assume,* unlikely as it may be, that Chomsky does not appear in this book because of some oversight or adventitious circumstance, rather than by deliberate exclusion, and look at something much more current in the speech and hearing field. It will be recalled that one of the books recommended as representing the latest and best thinking in this field is Gertrude L. Wyatt's *Language Learning and Communication Disorders in Children,* which was published only a few months ago (in 1969).

Again the picture is much the same. The name Chomsky does not appear in a four-page Index of Authors, nor is there any reference to his work in a 21-page Bibliography!

Since Dr. Wyatt has a background in both German and American theory, research, and practice in the field of speech and hearing, it is not surprising that she proceeds along lines rather similar to those followed by Luchsinger and Arnold, although there is somewhat more evidence of psychoanalytic thinking in the Wyatt book. But this does not, however, prevent the general point of view from being quite congruent with the learning-theory ("representational mediation theory") approach favored in the present paper. Since the Wyatt book bears many similarities to that of Luchsinger and Arnold, which we have already examined in some detail, only a few excerpts will be necessary here to establish the decidedly non-Chomskian tenor of this volume.

Under the heading of Basic Assumptions, at an early point in her book, Wyatt says:

> The following assumptions will provide the basis for our study of language learning and of developmental language disorders in children:
>
> 1. The acquisition of language by the child, though dependent upon maturation of the organism, is essentially a learning process occurring within an interpersonal matrix of reciprocal feedback between adult and child. During the early stages of this process the mother (or her substitute) serves as the primary model for the child's attempts at imitation of the language patterns specific for the given culture.
>
> 2. The optimum condition for successful language learning in early childhood is a continuous, undisrupted, and affectionate relationship between mother and child, manifested in frequent and appropriate communication, both nonverbal and verbal. Such communication is appropriate for the child if the mother takes her cues from the child's behavior and verbalizations and provides the child with a corrective feedback.
>
> 3. Language learning goes through a series of interrelated stages. Each new and higher stage of development represents fundamentally an

innovation, not merely an addition of certain characteristics to those of the previous level (Werner, 1957). . . .

4. Increasing mastery of language permits the child to sustain the relationship with the mother at a greater and greater distance in place and time. Once the child has reached the stage of internalizing the basic linguistic patterns of the model, he can reproduce them even if the model has been absent for some time (Mowrer, 1950b; Piaget, 1951; Shands, 1954). Eventually, autonomy of function will be reached when the child can dispense with the original model. He will then be able increasingly to modify the linguistic patterns at will, and he will turn to a variety of different models (people) for additional learning. Thus the child's interpersonal network of communication changes gradually from a dualistic to a pluralistic one. Together with the genetic endowment of each child, the vicissitudes— satisfactions and frustrations—of the primary dualistic speech relationship will affect the child's rate of learning to speak, the degree of skill he achieves at a given time, his expectancies concerning future speech partners, and thus his behavior in later speech situations. (p. 19 & p. 21)

Much later in her book, Wyatt introduces a concept which is seriously neglected in Chomsky's writings, namely, the concept of culture. This, of course, is not hard to understand, since Chomsky is a *nativist,* and culture presupposes that much human competence and skill is transmitted from generation to generation, not genetically, but by education, training, learning. Hence, we find Wyatt saying:

At the beginning of the book we proposed that the "medical model," which considers the child outside of his social context, is insufficient for an understanding of normal as well as of deviating language development. This statement does not imply an underestimation of the important contributions of the medical sciences to speech pathology and therapy. The so-called organic speech disorders—deficiencies in the biological equipment of the speaking and listening person—would never have been understood or ameliorated without the pioneering work of audiologists, otolaryngologists, neurologists, dentists, surgeons, and speech pathologists. However, a child's acquisition of language and the possible deviations in his language development cannot be understood through a merely biological approach.

Let us go back to Edward Sapir and remember his statement that language cannot be defined "as an entity in psychophysical terms alone, however much the psychophysical basis is essential to its functioning in the individual" (Sapir, 1921). Once we have accepted Sapir's thesis that speech is a noninstinctual, cultural function, a purely human method of communicating ideas, emotions, and desires by means of voluntarily produced symbols, we can no longer treat the social and cultural aspects of language behavior as mere epiphenomena, as is done so often in medically oriented textbooks. On the contrary, these environmental aspects must be perceived as variables of primary importance. If we think of a child's acquisition of language as a process occurring within a given communication system, of which the child is learning to become a part, it becomes

mandatory for research workers as well as for teachers and therapists to
pay as much attention to the kind of input the child is receiving as to the
biological equipment which enables him to receive, analyze, store, and
transform this input. (p. 289)

One can hardly imagine a general philosophy of language development and function more different from that of Chomsky and his
followers!

Assuming that the admittedly small sample of books we have
consulted from the field of speech and hearing are representative, no
further evidence is needed to show that this field has been influenced
only minimally, if at all, by the work of Chomsky and his associates.
One might interpret this fact as reflecting either insularity on the part of
speech and hearing writers—or wisdom and a sound sense of semantic
reality! In any case, it appears that workers in this field are not at all
inhibited or delimited in investigating and explaining both the simpler
and the more complicated aspects of language by their unawareness
(rejection?) of Chomsky, and that their sociocultural (psychological)
presuppositions provide, over and beyond due recognition of the bio-
logical-organic substructure of language, a dimension whose systematic
neglect by Chomsky constitutes a fatal shortcoming.

The Ambiguity of Chomsky's Present Status as a Linguist and Theoretician

Professor Karl V. Teeter is chairman of the Department of Linguistics at Harvard University, so is presumably qualified to judge and
rate, with considerable competence, the "visibility" and influence of
various other scholars in his field. At a meeting of the Indiana
University Linguistics Circle, in March, 1969, he opened an address
with the following observations:

> The late Bernard Bloch, in his obituary of Leonard Bloomfield which
> appeared in *Language* in 1949, tells us: "Every significant refinement of
> analytic method produced in this country since 1933 has come as a direct
> result of the impetus given to linguistic research by Bloomfield's book."
> We can go even further. Up until more recently, let's say 1960, every argu-
> ment for every claim in the theory and description of languages was in
> dialogue with Bloomfield and those who considered themselves his direct
> successors, Hockett, Harris, and Bloch himself heading the list. The
> measure of the success of the revolution in linguistic theory associated with
> the name of Noam Chomsky is the fact that, since about 1960, nearly the
> same thing can be said about American linguistic theory with the substitu-
> tion of the name Chomsky for Bloomfield. (p. 2)

Teeter's lecture was published in October, 1969, in *Language Science* (by the Indiana University Research Center for the Language Sciences); and in the November 15th, 1969, issue of *The New Yorker*, George Steiner begins a long and erudite article (under "Books") entitled "The Tongues of Men," in a similarly laudatory vein.[9] Here he says:

> Chomsky's "Syntactic Structures," which is to many the classic and most persuasive statement of his hypotheses, followed six years later [after the publication of Zellig Harris' "Methods in Structural Linguistics," in 1951]. Then, in 1958 came an important paper, "A Transformational Approach to Syntax," read at the Third Texas Conference on Problems of Linguistic Analysis in English, and "Some Methodological Remarks on Generative Grammar," published in the journal *Word* in 1961. In 1963, Chomsky contributed a severely technical and far-reaching chapter on "Formal Properties of Grammars" to Volume II of the "Handbook of Mathematical Psychology." "Current Issues in Linguistic Theory," a year later, marked the commanding prestige and wide influence of the whole Chomskian approach. "Cartesian Linguistics" (1966) is an interesting but in certain respects deliberately antiquarian salute to those French grammarians and philosophers whom Chomsky regards as his true forebears. His "Language and Mind" (Harcourt, Brace & World) was first delivered as the Beckman Lectures at Berkeley in January of 1967 and published a year later. (It has more recently been published as a paperback by Harcourt.) It represents both a summary of generative linguistics and a program for future work. Around this core of his professional writing lie explanatory or polemic interviews—notably with the English philosopher Stuart Hampshire, reprinted in B. B. C.'s *Listener* of May 30, 1968—and a number of recent lectures given in packed halls in Oxford, London, and Cambridge. (p. 217)

Although both Teeter and Steiner characterize Chomsky's stance as "revolutionary," they agree upon certain "continuities" between Chomsky and more traditional linguistic positions, particularly those represented by Chomsky's major teacher in this field, Professor Zellig Harris, of the University of Pennsylvania. More particularly on this score, Teeter says:

> The continuity from Bloomfield to Chomsky, first, is obvious in a formal sense. Chomsky is a direct student of an outstanding post-Bloomfieldian, Zellig Harris, himself an admirer and associate of Bloomfield. The continuity in content may at first glance appear less clear (we are so used these days to emphasizing the sharp discontinuities which, indeed, exist), but they are no less there, chief among them the adherence to sober and rigorous method and explicit statement (new being forgotten,

---

[9] This article contains no bibliography, so the citations are not referenced at the end of this chapter, unless made elsewhere.

one fears, by some of Chomsky's successors and contemporaries). Bloch
asserts in his obituary that "There is no doubt that Bloomfield's greatest
contribution to the study of language was to make a science of it," and I
think, given the slight exaggeration understandable in this genre of writing, that this remains a just appraisal. Bloomfield was an enemy of schools
and factional trends, as documented by the late Charles Fries in his article
(in *Trends in American and European Linguistics 1930–1960*) entitled
"The Bloomfield 'School,'" with sanitary quotation marks about the last
word of the title. Bloomfield abhorred sloppy thinking and ambiguous
statement, and was the first modern scholar so to stress the value of
methodological rigor. For a real continuity in thought, note Chomsky's
paean to rigor in the preface to his *Syntactic Structures*.

A second continuity, which runs directly through Harris, is interest in
syntax, by no means universal among Bloomfield's immediate successors.
Bloomfield was the first modern scholar to attack syntax with the same
emphasis on explicit statement he made part of his general approach. (p. 2)

But then a cleavage begins to appear between the Teeter and
Steiner articles, in two respects: (1) Since Teeter's article is entitled
"Leonard Bloomfield's Linguistics," it is not surprising that his
remarks concerning Chomsky play a rather secondary role in his paper
as a whole, whereas Chomsky is Steiner's focal concern; and (2)
Teeter's references to Chomsky, although episodic rather than central,
continue to be positive and generally approving, whereas the Steiner
analysis soon becomes challenging, and, at certain points, severely
critical. I had heard vague rumors of an anti-Chomskian reaction, but
here was the first concrete expression of any such tendency I had
encountered. We shall later have occasion to return, in a different
context, to the Teeter article; but for the time being let us consider that
it has served its purpose for us, and direct our attention exclusively to
the Steiner piece.

Steiner spends much of the body of his article merely describing and interpreting Chomsky's complex and otherwise not easily
comprehended postulations; but gradually questions and criticisms
begin to creep in.[10] One of the first of these appears on page 223:

[10] By what authority does one George Steiner, writing in *The New Yorker* without any
personal or scholarly identification whatever, take it upon himself to put Professor
Noam Chomsky in his place? According to *International Who's Who* (1969–70), the
only "George Steiner" notable enough to be listed is "an American writer and
scholar" who has studied and held fellowships in and received awards from some of
our best American, English, and French universities, and who is the author of a
number of books—largely literary in nature (in 1958 he received the O'Henry
Award)—including a volume entitled *Language and Silence* (1967). His addresses are
impressive ones: 32 Barrow Road, Cambridge, England, and the Harvard Club, New
York City. The author of the article in question is presumably this man. He was born
in 1929.

Chomsky's views on transformational grammars lead to certain inferences about the nature of the human mind and about the relation between being and perception. Except for purposes of study, these two planes of argument cannot really be kept apart. Nor ought they to be. The difficulty is that Chomsky sometimes argues as if they could, and then, at other—and often decisive—points, he buttresses his formal hypotheses with inferences that are philosophic and introspective in the old, loose sense. Formal logic tends to overlap with hunches that are occasionally quite nebulous.

Because of the complexity and obscurity of the Chomskian argument to which Steiner is alluding, I shall not attempt to give the full context of his next criticism but cite it only cryptically:

A sentence generated in this way has two distinct levels, and it is by virtue of this duality that Chomsky considers himself related to certain grammarians and logicians at work in the sixteen-sixties and after. "John loves Mary" is the *surface structure* of the sentence. It constitutes the sort of "physical signal," or phonetic articulation, to which we can perfectly well apply the traditional syntax we have learned in school: noun, verb, object, and so on. But this surface structure tells us little [argues Chomsky] and obviously differs from every language. "Far below," as it were, lies the *deep structure*, for which our phonetic expression has been generated and of which the spoken, audible sentence is in some respects a projection or mapping.

What is this purported deep structure like? On this point, crucial as it is to his entire theory of language, Chomsky is elusive and not always consistent. It might have been best, though by no means satisfactory, had he said that we cannot adequately describe in words a psychic system that somehow operates before or very far beneath language. In the Kantian sense, there might be a "final skin" of consciousness and self, which we cannot describe because we cannot step outside it. Instead, Chomsky offers suggestions that are often rather obscure and tangential. (p. 224)

How far can we probe into these deep structures and "settings" of consciousness? What kind of evidence are we looking for? Again Chomsky is elusive and inclines toward modest disclaimers. . . . Elsewhere . . . he is less circumspect. Linguistic universals, says Chomsky to Stuart Hampshire, must "be a biological property of the human mind." He adds, in a move strikingly reminiscent of those made by Freud when he was hoping for neurophysiological confirmation of his model of the subconscious (confirmation that never came), that there will "definitely someday be a physiological explanation for the mental processes that we are now discovering." (p. 227)

By way of summarizing the situation up to a mid-point in his article, Steiner (1969) says:

In a simplified, obviously abbreviated form, these are the theories Professor Chomsky has put forward over the last twelve years. No one since the great French-Swiss linguist Saussure, in the early part of the

century, and I. A. Richards, in the nineteen-thirties, has had more impact
on the study of language or done more to suggest that linguistics is indeed a
central discipline in the understanding of mind and behavior.[11] They have
been sharply queried by other linguists, *and there are now signs that the
Chomskian wave may be receding.* That such a recession might occur at a
moment when Chomsky's ideas are receiving their widest public and
"journalistic" echo would be a coincidence common in the history of
science and ideas. (p. 228, italics added)

At this juncture Steiner turns to a consideration of the particularly
severe criticisms which Professor Charles F. Hockett (*The State of the
Art,* 1968), of Cornell University, has directed toward Chomsky.
Steiner says:

> Hockett rejects the whole Chomskian model of the generation of
> grammatical sentences from hidden definite sets and rules. Chomsky's pic-
> ture of language, says Hockett, is absurdly over-abstract; it is a fiction pat-
> terned not on real human speech but on the artificial propositions and tau-
> tologies of formal logic. (pp. 228–229)

> There is no genuine evidence, argues Hockett, for anything like the
> deep structures that Chomsky postulates. There is, on the contrary, plenty
> of evidence that different languages handle the world in very different ways
> and that all languages have in them "sources of openness" that Chomsky
> ignores. His fundamental error, urges Hockett, is the belief that a study of
> semantics can ever be separated from a study of the actual grammar and
> lexicon of the relevant language or family of languages. (pp. 229–230)

> Hockett's charge that Chomsky leaves out the spontaneous, altering
> genius of actual speech touches on a larger philosophic dissent. This is well
> put by Dr. Yorick Wilks in a recent review of "Language and Mind". . . .
> In view of this impenetrability of "innate presettings," it is a very odd step,
> suggests Wilks, to pass from categories of grammatical description that
> may be "natural" and "deep" in Western languages to the assertion that
> there are universal mental patterns underlying *all* languages. (p. 330–333)

---

[11] Although I did not elaborate, until 1954, the notion that the sentence is perhaps,
basically, merely a conditioning device involving two (or more) signs rather than a
sign and a "thing" (as in the familiar laboratory conditioning situation), the idea had
occurred to me prior to 1948, before I left the position I had held for eight years at
Harvard University. While at that institution, I enjoyed generally amicable personal
relations with Professor Richards, and one semester we gave a joint seminar. But I
remember very vividly his distinctly unpleasant reaction when I once suggested to him
the idea of a conditioning paradigm for sentences. He laughed derisively and said the
whole idea was absurd. It was something of a compensation for that rebuke to see my
1954 paper, "The Psychologist Looks at Language," republished, some 20 years
later, as the lead chapter in Jakobovitz and Miron's *Readings in the Psychology of
Language* (1967).

Dr. Wilks' point about Chinese [having a sentence structure very different from that of European languages] relates immediately to my own main difficulties in regard to Chomsky's theory of language. Some four thousand languages are in current use on our crowded planet. There are numerous territories in Africa, Asia, and Latin America (not to mention corners of Switzerland) that are splintered by distinct, mutually incomprehensible tongues, though these territories are uniform in climate, way of life, and economic needs. These four thousand languages, moreover, are almost certainly the remnants of an even greater number. (p. 233)

I myself am unable to consider intellectually satisfactory or adequate to the truth any model or formula of human verbal behavior that does not in some way account for this fantastic multiplicity. Why four thousand or more languages, more languages than, say, there are human races or blood types? . . . To my mind, it is now the main job of linguistics, working with anthropology and ethnography, to get our actual language condition into clear focus . . . We must learn to ask the right questions about the deeply puzzling phenomenon of linguistic diversity. There *are* clues. But they do not, I think, point in Chomsky's direction.

The fundamental matter of language proliferation hardly turns up in the theory of generative and transformational grammar. (p. 234)

The linguistics of Noam Chomsky *could* account, and could account with beautiful economy and depth, for a world in which men would all be speaking *one* language, diversified at most by a moderate range of dialects. The fact that generative and transformational grammar would be beautifully concordant with such a result, that such a result is in some manner both natural and obvious to Chomsky's postulates, seems to me to cast serious doubts on the whole model. Like the great language mystics, who extend from Nicholas of Cusa to Jakob Böhme, Chomsky often seems to conjure up the radiant fiction of that single tongue spoken by Adam and his sons but forever lost and pulverized at Babel. In short, key features of the Chomskian language revolution appear to go against the grain of the linguistic situation in which the human race actually finds itself and in which it has existed as far as history and conjecture can reach back. (p. 235)

Within the limits of space available for Steiner's exposition and a certain hard core of inherent unintelligibility in Chomsky's writings, one must admit that this writer has made the most of his opportunities, and assaulted the House that Chomsky Built in a pretty devastating way. Because of my own extremely limited scholarly competence in the field of linguistics as such, I cannot qualify as an expert witness concerning the soundness of Steiner's criticisms; but I must say that, naively and psychologically, they make a lot more sense to me than do Chomsky's own pretentious and obscurantist ramblings. I have only one criticism of what Steiner actually says—and a criticism of something he does *not* say.

Near the outset of his paper, Steiner says:

> Chomskian generative and transformational grammar is one of those
> specialized conjectures which, by sheer intellectual fascination and range of
> implication, reach out to the world of the layman. Chomsky himself,
> moreover, is a *fluent expositor* and willing publicist of his technical work;
> at his best, he is an "explainer" in the tradition of Mill and T. H. Huxley.
> Thus a good deal of his professional argument is accessible in part, at least,
> to the outside. (p. 217, italics added)

I challenge the validity of almost every sentence in this quotation.
Granted that he is a "willing publicist," Chomsky is, in my estimation,
very far from a "fluent expositor." In plain truth, he is a bumbling and
clumsy writer (see earlier exhibits); and if many laymen as well as
professionals are "fascinated" and think they see great profundities in
his work, it is, I suspect, because of a fear akin to that of being caught
in the situation of not being able to see the emperor's "new clothes."
Steiner's remark about the great language mystics, who "extend from
Nicholas to Cusa to Jakob Böhme," I found most illuminating.
Chomsky, far from being a scientist, qualifies much better as a mystic—
and his appeal to others is, I suspect, essentially mystical, rather than
scholarly or scientific.[12]

As I have worked on this chapter, it has slowly dawned on me that
the plight of the linguist is not an enviable one. If he tries to make his
subject matter entirely objective and descriptive (analogous, let us say,
to astronomy), he is caught on one horn of a dilemma: he divorces language (which is incontrovertably a form of *behavior*) from the organisms
in which it originated and from which it emanates. And if he admits the

---

[12] This dilemma is well illustrated in Bloomfield's professional stance. This linguist
dismayed many of his contemporaries, who wished no "entanglements" with
psychology, by officially embracing early behaviorism. Teeter cites several articles in
which Bloomfield was severely taken to task for this, and it was a not uncommon
response to his work to hold that it was "vitiated by his adherence to behavioristic
psychology, with its trivialization of mental processes" (p. 3). But a little later Teeter
shows that Bloomfield was more intrigued than genuinely influenced by behaviorism
because it "was an exciting scientific phenomenon in the 1920s [and] valuable in its
insistence on rigorous method and checkable statements, just as was philosophical
positivism" (p. 4). And, despite his undoubted awareness of the behavioral basis of
language, Bloomfield himself swung over to the other horn of the dilemma when
pressed. Teeter says: "These considerations should also point the way toward an
understanding of why Bloomfield's adherence to behavioristic psychology did not
affect at least his linguistic practice. The fact is simply that his practice did not depend
on the findings of psychology and his famous book contains explicit statements to this
effect in the preface: '. . . we can pursue the study of language without reference to
any one psychological doctrine.' Many other quotes substantiating this view are given
by Fries in the article previously cited" (p. 4).

validity of the bio-psycho-social, *functional* approach, he is in danger of being *swallowed-up* by the behavioral sciences in general and psychology in particular. Linguistics, in the sense of the study of *language systems,* which is merely an extension of the study of language behavior at the personal and interpersonal level, makes excellent sense, and seems to be an eminently worthwhile enterprise; but as soon as "languages" are separated from their biological, psychological, and sociological contexts, such as enterprise becomes abstruse and arcane.[13]

The oversight in the Steiner piece previously mentioned has to do with a glaring inconsistency in Chomsky's argument which apparently did not disturb Steiner in the least. Beginning on the first page of his article (p. 217), Steiner says:

> The child [according to the point of view adopted by Skinner in *Verbal Behavior*] would learn language skills (what Chomsky was to call "competence") by some process of stimulus and response within a model fully comparable to that which has proved effective—or at any rate in part—in the "teaching" of lower organisms. The qualification is needed because there is of late some doubt about what Skinner's rats have in fact "learned."
>
> Chomsky found Skinner's proposals scandalous [!]—in the restrictions they seemed to impose on the complexity and freedom of human consciousness, as well as in their methodological naïveté. Skinner's alleged scientific approach, said Chomsky, was a mere regression to discredited mentalistic psychology. It could give no true account of how human beings, *who differ in this cardinal respect from all other known life forms,* can acquire and use the infinitely complex, innovative, and at all levels creative instrument of speech. Chomsky saw—and this has, I believe, been his most penetrating insight—that a valid model of linguistic behavior must account for the extraordinary fact that all of us perpetually and effortlessly use strings and combinations of words which we have never heard before, which we have never been taught specifically, and which quite obviously do not arise in conditioned response to any identifiable stimulus in our environment. Almost from the earliest stages of his linguistic life, a child will be able to construct and to understand a fantastic number of utterances that are quite new to him yet that he somehow knows to be acceptable sentences in his language. Conversely, he will quickly demonstrate his instinctive rejection of (that is, his failure to grasp) word orders and syntactic arrangements that are unacceptable, though it may be that none of these have been specifically pointed out to him. At every stage, from earliest childhood on, the human use of language goes far beyond all "taught" or formal precedent, and far beyond the aggregate of individually acquired and stored experiences. "These abilities," says Chomsky, "indicate that there must be fundamental processes at work quite independently of 'feedback' (tutelage

---

[13] As evidence that Chomsky's favorite subject, "transformational grammars," *can* be written about clearly and simply and *without* Chomsky's paradox-laden theoretical super- or should we say substructure, see Katsoudas (1966).

or correction] from the environment." The dynamics of human communication arises from within. (pp. 218–219)

Most starkly stated, the contradiction involved in the foregoing
passage is this: Of all living organisms, man is generally recognized as
the most flexible, plastic, docile (meaning "easily taught"), and *least*
subject to (controlled by) fixed, innate, instinctive, wired-in response
tendencies. This fact of man's superb capacity for variability (learning,
education, acculturation) means that he is indeed the most "creative"
and "innovative" of all creatures; and speech is a prime demonstration
of this propensity. Yet Chomsky "dehumanizes" this great achievement
by repeatedly affirming that language ("grammar") is based upon
(springs from) neurological mechanisms which he refers to as "native,"
"innate," "present," "instinctive." Or, to use Steiner's formulation,
"The dynamics of human communication [according to Chomsky]
arises from within." Hockett tightens the noose very neatly in his
charge that "the dispute is not between a mechanistic model and a free
or idealistic vision of the production of human speech, but 'between
two alternative mechanistics thories: Skinner's the simple one, and
Chomsky's the more complicated'" (Steiner, p. 230).

In a paper published in 1953 entitled "Freedom and Responsibility: A Psychological Analysis," I argued that the capacity to *change*
through learning is a crucial and basic aspect of freedom, psychologically considered; and, oversimplified though it be, Skinner's analysis of
language hinges critically upon a learning model and Chomsky's does
not. Yet Steiner says that Chomsky found Skinner's "proposals *scanda-
lous*—in the restrictions they seemed to impose on the complexity and
freedom of human consciousness, as well as their methodological
naïveté." Even though it be granted that Skinner's approach to language in *Verbal Behavior* is vastly oversimplified and in need of revision
and refinement, it at least pivots on the psychology of learning; and
Chomsky, as we can now see in retrospect, moves in a different and
quite wrong direction. What he manifestly should—or at least *could*—
have done, with his expertise in the field of linguistics, was to join in the
efforts which Osgood, Staats, myself, and others were making to develop
a psychology of learning that was sufficiently refined and powerful to
handle more and more complicated language problems; but what he did
instead was to pronounce anathema not only on Skinner's admittedly
too truncated theory but also upon *all* learning approaches and revert to
a conceptual scheme involving the antiquated notions of "innate ideas,"
"instincts," etc. This got Chomsky a lot of immediate attention and a
great reputation as an "innovator" and "discoverer"; but in the end he

has only a bundle of paradoxes, which can be perceived not only by psychologists but, increasingly, by the members of his own professional fraternity.[14]

A lot of verbal fog has now been cleared away, issues have been clarified; and, as the preceding discussion indicates, it looks as if both time for and toleration of the Chomskian absurdities are running out, and that the neobehavioristic approach described earlier in this paper (prominently involving mediational mechanisms) may be about to enter upon an energetic renaissance. At least, if we trace developments, as we have, from the 1954 monograph of Osgood and Seboek on the new would-be hybrid science of "Psycho-linguistics" to the article by Steiner in the November 15, 1969, *New Yorker*, this is the picture that seems to emerge.

Not only have Chomsky and his associates made the tactical error of identifying themselves with static (instinctual) rather than dynamic (learning) processes; they have gravely underestimated the psychological *and linguistic* continuity between various animal species, along evolutionary lines. These mistakes take two forms. (1) These writers speak (though not consistently) as if animal behavior were stereotyped as a result either of instinct or of conditioning and almost totally overlook the real though limited *spontaneous problem solving* ("innovation" and "creativity") that goes on in lower animals (Thorndike called it "trial-and-error learning"; Hull spoke of "habit formation"; Hilgard and Marquis used the expression "instrumental learning"); and (2) Chomsky and his school have drawn much too sharp a dividing line between verbal man and the presumably totally nonverbal remainder of the animal kingdom. Elsewhere (Mowrer, 1954), I have shown that there are four *levels,* or *types,* of "sentences": Thing–Thing, Sign–Thing, Thing–Sign, and Sign–Sign. The first three types are found in "a state of Nature," and are understood and sometimes *used* by

---

[14] Dr. Marjorie Marlin, a psychologist at the University of Missouri, in a personal communication, has made a neat and pertinent observation in this connection. Since man has specialized in and survived mainly by socially transmitted and acquired (learned, cultural) solutions to the challenge of existence, and since "lower" animals have relied much more heavily upon built-in (instinctive or morphological) adaptational mechanisms, it is surprising, if Chomsky's speculation is sound, that language emerged *in man,* the inventor and transmitter of cultural (learned) solutions, rather than in organisms which, in the evolutionary struggle, have relied more on fix, instinctual, organic prearrangements, of the type Chomsky postulates as undergirding and guiding language development and function in individuals. This, along with other examples appearing in the text of this paper, is representative of the innumerable paradoxes which beset and bedevil the whole Chomskian enterprise.

infrahuman organisms; and it is only the Sign–Sign or "true" sentence that is found exclusively in man[15]. It is true that the "distance" between the first three and the fourth of these types of "sentence" is considerable, yet they clearly lie on a continuum. It is, therefore, quite misleading and incorrect to suggest that "language" appears *de novo* in *Homo sapiens*. (See, for example, an article entitled "Teaching Sign Language to a Chimpanzee" by R. A. Gardner and Beatrice Gardner in the *Mental Health Digest* for November, 1969, and also my own paper "On the Psychology of Talking Birds" [Mowrer, 1950b]). What is obviously needed is a more detailed study of these existing continuities and further intensive study, on this firm base (which prominently involves the psychology of learning), of the incredible complexity and elaboration of human language ("linguistics"), but without losing sight of certain monumental simplicities which form the warp and woof of the *signaling and communication* processes throughout the world of sensate beings.

The Development of Mathematical Language

Since the foregoing was written, two more relevant arguments against Professor Chomsky's views have come to my attention. The first of these is to be found in Chapter VII, entitled "The Art of Counting," of *The Origins of Culture* (1958, Part I of *Primitive Culture*, 1871) by Sir Edward B. Tyler. I have long had an interest in the relation between learning theory and mathematical behavior (cf. Mowrer, 1962); and when recently, paging through *The Origins of Culture*, I came upon the chapter cited, I read it carefully and with much satisfaction. The first paragraph constitutes a summary of the chapter, and is reproduced herewith.

> Mr. J. S. Mill, in his "System of Logic," takes occasion to examine the foundations of the art of arithmetic. Against Dr. Whewell[16] who had maintained that such propositions as that two and three make five are "necessary truths," containing in them an element of certainty beyond that which mere experience can give, Mr. Mill asserts that "two and one are equal to three" expresses merely "a truth known to us by early and constant experience: an inductive truth; and such truths are the foundation

---

[15] Elsewhere in this volume, evidence is presented for believing that, with proper training, Sign–Sign or "true" language is possible in chimpanzees and gorillas (cf. Preface and Part IV).

[16] No reference provided by the author. Probably William Whewell (1794–1866), a prolific theologian and philosopher. Possible reference intended: *History of the Inductive Sciences*. London: J. W. Parker, 1857.

of the science of Number. The fundamental truths of that science all rest on the evidence of sense; they are proved by showing to our eyes and our fingers that any given number of objects, ten balls for example, may by separation and re-arrangement exhibit to our senses all the different sets of numbers the sum of which is equal to ten. All the improved methods of teaching arithmetic to children proceed on a knowledge of this fact. All who wish to carry the child's mind along with them in learning arithmetic; all who wish to teach numbers, and not mere ciphers—now teach it through the evidence of the senses, in the manner we have described." Mr. Mill's argument is taken from the mental conditions of people among whom there exists a highly advanced arithmetic. The subject is also one to be advantageously studied from the ethnographer's point of view. The examination of the methods of numeration in use among the lower races not only fully bears out Mr. Mill's view, that our knowledge of the relations of numbers is based on actual experiment, but it enables us to trace the art of counting to its source, and to ascertain by what steps it arose in the world among particular races, and probably among all mankind. (pp. 240–241)

It is at once evident that the point at issue here, between J. S. Mill and Dr. Whewell, is related to the controversy between the learning theorists and Professor Chomsky. Whewell and Chomsky champion the doctrine of "innate ideas," whereas Mill and the learning theorists stress "experience." In the chapter under examination, Tyler piles example upon example from various primitive societies which consistently show that "counting" (which is the beginning of mathematical operations) involves the use of "fingers and toes" or "heaps of pebbles or beans" (p. 246). And there seems to be not the slightest evidence that "such propositions as that two and three make five are 'necessary truths,' containing in them an element of certainty beyond that which mere experience can give." Is it not plausible to assume that mathematical language and "grammatical constructions" in general are one and the same phenomenon? Certainly both involve symbolic representation, which can be seen with special clarity in primitive mathematics.

Although originally published more than a century ago, Tyler's work is still highly respected and trusted. Professor Paul Radin, of Brandeis University, in the Introduction to *The Origins of Cultures*, remarks that in *Primitive Culture* Tyler "created practically from its foundations . . . the new science, modern anthropology," and that "no book on the subject has stood the test of time as well as his" (p. ix). Systematic analysis of the chapter "The Art of Counting" makes the notion of innate ideas in the realm of mathematics exceedingly unlikely, and substantially weakens the credibility of this concept in language generally.

"Out of the Mouths of Babes"

The body of this chapter was written in 1969. In 1971, D. L. Olmsted, Professor of Anthropology at the University of Indiana, was kind enough to send me a copy of his book, *Out of the Mouth of Babes,* with an inscription which reads in part, "in gratitude for one of the main ideas behind this project." His first allusion to this idea reads as follows:

> From the standpoint of language learning, the secondary reinforcement power acquired by the sound of the mother's voice is important in that it apparently (Miller and Dollard 1941, Mowrer 1960, Olmsted 1966) helps to guide the child's own production of vocal sounds. (p. 32)

On the next page Olmsted makes these additional salient observations:

> When the infant hears himself making sounds, the stimuli most similar are the sounds made by the mother. As we have seen, these already have acquired secondary reinforcing properties. Thus, the more similar the child's voice is to the mother's, the more secondary reinforcement he can supply for himself. The more his sounds deviate from the mother's the less reinforcement, so he has a constant incentive to imitate his mother's locutions. Of course, at first his attempts are more or less random, except as they are subject too the conditions that produce cooing; however, we would expect that they would gradually tend toward greater similarity with the mother's sounds, since the latter's voice has its secondary reinforcing power constantly renewed by re-pairing with primary reinforcement. All this is long before the child is attempting to produce regular utterances of the language and long before anyone in the family thinks he is learning anything about language. Now, as probably later, his parents will teach him many important things without knowing it and will fail in their attempts to teach him other, incompatible things, without understanding why. (p. 33)

This author then distinguishes between infantile "cooing" and "babbling." Here he says:

> This period of exercise [babbling] represents only a gradual increase from the "accidental" sounds of the cooing period and apparently has little to do with communication at first. At least, communication *with others* seems not to be involved. However, it is likely that the delivering of secondary reinforcement to oneself is a kind of communication, analogous to daydreaming in the older person. (p. 34)

> Between the babbling period and the later speaking period there seems to be one difference of crucial importance: *the role of auditory feedback cues from the infant's own behavior.* During babbling, under our assumptions about secondary reinforcement, the baby's main object is to obtain secondary reinforcement by sounding like the mother. Most of his

sound-production probably meets this standard fairly easily, since it doesn't have to make up meaningful utterances; he therefore gains no particular advantage from paying especial attention to how he sounds. However, when he begins, toward the end of this period (at about one-year of age, give or take a few months) to try to say something he has heard said, such as "Mama," "ball," "milk" or "blanket," he soon finds that just any old motions of the vocal apparatus will not do. Some of his productions get better results than others. These results (reinforcement) come in the form of maternal smiles, cries of delight, and increased attention generally, to say nothing of the possession of the thing (e.g., the ball) for which he asked or was thought to ask. In other words, for the first time, the child finds that he must *listen* to what he is saying with the object of matching it to what someone else has said. The closer the match, the better the results. The reinforcement is not now secondary pleasure in the sound of one's own voice, but much more direct in the form of food, attention and relief from frustration (e.g., getting the ball which has fallen from the crib). (pp. 34–35)

The evidence for these statements comes from the tape-recordings which were made of the 100 children of this study in their home environments, with the home noises, mothers' comments, interruptions by siblings, etc., as part of the record. (p. 37)

Both the tape-recordings and common observation reveal that this process is repeated over and over again and there is evidence to suggest that language-learning is markedly slower in children who do not have such help from a normal mother or mother-surrogate (Pringle & Bossio, 1958). A good model is essential; for example, twins, who spend much of their language years in each other's company, tend to learn more slowly than other children, because each gets less of the mother's attention and because they serve, to some extent, as (incorrect) models for each other. They thus learn more slowly and more of what they learn is incorrect (Day, 1932, Davis, 1937). (p. 38)

While it is clear that only human beings have the brains to learn and use language, with all its wonderful complexity, there is nothing in these early stages of language acquisition that is not explicable in terms of the learning theory that serves so well for research into non-linguistic human learning and animal behavior. In point of fact, it appears to be a more parsimonious and more powerful research tool than theories of child-language acquisition devised by extrapolating youthward from the linguistic behavior of adults. (p. 39)

Elsewhere in his 1971 book Olmsted repeatedly alludes to this conception of word learning in infants; but the foregoing quotations sketch, in outline, the essence of the "autism" theory of the first stages of language learning. Let us now turn and examine this writer's evaluation of Professor Chomsky's approach. Olmsted's discussion of this approach reads, in part, as follows:

Sometimes . . . neglect of the behavioral basis of the data has given rise to odd speculations. Consider, for example, the following passage from Chomsky (1965):

"A theory meeting these conditions would attempt *to account for* language in the following way. Consider first the nature of the primary linguistic data. This consists of an infinite amount of *information about* sentences. . . . For example, certain signals might be *accepted as properly formed sentences,* while others are classed as nonsentences . . . ."(p. 31) (italics added)

There are three difficulties with the quoted passage; they have been [italicized] in the above question. First, it is not clear what is meant by "to account for"; the topic is too extensive to go into here, except to record my own preference for *successful prediction* as the one really satisfactory confirmation of theories purporting to be about the data of science, as opposed to ones about logic and mathematics.

The second difficulty is of more immediate relevance. It should be apparent from the behavioral basis of language that primary linguistic data are not "information about sentences" but rather utterances themselves; one might perhaps call their perceptual effects secondary linguistic data. On the other hand, "information about sentences" appears to be a candidate for a place in a theory about the learning of metalanguage. In any event, "information about sentences" is very difficult to find, let alone study, particularly in the infant. What we get from him are cries and squalls and other articulatory products; if we infer from his speech that he possesses such and such "information about sentences", without wallowing in the data provided by his actual utterances, we risk suppressing much interesting information, and, in fact, the enterprise becomes an outline of the analyst's preferences in inferring "information" rather than a study of the child's behavior. And so in fact, runs the argument provided by Chomsky in the pages that follows: e.g., "A language-acquisition device that meets conditions (i)–(iv) is capable of utilizing such primary linguistic data as the empirical basis for language learning" (p. 32). (pp. 19–20)

McNeill (1966b) goes farther than Chomsky in attributing an analytical urge to the child:

"Suppose that a child has these basic concepts as part of his biological endowment. Suppose that he knows, for example, what the relation is between main verb and object." (p. 46)

"By assigning the basic grammatical relations a place in the child's innate linguistic endowment, we assume them to be universal . . . Thus a child who knew them could commence acquiring any natural language by striving to discover how each of these relations is expressed vocally." (p. 47)

These formulations of McNeill's are difficult to test, since the task of examining an infant to see if he "knows" the relation between verb and object will strike anyone who has ever worked with babies as, at least, unprecedented. Such an assumption—however silly it may seem—would do no harm were it not for two consequences: first, it tends to turn attention away from the problem of studying the child's learning of basic grammatical relations by assuming that they are innate; secondly, it results in the attribution to the child of a "striving to discover" how these relations are "expressed vocally." The latter attribution not only introduces, non-parsimoniously, cognitive motivation for which there is no other evidence aside from the data it is supposed to explain, but it also helps prepare the way for consideration of the child as a kind of data-processing mechanism, rather than an organism. McNeill borrowed from Chomsky the notion of the LAD (Language Acquisition Device), and his discussion revolves around the efforts of the LAD to acquire language, though parallels are frequently drawn between the LAD and the child. (p. 21)

Here, then, in Olmsted's work is to be found another acceptance of the approach to language acquisition based on learning theory rather than on the suppositions of Chomsky, McNeill, and others. Olmsted and Tyler both represent the field of anthropology rather than linguistics, narrowly conceived; but this fact does not reduce the credibility of their inductive generalizations. Quite the contrary! However, any hypothesis which has been accepted by as many writers as those who have joined ranks with Chomsky cannot be lightly dismissed. No matter how substantial the empirical support (which has been reviewed in the preceding pages) for the learning-theory approach to language, one must hold the inductive view of language acquisition and use with some tentativeness. There are at present some indications that the excitement over and interest in Professor Chomsky's speculative system are receding, whereas the support for and acceptance of the experiential or inductive approach is holding its own and perhaps even gaining ground.

References

Bandura, A. Social learning through imitation. In M. R. Jones (Ed.), *Nebraska symposium on motivation*. Lincoln: University of Nebraska Press, 1962.

Bandura, A. Influence of Model's reinforcement contingencies on the acquisition of imitative responses. *Journal of Personality and Social Psychology*, 1965, *1*, 589–595.

Bandura, A., & Walters, R. H. Social learning and personality development. New York: Holt, Rinehart, & Winston, 1963.

Bar-Hillel, Y., Kasher, A., & Shamir, E. *Measures of syntactic complexity*. Report for U.S. Office of Naval Research, Information Branch, Jerusalem, 1963.

Bellugi, U., & Brown, R. (Eds.). *The acquisition of language. Monographs of the Society for research in child development*, 1964, Vol. 29.

Berlyne, D. R. *Structure and direction in thinking*. New York: Wiley, 1965.

Berlyne, D. R. Mediating responses: A note on Fodor's criticisms. *Journal of Verbal Learning and Verbal Behavior*, 1966, *5*, 408–411.

Bever, T. G., Fodor, J. A., & Weksel, W. On the acquisition of syntax: A critique of "contextual generalizations." *Psychological Review*, 1965, *72*, 467–482.

Block, B. Leonard Bloomfield. *Language*, 1948, *25*, 87–98.

Bloomfield, L. *Language*. New York: Henry Holt, 1933.

Brown, R. W., & Dulany, D. E. A stimulus-response of language and meaning. In P.

Henley (Ed.), *Language, thought and culture.* Ann Arbor: University of Michigan Press, 1958.

Chomsky, N. *Syntactic structures.* The Hague: Mouton, 1957.

Chomsky, N. Review of Skinner's verbal behavior. *Language,* 1959, *35,* 26–58. (a)

Chomsky, N. On certain formal properties of grammars. *Information and Control,* 1959, *2,* 137–167. (b)

Chomsky, N. On the notion "rule of grammar." In *Proceedings of Symposia in Applied Mathematics, American Mathematical Society,* 1961, *12,* 6–24.

Chomsky, N. *Current issues in linguistic theory.* The Hague: Mouton, 1964.

Chomsky, N. *Aspects of the theory of syntax.* Cambridge, Mass.: The M.I.T. Press, 1965.

Cudworth, R. *A treatise concerning eternal and immutable morality.* London: J. & J. Knapton, 1731.

Davis, E. A. *The development of linguistic skill in twins, singletons with siblings and only children from age five to ten years.* Institute of Child Welfare Monograph Series. No. 14. Minneapolis: University of Minnesota Press, 1937.

Day, E. J. The development of language in twins: I. A comparison of twins and single children. *Child Development,* 1932, *3,* 179–199.

De Laguna, Grace. *Speech: Its function and development.* New Haven: Yale University Press, 1927.

Descartes, R. Notes directed against a certain programe. In E. S. Haldane & G. T. Russ (Translators), *The Philosophical works of Descartes* (Vol. I). New York: Dover, 1955. (Originally published, 1647).

Diebold, A. R. A survey of psycholinguistic research, 1954–1964. In C. E. Osgood & T. A. Sebeok (Eds.), *Psycholinguistics—A survey of theory and research problems.* Bloomington: Indiana University Press, 1965.

Dixon, T. R., & Horton, D. L. (Eds.). *Verbal behavior and general behavior theory.* Englewood Cliffs, N. J.: Prentice-Hall, 1968.

Fodor, J. A. Could meaning be an r_m? *Journal of Verbal Learning and Verbal Behavior,* 1965, *4,* 73–81.

Fodor, J. A. More about mediators: A reply to Berlyne and Osgood. *Journal of Verbal Learning and Verbal Behavior,* 1966, *5,* 412–415.

Forster, K. I. Left to right processes in the construction of sentences. *Journal of Verbal Learning and Verbal Behavior,* 1966, *5,* 285–291.

Foss, D. M. Mimicry in mynas (*Gracula religiosa*): A test of Mowrer's theory. *British Journal of Psychology,* 1964, *55,* 85–88.

Fries, C. C. The Bloomfield "School." In C. Mohrmann, A. Sommerfelt, & J. Whatmough (Eds.), *Trends in European and American linguistics; 1930–1960.* Antwerp: Spectrum Publishers, 1961.

Gardner, R. A., & Gardner, B. Teaching sign language to a chimpanzee. *Mental Health Digest,* 1969, *1,* 4–8.

Garrett, M., & Fodor, J. A. Psychological theories and linguistic constructs. In T. R. Dixon & D. L. Horton (Eds.), *Verbal behavior and general behavior theory.* Englewood Cliffs, N. J.: Prentice-Hall, 1968.

Goss, A. E. Verbal mediation response and concept formation. *Psychological Review,* 1961, *68,* 248–274.

Greenberg, J. H. (Ed.), *Universals of language; report.* Cambridge, Mass.: The M.I.T. Press, 1963.

Gregory, H. H. (Ed.), *Learning theory and stuttering therapy.* Evanston, Ill.: Northwestern University Press, 1968.

Griffith, C. R. *General introduction to psychology.* New York: Macmillan, 1924.

Grosslight, J. H., & Zaynor, W. C. Verbal behavior and the mynah bird. In *Research in verbal behavior and some neurophysiological implications*. New York: Academic, 1967.

Herbert of Cherburg. *De veritate*. (M. H. Cucré, Trans.). University of Bristol Studies, No. 6, 1937.

Hilgard, E. R., & Marquis, D. G. *Conditioning and learning*. New York: Appleton-Century-Crofts, 1940.

Hockett, C. F. *Language, mathematics, and linguistics*. The Hague: Mouton, 1967.

Hockett, C. F. *The state of the art*. The Hague: Mouton, 1968.

Hull, C. L. Knowledge and purpose as habit mechanisms. *Psychological Review*, 1930, *37*, 511–525.

Hull, C. L. *Principles of behavior*. New York: Appleton-Century-Crofts, 1943.

Jakobovitz, L. A. Implications of recent psycholinguistic developments for the teaching of a second language. *Language Learning*, 1968, *18*, 89–109.

Jakobovitz, L. A., & Miron, S. (Eds.), *Readings in the psychology of language*. Englewood Cliffs, N. J.: Prentice-Hall, 1967.

Jenkins, J. J. Mediated asociations: Paradigms and situations. In C. Cofer & B. Musgrave (Eds.), *Verbal behavior and learning*. New York: McGraw-Hill, 1963.

Jenkins, J. J. Mediation theory and grammatical behavior. In S. Rosenberg (Ed.), *Directions in psycholinguistics*. New York: Macmillan, 1965. (a)

Jenkins, J. J. Comments on pseudomediation. *Psychonomic Science*, 1965, *2*, 97–98. (b)

Jenkins, J. J., Foss, D. J., & Odom, P. B. Associative mediation in paired-associates learning with multiple controls. *Journal of Verbal Learning and Verbal Behavior*, 1965, *4*, 141–147.

Johnson, N. F. Sequential verbal behavior. In T. R. Dixon & D. L. Horton (Eds.), *Verbal behavior and general behavior theory*. Englewood Cliffs, N. J.: Prentice-Hall, 1968.

Johnson, R. C., & Medinnus, G. R. *Child psychology: Behavior and development* (2nd ed.). New York: Wiley, 1969.

Kainz, F. *Psychologie der Sprache* (4 vols). Stuttgart: Enke, 1941–1956.

Kainz, F. Alalia ex separatione. *Zeitschrift fuer Experimentelle Angewandte Psychologie*, 1959, *40*, 6.

Katsoudas, A. *Writing transformational grammars: An introduction*. New York: McGraw-Hill, 1966.

Katz, J. J. *The philosophy of language*. New York: Harper, 1966.

Kellogg, W. H., & Kellogg, L. A. *The ape and the child*. New York: Whittlesey House, 1933.

Kendler, H. H., & Kendler, J. A. Vertical and horizontal processes in problem solving. *Psychological Review*, 1962, *69*, 1–16.

Lair, Winifred S. *Psychoanalytic theory of identification*. Ph.D. dissertation, Harvard University, 1949.

Lashley, K. S. The problem of serial order in behavior. In L. A. Jeffress (Ed.), *Cerebral mechanisms in behavior: The Hixon symposium*. New York: Wiley, 1951.

Lenneberg, E. H. *Biological foundations of language*. New York: Wiley, 1967.

Luchsinger, R., & Arnold, G. E. *Voice-speech-language—Clinical communicology: Its physiology and pathology*. Belmont, Calif.: Wadsworth, 1965.

McNeill, D. Speaking in space. *Science*, 1966, *152*, 875–880. (a)

McNeill, D. Developmental psycholinguistics. In F. Smith & G. A. Miller (Eds.), *The genesis of language: A psycholinguistic approach*. Cambridge, Mass.: The M.I.T. Press, 1966. (b)

McNeill, D. On theories of language acquisition. In T. R. Dixon & D. L. Horton

(Eds.), *Verbal behavior and general behavior theory.* Englewood Cliffs, N. J.: Prentice-Hall, 1968.

Meyer, M. F. *The fundamental laws of human behavior—Lectures on the foundations of any mental or social science.* Boston: R. G. Badger, 1911.

Mill, J. S. *System of logic.* London: J. W. Parker, 1843.

Miller, G. A. Psycholinguistics. In G. Lindzey (Ed.), *Handbook of social psychology* (Vol. 2). Cambridge, Mass.: Addison-Wesley, 1954.

Miller, G. A. Some preliminaries to psycholinguistics. *American Psychologist,* 1965, *20,* 15–20.

Miller, G. A., & Chomsky, N. Finitary models of language users. In R. D. Luce, R. Bush, & E. Galazitev (Eds.), *Handbook of mathematical psychology.* New York: Wiley, 1963.

Miller, G. A., & Isard, S. Free recall of self-embedded English sentences. *Information and Control,* 1964, *7,* 292–303.

Miller, N. E., & Dollard, J. *Social learning and imitation.* New Haven: Yale University Press, 1941.

Mowrer, O. H. *Learning theory and personality dynamics.* New York: Ronald, 1950. (a)

Mowrer, O. H. On the psychology of "talking birds"—A contribution to language and personality theory. In O. H. Mowrer (Ed.), *Learning theory and personality dynamics.* New York: Ronald, 1950. (b)

Mowrer, O. H. The autism theory of speech development and some clinical applications. *Speech and Hearing Disorders,* 1952, *17,* 263–268.

Mowrer, O. H. Freedom and responsibility: A psychological analysis. *Journal of Legal Education,* 1953, *6,* 60–78.

Mowrer, O. H. The psychologist looks at language. *American Psychologist,* 1954, *9,* 660–694.

Mowrer, O. H. *Learning theory and behavior.* New York: Wiley, 1960. (a)

Mowrer, O. H. *Learning theory and the symbolic processes.* New York: Wiley, 1960. (b)

Mowrer, O. H. A psychologist views (with alarm) the mathematical concepts of "multiplication" and "division." *The Arithmetic Teacher,* 1962, *9,* 3–9.

Mowrer, O. H. The psychologist looks at language. In L. A. Jakobovitz & M. S. Miron (Eds.), *Readings in the psychology of language.* Englewood Cliffs, N. J.: Prentice-Hall, 1967.

Mowrer, O. H. A resume of basic principles of learning. In H. H. Gregory (Ed.), *Learning theory and stuttering therapy.* Evanston, Ill.: Northwestern University Press, 1968.

Mowrer, O. H., & Viek, P. Language and learning: An experimental paradigm. *Harvard Educ. Rev.,* 1945, *15,* 35–48.

Olmsted, D. L. A theory of the child's learning of phonology. *Language,* 1966, *42,* 2, 531–535.

Olmsted, D. L. *Out of the mouth of babes: Earliest stages in language learning.* The Hague: Mouton, 1971.

Osgood, C. E. *Method and theory in experimental psychology.* New York: Oxford University Press, 1953.

Osgood, C. E. A behavioristic analysis of perception and language as cognitive phenomena. In *Contemporary approaches to cognition.* Cambridge: Harvard University Press, 1957. (a)

Osgood, E. E. Motivational dynamics of language behavior. In *The Nebraska symposium on motivation.* Lincoln: University of Nebraska Press, 1957. (b)

Osgood, C. E. On understanding and creating sentences. *American Psychologist,* 1963, *18,* 735–751.

Osgood, C. E. Meaning cannot be an r_m? *Journal of Verbal Learning and Verbal Behavior,* 1966, *5,* 402–407.

Osgood, C. E. Toward a wedding of insufficiencies. In T. R. Dixon & D. L. Horton (Eds.), *Verbal behavior and general behavior theory.* Englewood Cliffs, N. J.: Prentice-Hall, 1968.

Osgood, C. E. Is Neo-Behaviorism up a blind alley? Urbana: University of Illinois, 1969. (mimeograph)

Osgood, C. E. Where do sentences come from? Urbana: University of Illinois, 1970. (mimeograph)

Osgood, C. E., & Miron, M. S. (Eds.). *Approaches to the study of aphasia: A report of an interdisciplinary conference on aphasia.* Urbana: University of Illinois Press, 1963.

Osgood, C. E., & Sebeok, T. A. (Eds.). *Psycholinguistics: A survey of theory and research problems.* Baltimore: Waverly Press, 1954. (a)

Osgood, C. E., & Sebeok, T. A. (Eds.). *Psycholingusitics: A survey of theory and research problems.* Supplement to *Journal of Abnormal and Social Psychology,* 1954, *49,* 203ff. (b)

Osgood, C. E., Sebeok, T. A., & Diebold, A. R. *Psycholinguistics.* Bloomington: Indiana University Press, 1965.

Paskal, Vivian. The value of imitative behavior. *Developmental Psychology,* 1969, *1,* 463–469.

Patterson, G. R. Behavioral techniques based upon social learning. In C. M. Franks (Ed.), *Behavior modification: Appraisal and Status.* New York: McGraw-Hill, 1969.

Pavlov, I. P. *Conditioned reflexes.* (G. V. Anrep, Trans.). London: Oxford University Press, 1927.

Pei, M. *The story of language.* New York: Lippincott, 1949.

Piaget, J. *Play, dreams, and imitation in childhood.* New York: Norton, 1951.

Pichon, E., & Borel-Maisonny, S. Psychophysiologie du langage. *Folia Phoniatrica,* 1947, *1,* 38, 124.

Pool, I. S. (Ed.). *Trends in content analysis; papers.* Urbana: University of Illinois Press, 1959.

Pringle, M. L. K., & Bossio, V. A study of deprived children. Part 2: Language development and reading attainment. *Vita Humana,* 1958, *1,* 142–170

Razran, G. H. S. Conditioned responses in children: A behavioral and quantitative critical review of experimental studies. *Archives of Psychology,* 1933, No. 148.

Russell, B. *Philosophy.* New York: W. W. Norton, 1927.

Sapir, E. *Language, an introduction to the study of speech.* New York: Harcourt, Brace, & World, 1921.

Saporta, S. *Psycholinguistics—A book of readings.* New York: Holt, Rinehart & Winston, 1961.

Sebeok, T. A. (Ed.). *Style in language.* Cambridge, Mass.: The M.I.T. Press, 1960.

Semon, R. W. *The Mneme.* London: Allen & Unwin, 1921.

Shands, H. C. Anxiety, anaclitic object, and the sign function: Comments on early developments in the use of symbols. *American Journal of Orthopsychiatry,* 1954, *1,* 84–97.

Sheldon, W. H. *The varieties of human development.* New York: Harper, 1940.

Shipley, W. C. An apparent transfer of conditioning. *Psychological Bulletin,* 1933, *30,* 541. (Abstract)

Simon, C. T. The development of speech. In L. E. Travis (Ed.), *Handbook of speech pathology*. New York: Appleton-Century-Crofts, 1957.

Skinner, B. F. *Verbal behavior*. New York: Appleton-Century-Crofts, 1957.

Slobin, D. I. The acquisition of Russian as a native language. In F. Smith & G. A. Miller (Eds.), The genesis of language: A psycholinguistic approach. Cambridge, Mass.: The M.I.T. Press, 1966.

Staats, A. W. *Learning, language, and cognition*. New York: Holt, Rinehart & Winston, 1968.

Staats, A. W. Integrated-functional learning theory and language development. In D. I. Slobin (Ed.), *The ontogenesis of grammar: A theoretical symposium*. New York: Academic, 1971.

Staats, A. W., & Staats, C. K. Attitudes established by classical conditioning. *Journal of Abnormal and Social Psychology*, 1958, *57*, 37–40.

Steiner, G. *Language and silence: Essays on language, literature, and the inhuman*. New York: Atheneum, 1967.

Steiner, G. The tongues of men. *The New Yorker*, November 15, 1969.

Stewart, G. R. *Man, an autobiography*. New York: Random House, 1946.

Teeter, K. V. Leonard Bloomfield's linguistics. *Language Sciences*, 1969, October, 1–6.

Thorndike, E. L. *Man and his work*. Cambridge: Harvard University Press, 1943.

Tolman, E. C. *Purposive behavior in animals and men*. New York: Appleton-Century-Crofts, 1932.

Tyler, E. B. *The origins of culture*. (Introduction by Paul Radin). New York: Harper, 1958.

Urban, W. M. *Language and reality—the philosophy of language and the principle of symbolism*. New York: Macmillan, 1939.

Walters, R. H. Some conditions facilitating the occurrence of imitative behavior. In E. C. Simmel, R. A. Hoppe, & G. A. Milton (Eds.), *Social facilitation and imitative behavior*. Boston: Allyn & Bacon, 1968.

Wassermann, J. *Caspar Hauser*. (C. Newton, Trans.). New York: Liveright, 1963.

Weir, R. H. *Language in the crib*. The Hague: Mouton, 1962.

Werner, H. *Comparative psychology of mental development* (2nd rev. ed.). New York: International Universities Press, 1957.

White, S. H. Evidence for a hierarchial arrangement of learning processes. In L. P. Lipsitt & C. C. Spiker (Eds.), *Advances in child development and behavior* (Vol. 2). New York: Academic, 1965.

Winnen, L., & Winnen, W. Uber einen Fall von Vokalsprache bei einigen Zwillingen. *Folia Phoniatrica*, 1958, *10*, 182.

Wyatt, G. L. *Language learning and communication disorders in children*. New York: Free Press, 1969.

Yngve, V. H. A model and a hypothesis for language structure. *Proceedings of the American Philosophical Society*, 1960, *104*, 444–466.

Addendum

Repeatedly in the preceding chapter and elsewhere in this book, the statement has been made that the autism theory of vocal imitation operates "in talking birds and babies alike." But elsewhere research findings have reported that under controlled laboratory conditions, myna birds, who as pets readily learn to repeat human utterances, fail to do so in experimental settings. This finding has been interpreted as invalidating the autistic theory of imitation, not only in birds, but also in human infants. In Figures 2 and 3 (pp. 108, 109), empirical evidence is presented which dramatically validates the autism theory with laboratory rats as subjects; and various students of early human development have been cited who feel that the theory is highly applicable to human infants. A part of the difficulty seems to come from the fact that in a state of nature, the vocalizations of birds, especially during the nesting season, have to do with the establishment and maintenance of "territoriality" and that their imitative vocalizations may be more instinctive than learned, as the autism theory of imitation assumes.

Also, it should be pointed out that the autism theory applies to a very early, perhaps the *first,* form of imitation to appear in human infants; and its proponents do not at all exclude other forms of imitative activity or "play" which occur at later stages. One of the best ways to establish rapport with and responsiveness in small children (one to three years of age) is to *imitate them,* vocally, manually, posturally, etc. This approach has been described in detail by E. B. Holt in *Animal Drive and the Learning Process* (New York: Henry Holt, 1931, see especially pp. 117–120). See also a paper by J. McV. Hunt entitled "The Psychological Development of Orphanage Reared Infants: Intervention with Outcomes (Terhan)" (*Genetic Psychology Monographs,* 1976, *94,* 117–226, especially pp. 211–212). What happens in this type of situation is relatively complicated but can, I believe, be quite satisfactorily accounted for in terms of a refined and flexible theory of learning.

The most comprehensive discussion of various forms of imitation is to be found in Chapter 2 (pp. 47–108) of *Social Learning and Personality,* by Albert Bandura and Richard H. Walters (New York: Holt, Rinehart & Winston, 1963), to which the reader is referred.

Language Abuse and Psychopathology

It is most remarkable that so much has been written on the psychology of language, the philosophy of language (logic), and linguistics, and so little on that common, and deliberate, misuse of language called *deception*. From my own collection of books in this area, I have just taken 10 of the best known off the shelf: Bloomfield's *Language* (1933); Korzybski's *Science and Sanity* (1933); Miller's *Language and Communication* (1951); Morris's *Signs, Language, and Behavior* (1946); Ogden & Richards's *The Meaning of Meaning* (1938); Osgood's *Method and Theory in Experimental Psychology* (1953); Piaget's *The Language and Thought of the Child* (1952); Schlauch's *The Gift of Tongues* (1942); Skinner's *Verbal Behavior* (1957); and Zipf's *Human Behavior and the Principle of Least Effort* (1949). Would you believe it? In the subject index of not a single one of these volumes is there any reference to the phenomenon of *deception*! Korzybski has four references to *lying*, and Morris one.

In the history of the race the infamy of deception or misrepresentation has been dramatized by reference to the Devil as The Prince of Lies. Parents have proverbially told their children, "Whatever you do, never lie to your parents." And Anant (1966) quotes Oliver Wendell Holmes as saying: "Sin has many tools, but a lie is the handle that fits them all." Yet scholars in the field of communication and language either ignore the phenomenon altogether, or make only passing reference to it. Morris's reference to lying consists of a rather vapid eight-line footnote. And the only one of Korzybski's four references to it that has any "punch" is the following: "A theory of sanity must draw attention to problems involving 'truth,' 'falsehood,' 'repressed.' . . . We must investigate the effect false (or repressed) statements may have on the working of the nervous system" (p. 529).

In the "research" just described, I also examined *Selected Writings of Edward Sapir in Language, Culture, and Personality* (edited by D. G. Mandelbaum, 1958), only to find that this volume has no subject index. And then it occurred to me to wonder if I had done much better in my own book, *Learning Theory and the Symbolic Processes* (1960). Here I found no reference in the subject index to *lying*, but two references to *deception*.

In 1964 I published a small volume entitled *The New Group Therapy*, and in its subject index there are five extended references to the topis of *deception*, indicating a growing interest in this abuse of language as I became more and more immersed in the subject of personality disorder and group therapy (Mowrer, 1972).

It was, then, through the "backdoor" of psychopathology that I became interested in deception, not from the study of language *per se*. And between 1960 and 1970 I published nine papers having to do with deception, guilt, and various forms of personality disorder.

During the same decade, paradoxically, it became increasingly clear that at least the more serious forms of personality disturbance have a genetic or constitutional basis (Rosenthal, 1970). How, therefore, was one to reconcile the seeming inconsistency arising from the fact that psychosocial factors (including deception and guilt) are influential in this realm, and the very substantial evidence that biogenetic factors are also of critical importance here? This has been done in the form of what is now commonly known as the *diathesis–stress hypothesis*, which, reduced to simplest terms, says that the overt manifestation or "outbreak" of psychopathology is a function of (a) the individual's constitution or hereditary predisposition *and* of (b) the life stresses which the individual experiences. It is well established that guilt and alienation are potent forms of stress and that, to paraphrase Freud, deception is the "royal road" to alienation. Thus, causation in the field of psychopathology is said to be "multiple" or "interactive"; and the more genetically disposed a given individual is to a particular form of personality disorder, the more urgent it is that he avoid the strains and stresses that derive from deception, guilt, and other interpersonal sources.

The 6 papers which constitute Part III of this book present, from varying points of view, the reasons why truthfulness and integrity are conducive to mental health; and related considerations will be found in a treatise entitled "Belated Clinical Recognition of the 'Pathogenic Secret'" (Mowrer, 1970). It is also an interesting coincidence that Marcel Eck (1970) has just published a book entitled *Lies and Truth*; but as yet I have been able to examine its contents only sketchily. In another paper (Mowrer, 1972), I have summarized some of the evidence (see also Rosenthal, 1970) for the operation of genetic and biochemical factors in this realm. But the point which is of primary importance from the standpoint of the present volume is that the way in which a person uses *or abuses* language is almost certain to exert, for good or for ill, a major influence upon his life adjustment; and in some instances it appears that this influence may be of critical significance. In light of these circumstances, it is all the more astonishing that most writers on the subject of language have paid so little attention to the practice of deception and its often fateful consequences.

References

Anant, S. S. Integrity therapy and the Sikh religion. *Insight: Quarterly Review of Religion and Mental Health.* 1966, *5*, 22–29.

Bloomfield, L. *Language.* New York: Henry Holt, 1933.

Eck, M. *Lies and truth.* London: Macmillan, 1970.

Korzybski, A. *Science and sanity: An introduction to non-Aristotelian systems and general semantics.* New York: International Non-Aristotelian Library, 1933.

Mandelbaum, D. G. (Ed.). *Selected writings of Edward Sapir in language, culture, and personality.* Berkely & Los Angeles: University of California Press, 1958.

Miller, G. A. *Language and communication.* New York: McGraw-Hill, 1951.

Morris, C. *Signs, language, and behavior.* New York: Prentice-Hall, 1946.

Mowrer, O. H. *Learning theory and the symbolic processes.* New York: Wiley, 1960.

Mowrer, O. H. The new group therapy. Princeton, N.J.: Van Nostrand, 1964.

Mowrer, O. H. Belated clincal recognition of the "pathogenic secret." University of Illinois, 1970. (Mimeographed)

Mowrer, O. H. *Integrity groups: Principles and practices.* Counseling Psychologist, 1972, *3*, 7–87.

Ogden, C. K., & Richards, I. A. *The meaning of meaning.* New York: Harcourt, Brace, 1938.

Osgood, C. E. *Method and theory in experimental psychology.* New York: Oxford University Press, 1953.

Piaget, J. *The language and thought of the child.* New York: Humanities Press, 1952.

Rosenthal, D. *Genetic theory and abnormal behavior.* New York: McGraw-Hill, 1970.

Schlauch, Margaret. *The gift of tongues.* New York: Modern Age Books, 1942.

Skinner, B. F. *Verbal behavior.* New York: Appleton-Century-Crofts, 1957.

Zipf, G. K. *Human behavior and the principle of least effort.* Cambridge, Mass.: Addison-Wesley, 1949.

How White Is a 'White Lie?'

It is no accident that one of the first articles I wrote on deception appeared in The Grapevine *(1962, 4, 10–15), published by Alcoholics Anonymous. It is a common saying in AA circles that every alcoholic is a "liar," and that he cannot get sober until he gets honest. Accordingly, six of The 12 Recovery Steps of AA (1, 4, 5, 8, 9, 10) have to do either with the admission of past deception, or amendment of the injustices and harm thus done to others. In 1962 there was still very little emphasis in professional circles on what Ellenberger (1966) has recently, and very aptly, called "the pathogenic secret." But long before 1962 it was already apparent that Alcoholics Anonymous was a "going concern," and I was glad to give "clinical" witness to the harmfulness of deception (and the healing power of truth), and to have this brief piece accepted for publication in* The Grapevine.*

The only other thing I would add here is that this article was written while I still believed in a monistic, rather than a multiple (or interactive), theory of personality disorder. The thought I would therefore emphasize here is that lying is not good for anyone, but that some persons (because of constitutional differences) can tolerate more intrapsychic and interpersonal stress than others—and can thus "get by" with deceptive practices which, for others, are utterly devastating. In other words, there are "individual differences" in the capacity to tolerate the stress produced by lying; but it produces some stress in everyone.

A recent issue of a popular magazine carried an article entitled "The Whole Truth about Lying," by Herman E. Krimmel. "You are a liar! So am I, and so is everyone else," it begins.

There are, according to Mr. Krimmel, two kinds of lying. One is admittedly malignant, destructive, hurtful. But the individuals who

171

engage in it are really "sick" and not to be held accountable. "Reality is so painful to its victims that they retreat behind a protective wall of deceit. Usually they cannot help themselves and are unable to distinguish truth from falsehood."

We used to think, naively perhaps, that those who were taken in and exploited by swindlers, confidence men, and other "psychopathic liars" were "the victims." Now we have become so civilized and "scientific" that the victims are said to be the liars themselves, victims of a "severe illness"—and unable to "help themselves." Here Mr. Krimmel is simply echoing the now widely held view that if you are "sick"—or, better, "sick, sick, sick,"—you can, literally, get away with murder, not to mention the mere mishandling of truth.

Since Mr. Krimmel is not himself a psychiatrist or professionally affiliated in any other way with the field of psychopathology, we should perhaps not try to take too seriously what he has to say about "malignant" lying and consider, instead, his views on normal, ordinary, healthy lying: the kind you do, inevitably, if you are intelligent, have your own best interests at heart, and are compassionate and considerate of others.

Such lying is declared to be "innocent, quite innocuous, essential to contemporary living, mandatory to get along in society, appropriate." And the final clincher given for this point of view is a quotation from an unidentified lawmaker from New Mexico, to the effect that freedom to lie is a fundamental right: "I say" (imagine you hear Senator Claghorn speaking and it comes out about right) "I say you have a right to lie to whomever you please."

Let us consider first the *lighter* side of this beguiling argument. Under the sway of Freudian psychoanalysis, we psychologists and psychiatrists tried for several decades to believe that the painful discrepancy which is found in every case of so-called neurosis or functional psychosis between an individual's moral standards and his actual conduct or performance has arisen, not because his performance has been inferior or "bad," but because his standards are unrealistically high. In short, according to this view, people fall "ill" because they are trying to be *too good*. And Mr. Krimmel is making what he may regard as a faithful application of this philosophy when he says, we shouldn't be too hard on ourselves if we lie or cheat a little—or is it just "a little"?—now and then.

The alternative view which is now in process of emerging is as follows. As long as neurosis was attributed to a too severe, too demanding conscience, it was perhaps logical enough to say that the individual himself was "not responsible" for his personality problems. Obviously we get our consciences from our parents and other representatives of adult society; and if we end up with *too much* conscience, it is clearly *their* fault, rather than ours.

But we are now, for a variety of reasons, beginning to suspect that the real problem is not that our standards are too high, but that we fail or refuse to *live up to them*. If *this* is the situation, then the responsibility or "blame" comes back squarely upon ourselves. And we are beginning to ask: Why, then, do we human beings permit ourselves to engage in such unfortunate, costly, self-destructive actions? Why, in other words, are we so weak and "evil"?

If it were true that so-called neurotics are "disturbed," not because of anything *they* have done but because of what has been *done to* them, it would clearly be someone else's responsibility to "diagnose and treat" them—an inference which has created what Dr. Szasz aptly calls "the healing industry," but has not, it seems, created a whole and happy people. So we are beginning to assume, instead, as the current slogan of the National Association of Mental Health puts it, that "mental health is everybody's business," and are asking just how, as individuals, we can *be* responsible, competent, informed, strong, effective, businesslike in this area.

When the problem is reformulated in this way, the hypothesis that is most likely to be advanced is that we permit ourselves to indulge in "inferior," "low," "degrading," behavior, with the familiar sequence of guilt and the self-administered suffering which we call "mental disease," because we have a *weak will*. And at a grossly descriptive level, this assumption is true. However, it does not tell us what "will power" or strength of character is, or how we lose or regain it.

Psychiatrists, psychologists, and other social scientists are now beginning to realize that will power, i.e., the capacity to make the right decisions and to *act* upon them, is a function of whether one is *in or out of community*. This means, quite simply, that if we follow the policy of keeping our lives always "open to inspection," we find that our "wills" are surprisingly strong.

Conscience has been defined, somewhat wryly but not inaccurately, as that still, small voice that tells us when someone is *watching*. But if we adopt a policy of secrecy and deception, so that others *can't* "watch" us, then we have no "resistance to temptation," and our "wills" progressively deteriorate.

One of the commonest manifestations of "neurosis" is a feeling of "depersonalization," that is, a tendency not to "seem" quite like oneself, and a generalized sense of "unreality." What could be better calculated, really, to produce such a state than the practice of consistently denying who one is, by lying, pretending, boasting? Yet Mr. Krimmel and the authorities he cites would apparently have us believe that lying is not wrong or dangerous, but is instead normal and healthy—at least if "used in moderation."

In psychosis a common symptom is a weakening or loss of "ego boundaries," by which is meant an inability on the part of the patient to discriminate clearly between his own thoughts and feelings and those of other persons. In a technical article John Shlein (1961), of the University of Chicago, tells of a young male schizophrenic who believed he had a "machine" in his head which "broadcast" his thoughts, in such a way that *others could know about them.* And the delusion that other people are "reading my mind" is very common indeed. Such a condition is obviously highly "abnormal," and a person manifesting it is "very sick"; but Dr. Shlein suggests the interesting possibility that this sort of "symptom" is really a primitive and automatic ("unconscious") protective device, aimed at ending the policy of secrecy and isolation in the life of a chronically duplicitous individual. [John Shlein is now at Harvard University.]

After all, if others can read your mind or if your thoughts are going to be "broadcast," your life becomes, in effect, an "open book," and nothing *can* any longer be hidden. If this is "nature's" ultimate way of dealing with liars, we surely take an awesome responsibility upon ourselves when we condone or deliberately advocate lying as a regular, or even occasional, personal strategy.

Mr. Krimmel and those who share his disingenuous philosophy seem to be advocating that we revise the Ten Commandments, at least to the extent of eliminating the one which admonishes us not to bear false witness. This may seem like a relatively innocent and not too unreasonable suggestion; but we need to realize that such a proposal is, in effect, an open invitation to disregard the *other nine*; for if we have no compunction about lying, what "protection" do we have against the temptation to perform *any action* which may seem to be to our immediate advantage, since we hope, by the strategy of deception and denial, to avoid the more remote—and possibly less agreeable—consequences.

I personally am no arch conservative, and when a law or ethical rule has truly outlived its usefulness, I am as glad to see it go as anyone. But we are on unsound grounds when we argue that the injunction against bearing false witness is outmoded. Instead of our eliminating the Ninth Commandment, as Mr. Krimmel proposes, I would like to see it *raised* to a much higher position in the Decalogue. For if we can but observe *it*, the danger of our violating the remaining Commandments is materially lessened.

Sir Walter Scott, in "Lochinvar," neatly captures the essential idea here when he says: "Oh what a tangled web we weave when *first* we practice to deceive."

We all know, of course, how hopeless, trapped, and boxed in neurotic and psychotic persons characteristically feel. But they are living in a self-created prison; and it is quite wonderful to see what a difference it makes if and when they adopt a new policy of openness, not just with a "therapist," but with "significant others," which is Harry Stack Sullivan's apt phrase for those in our lives who "count most" (which means not only those on whom *we* are most dependent but also those who *count on us*).

The universal testimony of those who have tried and persevered in such a policy is that, very soon, "things begin to happen." Since others who would like to help a person who is in trouble cannot do so unless they *know* what the trouble is, it is small wonder that the situation remains pretty static and stagnant as long as deception and denial are systematically practiced.

When I was in government service during World War II, there was a sign in one of our offices which read: "Remember the turtle: He makes progress only when his neck is out." We have our "neck out" only when we are being open and honest; and when we shift from the strategy of *hiding our head* (in our fear and shame), it is remarkable how much "progress" we do begin to make.

Our journey back to integrity and self-respect may be a painfully long one. But this, and apparently *only* this, is the "switch" that makes such a journey possible; and the "minor" victories that we experience along the way will be sufficiently rewarding to give us the strength for the next step, and the next, and the next, if we but make a "good beginning."

References

Ellenberger, H. F. The pathogenic secret and its therapeutics. *Journal of the History of Behavioral Sciences*, 1966, *2*, 29–62.

Shlein, J. A client-centered approach to the psychoses. In A. Burton (Ed.), *Psychotherapy of the psychoses*. New York: Basic Books, 1961.

Truth in Communication

In October, 1964, the Journal of Business Communication *published an article by Professor Bernard Sarachek, of Rutgers University, entitled "An Honest Appraisal of Honesty in Communication" (pp. 11–17). The thesis of this article follows:*

> Simply stated, the successful communicator is one who knows exactly how much of his information and intentions to communicate to others. He knows the extent to which he must distort or color his information in order to induce others to accept the attitudes he desires. For the successful communicator, ethical communication and effective communication need not be treated as synonymous terms. (pp. 11–12)

Professor Paul M. Dauten and I were invited to write commentaries on the Sarachek article. Mine (originally published in the Journal of Business Communication, *1964, 2, pp. 18–23), is reproduced below. But first this observation: In light of the folk wisdom of the ages, as well as the abundant "clinical" evidence concerning the practice of dishonesty, it is little short of incredible to find the practice of deception openly advocated by a member of a "community of scholars" (university) who are dedicated to the pursuit and perpetration of the truth; yet anyone would be naive indeed who did not know that in the field of "advertising" deception is pervasively, though covertly, practiced. One sometimes wonders if we wouldn't be better off if all advertising were eliminated. Yet in some ways we depend upon it, and even seem to like it.*

Having been invited to comment on Professor Sarachek's article, "An Honest Appraisal of Honesty in Communication," let me say that I write as a psychologist who is interested in getting, and keeping, people *out* of mental hospitals, rather than talking them into buying things they do not really want or doing things which are against their own best interests.

From one point of view, our approaches and objectives are antithetical, but they are not unrelated. Some of the strategies which Professor Sarachek regards as most successful in promoting anything from pretzels to "personalities" are also effective, it seems, in bringing human beings into the state of estrangement, anomie, and self-loathing which we call insanity. Thus we can agree upon the salient power and importance of communication and upon the responsibility we bear to understand and use it well; but we do not at all agree upon the social purposes and applications which legitimize the use of such knowledge as we may have of this phenomenon.

Mental Illness and Language

Once each week a few colleagues and I go to a state hospital and take part in a special group-therapy project; and each day we are there some of us spend an hour or so "recruiting" on the female admissions ward. Over and over again, I have been impressed by the regularity with which newly received mental patients show anomalies and disorders of the communicative process. The situation we encountered on a recent visit is typical.

Two middle-aged women in the group, on this particular morning, talked a great deal but *said* very little. They concealed the truth about themselves by talking irrelevantly, trivially. There was another patient who had decided that the best way to keep *her* secrets was not to talk at all. One younger woman kept others at a distance and "threw them off" by talking psychotic nonsense; and the others exhibited verbosity, mutism, or "word salad" in varying degrees. The only remaining person who could "talk straight" and tell you exactly who he was was the young clergyman who had come with me. Significantly, he was *not* a "patient." So I submit that the most important single criterion of whether one "belongs" in or out of a mental hospital is the way he uses, or abuses, language. Language is truly a gift of the gods; and when we do evil, perverse things with it, let us not be surprised if strange agonies are visited upon us.

Aside from the "face validity" of the thesis that insanity is associated with peculiarities and abuses of the communication function, there is this additional source of evidence. On the occasion just described, I went on to suggest that the tensions, nervousness, and vague fears which were complained of could all be reduced to the simple danger of being "found out," *known*. But this was categorically denied. Instead, the common explanations were: "I got sick." "I worked too hard." "People were mean to me." Anyone who could, at this stage, say "I goofed—lied, stole, cheated" would already be on his or her way out of the hospital; and the major thrust of our special therapy groups is to help persons become radically honest about themselves, and charitable with respect to others.[1] If and as a person can move in this direction, he moves toward security, and sanity; and when I see anyone deliberately advocating such liberties with the truth, and such calculated indifference to the welfare of others, as does Professor Sarachek, I shudder. He ought to have the responsibility for rehabilitating some of the practitioners of his dubious arts who "graduate" into mental hospitals.

Misrepresentation as a Source of Guilt

Recently I have become deeply interested in that form of group therapy which has proved most effective in dealing with alcoholism. I refer, of course, to the program of Alcoholics Anonymous. And what is the heart of that program? It is the recovery of personal honesty, accountability, responsibility, according to AA's familiar steps:

> Admitted we were powerless over alcohol. . . . Made a searching and fearless moral inventory. . . . Admitted the exact nature of our wrongs. . . . Were entirely willing to have all our defects of character, shortcomings removed. . . . Made a list of all persons we had harmed, and became willing to make amends to them all. . . . Made direct amends. . . . Continued to take personal inventory and when we were wrong promptly admitted it. . . . Having had a spiritual awakening as the result of these steps, we tried to carry this message to alcoholics, and to practice these principles in all our affairs.

Compare Professor Sarachek:

> By using emotion-laden words, the message sender can obscure much actual information while conveying the feeling of disclosing much more information than he actually does. (p. 13) . . . They create the impression among the message recipients of [our] having passed along more information or different information than the actual information or different information than the actual information content of the message. Thus, they

---

[1] This was written at a time when I took it for granted that one could be mentally deranged because of organic difficulties, such as arteriosclerosis or brain tumor. But I assumed that the so-called "functional psychoses," schizophrenia and cyclothymia, were indeed functional in the sense of resulting from the mismanagement of one's life. Evidence now available (Rosenthal, 1970; Mowrer, 1976) makes it unmistakably clear that genetic factors play a role in these disorders, although, as previously suggested in this volume, *stress* also enters into the picture. The connection between a "clear conscience" and the ability to relax and sleep well is proverbial.

[emotion-laden words] are effective tools in molding attitudes, opinions
and behavior. (p. 14) . . . An effective communication is one that induces
message recipients to respond in a manner intended by the message sender.
To be effective, communication need not imply the full and honest flow of
information between sender and recipients. Rather, there may be times
when the motivating power of messages can be enhanced by restricting the
information content of the message, and by coloring or distorting the
contents of the messages. (p. 17)

I now know quite a lot of men and women in AA, and it is my
casual impression that the advertising business contributes more than its
share of members. This might well be expected, for misrepresentation
always creates the danger of being exposed; and this danger generates
chronic apprehension, insecurity, and guilt, which are deadened, temporarily, by alcohol. AA experience confirms this thesis, so to say, in
reverse; it shows that the best way to get sober is to get honest, thus
confirming the supposition that dishonesty, and the fear it creates,
directly encourages the excessive use of alcohol. I do not have precise
statistical proof that advertising personnel are especially prone to
alcoholism; but there's not much doubt how an empirical study of this
problem would turn out. I've heard advertising men themselves say that
this is the business which will most quickly produce "gold-plated
ulcers." It also intensifies the "taste" for alcohol—and provides the
wherewithal to satisfy it.

Dishonesty, No Real Advantage

After reading Professor Sarachek's article, one can only wonder
what his motivation was for writing it. If he was attempting to be
honest, then he is not practicing what he preaches. And if he was being
consistent with his thesis that dishonesty is a fine thing, we have no
reason to take him seriously, *trust* him. One might wish that the whole
piece were a hoax, a kind of satire on dishonesty, a *reductio ad
absurdum*. But the indications are that this was not the author's intention. Ostensibly, he wishes to be taken seriously, believed; but since he
is a professed and practiced deceiver, we would not be particularly
"sharp" if we did not suspect and look for deception. Such a search is
not unavailing.

Professor Sarachek says he recognizes that many people feel that
dishonesty is dangerous, but he thinks the risk is overestimated. He
says:

So long as message recipients need not inevitably discover that the
sender held back or misrepresented his hidden meaning, communication

need not be completely honest or unrestricted. Indeed, even if message recipients do discover that the information content of the sender's message does not match his hidden meaning, complete honesty is still not an essential part of effective communication. Individuals are much more concerned with what is being said and done *today* than with the consistency between past and present acts and statements. All that is necessary for effective communication is that the message recipients maintain a sense of confidence in the message sender. (p. 15)

We notice that the quotation (from an author who advocates "the Golden Rule of good communication") is built around the implicit assumption that less than fair, honest or ethical standards of communication will eventually be discovered by others. Otherwise, why should there be any danger of a loss of faith, confidence, loyalty? This implicit assumption may be either true or false. In any event, the author does not establish the realism of such an assumption. (p. 17)

This rejoinder is manifestly *weak,* and it systematically neglects a wide range of evidence which could easily be adduced to the contrary. History pretty consistently shows that, in the long run, honesty *is* the best policy, even in the realm of business and politics. And it is becoming ever more apparent that, in purely personal relations, dishonesty is particularly costly.

One way or another, I have occasion to talk to a number of men and women whose marriages are "on the rocks," and consistently they report a "breakdown of communication." This, of course, is just a euphemism for the fact that they have been *lying* to each other—no doubt with the loftiest of motives, but lying, nevertheless. And the only solution to such a sad state of affairs, short of divorce (with its dismal implications), is a restoration, step by step, of mutual trust through radical honesty.

It is hard for me to believe that studied techniques for man-handling the truth, which have such disastrous results in that most intimate of human relationships, can have anything but a similarly eroding effect in the "marriages" (contractual agreements, "transactions") we have with others in the less personal areas of our lives. It is commonly said today that our whole society is "sick." And I suggest that slick talk about how to gain some paltry immediate advantage by deceiving others (and ultimately ourselves!) has played no small role in bringing this unhappy condition about.

Truth and Healing

The other major deception which we find in the Sarachek article is implied by this concluding sentence: "Paradoxically, this admission [of deliberate deception, distortion, dishonesty] leads to a more honest description of effective communication than that of the 'Golden Rule' of free and honest communication." If one is going to practice dishonesty, it would seem to be to his decided advantage for other persons not to know about it; and a good way to avoid suspicion on this score is, indeed, to *talk* about the "Golden Rule" as here defined. Professor Sarachek's assumption seems to be that most writers who stress this Rule do not themselves observe it, and that it is thus mere pious verbiage and camouflage. Rather than be guilty of *this* crime, Professor Sarachek says he would rather *admit* to being a liar. (Is this in order to gain our confidence so that he can swindle us in some larger way? Or is it a partial "confession" born of a guilty conscience—an admission of reprehensible conduct which is made in the hope of gaining "acceptance," without the necessity for restitution and reform?)

But there is a third possibility which is considerably more attractive and less complicated than either of the two which have just been considered, namely, to preach the truth and practice it, too! Our author's objection to this procedure would, of course, be that it's not "effective," in the sense that if you tell the "unvarnished truth," you cannot so easily manipulate and influence others. If we are trying to influence others to our own advantage and their disadvantage, then this is indeed the case: the truth is *not* "effective." But if we are trying to heal and *help* others, it is an instrument of great power, of unparalleled effectiveness. It has been our experience that the most profound influence that one person can have upon another, in a rehabilitative relationship, is that which comes from absolute and utter personal candor, undefensiveness, and openness on the part of the helping person. And one of the reasons why so much professional "therapeutic" effort is unavailing is that it involves techniques and tricks which are designed to produce honesty *in others*, by persons who themselves do not exhibit it. "Do as I say, not as I do" might well be their motto.

May I suggest another aphorism? "When in doubt, try getting by with the truth!"

References

Mowrer, O. H. Changing conceptions of "neurosis" and the small-groups movement. *Education*, 1976, *97*, 24–62.
Rosenthal, D. *Genetic theory and abnormal behavior*. New York: McGraw-Hill, 1970.

Stage Fright and Self-Regard

It is the main thesis of this paper that if dishonesty and secret guilts make people "uneasy" with others (lest their secrets be detected), it follows that such uneasiness will be accentuated before an "audience." But thus far we have cited only informal evidence that dishonesty and guilt-riddenness are the predominant characteristics of so-called neurotic and functionally psychotic persons. At this point, it is therefore appropriate to call attention to a monograph entitled "New Evidence Concerning the Nature of Psychopathology" (Mowrer, 1968), in which upwards of a dozen empirical investigations are reviewed, all of which show that on a scale of "socialization," the neurotic, while not falling as low as the sociopath, is considerably lower than the normal person. This finding is at variance with Freud's widely accepted theory that the neurotic is the most highly socialized (inhibited) type of person, the sociopath the least socialized, with the normal person falling somewhere in between. Hence, the theory that stage fright is simply an augmentation of one's fear of having one's concealed misdeeds discovered when many people are looking at and watching one.

Out of this reasoning comes the suggestion that perhaps group therapy, in which one gradually gets rid of guilty secrets, would be an excellent form of training for public speaking. The fact that members of Alcoholics Anonymous often become excellent public speakers seems to arise from the fact that they are first encouraged to "tell their story" to just one person (the Fifth Step), and then speak honestly about themselves to larger and larger audiences.

The paper which follows was presented in December, 1964, at the annual convention of the Speech Association of America in Chicago, and was published in Western Speech *(1965, 29, 197–200).*

The subject of stage fright is often approached in terms of rather superficial fears which, it is assumed, will wear off or disappear as the person becomes more experienced in the role of public speaker. I am sure that this view of the matter has some validity, that it is applicable in some cases and perhaps has a limited applicability in all cases. But I would invite your attention to a more fundamental aspect of the problem, one which, we may say, has to do with the whole person, his self-concept, and his general strategy in relating to others.

For many years I have been interested in the subject of psychopathology; and it seems to me that stage fright is in many instances merely a concentrated, "localized" version of the anxiety, the fear, the panic which we see in more chronic form in so-called neurosis and the functional psychoses. It was Shakespeare, was it not, who likened the whole world to a stage, on which we are actors—and on which, we may add, "stage fright" is the "loss of nerve," the fearful apprehension which we think of as the essence of personality disorder in general. Patients in mental hospitals will often tell you that they are pervasively "afraid of people," that is, that they are fearful not just when they face a formal audience, but also when they meet or interact with others in even the most commonplace circumstances; and "retreat" and "withdrawal," in one form or another, is the way in which they manifest their uneasiness. The most plausible interpretation of this kind of fear that I know is to the effect that such persons are suffering from guilt, that is, a knowledge that they have behaved in socially inappropriate ways, have concealed the fact of their misbehavior from others, and are now fearful lest they be found out, "seen through," and called to account.

There is, of course, nothing new in the assumption that the central problem in personality disturbance is guilt. Freud assumed, quite correctly it seems, that the neurotic is suffering from a discrepancy between the standards he holds for himself and his actual conduct. But Freud's supposition was that this painful discrepancy arises, not because a person's performance has been too low, but because his standards are too high, and ought, with the aid of psychoanalytic treatment, to be lowered. However, many investigators are now coming to see that this is a misleading "diagnosis" and that the problem is one of *real* guilt rather than mere guilt *feelings*. If one were dealing with guilt feelings, feelings which are unrealistic and false, then one might indeed think of them as subject to extinction, habituation, "wearing off" with the passage of time and continued experience. But real guilt does not behave in this manner. Here the sense of "danger" is realistic and durable. The mere fact that one has not been found out or caught to date is no guarantee that he will not be tomorrow, or the next day—and the possibility of punishment is, so to say, "always there."

Now if the foregoing is a reasonably accurate and sound way of viewing the chronic personal insecurity which we see in neurosis (Erikson's term "identity crisis" is, it seems, a far more apt one), and if stage-fright is simply an acute, "peak" expression of this state, it will perhaps be illuminating to look at this phenomenon explicitly in terms of the hypothesis that real, current, unresolved personal guilt is the basic problem. If a somewhat insecure person is afraid of being "seen through," what more vulnerable or threatening situation than that of being before an audience with all eyes upon him? He is being watched, scrutinized, "examined," in a way that otherwise rarely occurs; and if there are guilty secrets in a person's life, such a situation is obviously precarious. Eyes (with their implications of watchfulness, inquiry, attention) are a proverbial symbol of *conscience*; and if one is on bad terms with this part of his personality and is trying not to "think about" what it is that conscience has "against" him, an audience, with its concentrated gaze, is a powerful reminder of his moral vulnerability.

Too often, I suspect, public speaking is taught as an act or performance which one "puts on." And there are, to be sure, times when one must play a role, not only in frankly dramatic presentations and entertainments, but also in teaching and lecturing on many other occasions. But I suggest that in the preparation of students for public appearances of all kinds, it would be a wonderful thing if they could be led through a "graded series" of self-disclosures and self-authentications, which would help resolve real guilt in their lives, and thus lay the basis for a genuine security and confidence in the presence of an audience, whatever the occasions.

Let me give an illustration of what I have in mind. As is well known, Alcoholics Anonymous is today proving far more effective in dealing with the problem of alcoholism than any other approach. And AA is producing "public speakers" by the score. How, precisely does this program operate, and why was it evolved? The philosophy of alcoholism which AA accepts holds that this addiction comes about because of chronic deception and untruthfulness in the life of the afflicted individual. All alcoholics are assumed to be "phoney," and a large part of the AA program is devoted to helping its members "get honest." This is done, in the first place, by means of *encouragement*. That is, newcomers hear the testimony of older members concerning their own past deviant actions and deceptions, and how they got rid of the compulsion to drink when they became more responsible, reliable, and "open."

And how does the program of honesty begin for the new member, himself? In addition to being admonished to "attend meetings," he is given a sponsor, who works particularly close with him by way of providing encouragement and guidance. And eventually the new member is urged to take the "Fifth Step," either with the sponsor or someone else, which is in effect in act of personal confession. This takes the form of "admitting the exact nature of our wrongs to God, to ourselves, and to another person." At this point the "audience" is, from one point of view, still not very large; but it is larger than it has previously been, and this is a real therapeutic gain.

Then, in the Twelfth Step of the program, the member is urged to "carry the message" to other alcoholics. And what is "the message"? It is the notion that covertness, secrecy, phoniness will drive a man to drink (as well as crazy), and that AA has a program which helps one move from secrecy to openness, from destructive privacy to "public speaking." For not only does the AA member "tell his story" in connection with the Fifth Step and in his "Twelfth-Stepping" with other alcoholics. He is also schooled in speaking about his experience with his own AA group; and little by little he begins to be invited to speak to other local groups, and then perhaps at regional or even national conferences.

By and large, AA speakers, although not always particularly literate or brilliant, make very moving and effective presentations. They do not use manuscripts and rarely even have recourse to notes. They don't need to. They are speaking directly out of their own experiences, which they can never forget, and they are speaking truthfully. I have often heard AA speakers admit to being scared. But they keep going, and I have never seen one of them break down or have to leave the platform disorganized.

If I were teaching public speaking, I think I would do it in the context of "group therapy," as AA does. I would start with interviews with individual students, sharing deeply out of my own life with them and inviting them to do the same with me. Then I would begin to enlarge the "audience," from one to three or four. And then, with perhaps some safeguards taken out of consideration for others, each person would be encouraged to "tell his story" before the class as a whole. This, in my judgment, would be a highly efficient and reliable method for producing secure and effective public speakers. I have sometimes remarked that AA is turning out better "evangelists" than any theological seminary I know. It is also, I suspect, producing more effective public speakers than most formal classes in the subject.

This approach to the problem may seem so unconventional as not to be feasible. But in composition courses, students are not infrequently asked to write frank autobiographies. And I see no reason why, in other courses, they could not learn to speak autobiographically, in an authentic and liberating way. An attack of uncontrollable stage fright is, itself, a kind of involuntary, inexplicit "confession." A part of the personality is thus trying to make an "admission" of some sort which another part is trying to block. How much better, then, to go right to the heart of the matter and deal with the guilt and fear-engendering secrets directly, voluntarily, instead of having them dumbly "acted out" in incapacitating "stage fright." The best way I know to deal with the problem of impaired identity, that is, an "identity crisis," is to become able to say who one genuinely is—to speak publicly, rather than privately or not at all.

On another occasion, I have suggested that stuttering may have much the same "dynamics" as is here posited for stage fright: namely, that the individual is trying to stifle and at the same time make an admission of some sort (see Chapter 12). The result is that he says neither what he consciously intends, nor what another part of him is trying to reveal. Although I myself have never been a stutterer, I have repeatedly had the experience of getting up to talk before an audience, feeling nervous, making a slip or "goof," and then feeling embarrassed, yet strangely relieved. I can only infer that I had come to the situation with some pretention which I thus involuntarily "corrected." By my slip or blunder, I "admitted" that I perhaps "wasn't so much" after all. When I eventually came to see this as a pattern and began to practice a little self-conscious humility, I found that the involuntary self-revelations did not occur nearly so often.

In thus stressing the concealment of one's true identity and its involuntary disclosure in stage fright, I do not wish to deny or neglect other variables. Lack of adequate preparation, legitimate fear of failure, and stress caused by extraneous circumstances may certainly interfere with smooth performance in a public speaking situation. I remember, a few years ago, having to go directly from a situation in which I had become very angry, to make a public presentation. At one point my train of thought was interrupted, and I just had to admit that I had "blocked." One interpretation could be that in an effort not to show the anger which had been generated in the other situation, I was "overcontrolling" in the lecture. But one could also view the blocking as a kind of automatic admission of the not too dignified hassle I had just been involved in, and as a form of self-punishment for not having conducted myself with greater dignity and restraint.

I hope that these reflections will sufficiently interest speech teachers and researchers that they will put them to empirical test. On the basis of evidence drawn from other fields, I believe this approach to the problem of stage fright will be found to have considerable validity and power.

Reference

Mowrer, O. H. New evidence concerning the nature of psychopathology. In M. J. Feldman (Ed.), *Studies in psychotherapy and behavior change.* Buffalo, N. Y.: University of Buffalo Press, 1968.

How to Talk about Your Troubles

This chapter was first prepared and widely circulated as a small booklet designed to provide basic information for persons who had expressed a preliminary interest in Integrity Groups. However, in order to bring its contents to the attention of more professional readers, this piece was published under the title of "Integrity Therapy: A Self-Help Approach" in Psychotherapy: Theory, Research and Practice *(1966, 3, 114–119). It is reproduced here under its original title.*

On page 191 a statement appears which calls for emendation: namely, "It is the truth we ourselves speak, rather than the treatment we receive, that heals us." Two corrections are indicated here. In the journal version of this paper, the title was: "Integrity Therapy: A Self-Help Approach." The term "self-help," although widely used in this context, is inaccurate and misleading. A much better expression is "mutual help." It is not only what the individual himself says and does that helps, but also the encouragement and "feedback" he obtains from other members of his group. Also, one is justified in speaking of "treatment" (rather than "self-help") when one is receiving appropriate and helpful psychotropic drugs or medication.

From reading the following article, one could easily get the impression (which was indeed at one time our position) that all psychopathology which does not involve manifest organicity is due to deception-induced alienation. We now recognize the role of predisposing genetic factors in certain other types of personality disorder (see Footnote 1). But even when these factors are present, one may depend upon it that the practice of honesty and integrity will do no harm. In point of fact, the stress induced by deception and irresponsibility might be just the force needed to "trigger" the genetic predisposition.

Somehow the notion has gotten about that if one is emotionally disturbed, the only thing one can do is to seek professional help. This

view, I believe, rests on a misunderstanding of the origin and nature of
the condition in question. Sometimes it is called a "neurosis," with the
implication that one's nerves are "bad" and need treating, most logically perhaps by a physician. Sometimes it is assumed that the difficulty
lies deep in an "unconscious" part of the mind which only a
psychologist or psychoanalyst knows how to "reach." And sometimes
the difficulty is interpreted as a sin against God, in which event the
services of a theologian might seem indicated. Still another possibility is
that the chronic state of tension and apprehension with which we are
here concerned arises from a "bad conscience," that is, from some
unworthy act or acts committed and concealed, or some slighted obligation.

What is most clearly needed, if the latter understanding of the
situation is valid, is the determination and strength to *admit*, to the
"significant others" in one's life, the exact nature of one's wrongs—and
then get about the business of correcting them. For this there is no need
of an expert or specialist. And when there is recourse to one, it is
frequently with the motivation of finding an "out" which will avoid the
necessity of coming to grips with the problem on its own terms.

The most frequent objection I hear to the notion that it is useful to
talk about one's emotional problems to relatives and friends is that
"they are not interested in hearing about your problems—they just do
not have the time or the patience to listen to you." One is likely to be
lulled into disastrous inaction by this half truth, for it provides an
excuse for not doing something which, although radically effective, is
temporarily painful. And the professional "listeners," in both psychiatry and religion, are also loth to encourage such a venture, lest it be
discovered that one can get along without them. "That's right!" most
professionals say. "Others *aren't* interested in listening to your difficulties. Nor will they really understand or know how to 'treat' you. So,
consult us instead!"

If "secret confession" to psychiatrists and priests had a really good
record of accomplishment, we should be glad enough to be spared the
embarrassment of having the "ordinary" people in our lives know who
we are. But that record is *not* good; and, reluctantly many people today
are experimenting with *open* confession of one kind or another. After
all, *secret* confession is a contradiction in terms—secrecy is what makes
confession necessary. And it is not surprising that the attempt to cope
with unresolved personal guilt by means of continued furtiveness does
not work out very well. Should we actually expect much to come of letting a priest, minister, psychiatrist, psychologist, social worker, or some

other "specialist" hear our sins, if we continue to live the Big Lie with the people who really matter to us?

As a result of my ongoing experience with group therapy, both in a mental hospital and in ordinary community settings, I am persuaded that healing and redemption depend much more upon what we say about ourselves *to others, significant others*, than upon what others (no matter how highly trained or untrained, ordained or unordained) say *to us*. It is the truth we ourselves speak, rather than the treatment we receive, that heals us.

This article emphasizes the opportunities for change and restoration which constantly surround everyone. I mean, opportunities for improving the quality of relationships with family members, friends, working associates, and the "strangers" we meet in those groups which are specially designed to provide practice in "getting honest"—and "getting well." Some suggestions will also be made about how one can best aid individuals when they try to be candid and tell us who *they* are.

If one talks about one's troubles in the sense of merely *complaining* about how bad one feels, then others are indeed likely to get bored and withdraw. Why shouldn't they? We're not giving them any information about the real source of our difficulties; and there isn't much they *can* do to help us, in a basic or lasting way. They may try reassurance, suggest a "drink" (or some more modern type of tranquilizer), or recommend a "good psychiatrist."[1] None of these alternatives is likely to be permanently effective, so one's friends, understandably, get discouraged and disappear—physically if they can, or, if this isn't possible, they simply stop "hearing." Thus it is easy to blame others if nothing comes of "talking" to them. The question is: Can it be that the fault is more nearly ours, in that we haven't talked about the right things, in the right way?

It has been my consistent observation that if, instead of complaining, one tries *confessing*, others do not get impatient, and genuinely useful things start happening. When we stop talking about how much we hurt and get down to the (good and sufficient) *reasons* for our dis-

---

[1] The preceding sentence was written before I became fully aware of the extent and convinced of the validity of the evidence for genetic factors in certain types of personality disorder. I therefore denigrated both the psychotropic drugs and their dispensers (psychiatrists). I would still hold that no one gets "well" until he also gets honest (if he has been dishonest to any seriously damaging, alienating extent), but I would also now assume that in many instances confession and restitution alone are not enough to restore psychic equilibrium; there are biochemical (enzymic) imbalances which also need to be corrected.

comfort, the effect is dramatically different. In the first place, it permits us to be brief, to "get to the point" quickly. We can go on forever about how bad we *feel*, but even the wickedest of us can, if we choose, be fairly concise about how bad we have *been*. Others are rarely bored with a sincere confession, because they intuitively recognize its importance; and they don't feel helpless, either. When we let them know what is really "bugging" us, they can begin responding relevantly. We don't have to talk endlessly, now. The truth is out, and others have something to "work on"—and so do we! Although there will be a time of shame and sorrow, peace and strength will ultimately follow, if, after confession, we *act* as we should.

When we are presenting a shell of pretense and hypocrisy to the world, we come to feel that people in general are dull, uninteresting, and uninterested. Life itself, our very existence and experience of self, ceases to be meaningful, or even tolerable. How *can* others interact authentically, validly, meaningfully with us when we are giving them only limited and perhaps systematically distorted data? It is a never-ending delight to see how warmly, intelligently, and helpfully people respond to a previously inauthentic, "neurotic" person when he begins to "come out of his shell." Now others know what his problem is and can become specifically helpful. As long as one lets others know only what his "symptoms" are, all they can do in return is "symptom therapy." But when they hear what one has *done*, and perhaps is *still* doing, to cause and deserve the symptoms, others—even the most ordinary others—can give real support and help.

So, if one wants basic, enduring change in his life, one must stop complaining about how much he *hurts* and try admitting who he *is*.

There are, it seems, two ways of "confessing," of being honest—honest about oneself and "honest" about others. When someone says, "I'm going to be frank with you," he means he is going to be frank, honest *"about you."* He is displeased about something (probably his own shortcomings), and is going to "take it out" on whoever happens to be available at the moment.

Others undoubtedly have had an influence upon all our lives; but it is hard to change oneself by changing them. Small children are, to be sure, often disorganized because their parents are; and if the parents will straighten out their lives, the children's difficulties tend to disappear. But no adult need continue to act as if he were still a helpless, irresponsible child who is at the mercy of others.

At the hospital where I am associated with a group-therapy project, we recruit new members for our groups on the admissions ward. One newly admitted patient spoke at length about how she had been "railroaded" into the hospital, how everyone was "against" her, and what a blameless life she herself had led. When we eventually asked the next woman how she happened to be in the hospital, she replied, simply: "I goofed." It is not difficult to predict which of these two women is going to leave the hospital first.

There is a fateful difference between "the shamers" and "the blamers." Those who can say, "*I* am to blame and am ashamed" have a far brighter prospect, not only of leaving a mental hospital but of remaining out of one, than do those who use others as scapegoats.

Not many years ago there was a widespread tendency in mental hospitals for the professional staff to lead patients to believe that their difficulties had arisen primarily as a result of the way they had been treated by others, and to encourage relatives and friends of patients to try to be *nicer* to them when they "came out." Our observation is that it's *the patient* who needs to learn to be "nicer," more self-critical, responsible, and open, and that as this change comes about, the response he gets from those about him improves automatically.

In our groups, people quickly come to appreciate all this, and when someone makes a painful but liberating self-disclosure, there is no attempt either to condemn or "forgive" that person. Instead the emphasis is upon what the person is doing, here and now, by way of trying to become more honest and authentic. But sometimes people who are new to this philosophy follow a less helpful practice. Not long ago a small group of people were meeting in my home; and in the course of one man's account of his life, he related an incident about which he felt deep guilt and shame. At this point one or two newcomers to the group tried to reassure this man, with such comments as: "Oh, that wasn't so bad. Lots of people have done worse things than that. Forget it!" The man rightly refused to take comfort from these well-intentioned but idle reassurances. He said that he had been saying much the same sort of thing to himself for years, and it hadn't helped. Now he wished to speak candidly, take full responsibility for his life, and have the transforming power that can come in no other way.

Our earlier point was: don't complain, confess. But, as we now see, there are two ways of confessing: one can confess others' sins, *or* one's own. Only the latter procedure is likely to be truly helpful. If one is honestly self-critical, the chances are that others will respond with very similiar behavior.

Another common question is: "But if I let others know me as I know myself, won't they reject, criticize, gossip about, or otherwise punish me?" someone will ask. "That is, if I let others know my sins and shortcomings, won't they just 'throw them up' to me and make me feel worse, rather than better?"

Perhaps the first thing to note here is that if one has been behaving badly, one of the strongest incentives for *change* is to have the eyes of others on one, to bring oneself "under suspicion." With striking regularity, persons who become deeply open with a group find that their "will power" is mysteriously strengthened. (Not only do they change with respect to the problems which brought them into the group; they also, for example, often stop smoking and make alterations in other areas of their lives which they originally did not know they *could* change. Smoking, drinking, and pill-taking are rendered considerably less attractive when one deals with the guilt in one's life in more basic ways.) Through secrecy one is shielded from group sanctions, so it is not surprising that, while practicing secrecy, one is commonly helpless in the face of temptation. One is "weak" because one does not allow the strength, concern, *and discipline* of others to operate to advantage. Confession indicates willingness to live "under the judgment" of one's fellows. It would seriously defeat the purpose of this whole procedure if one asked and received "forgiveness" and "acceptance," in the sense of no questions asked and nothing expected or demanded.

Of course, if one attempts to become honest in the presence of persons who have a similar need but no intention of doing anything about it, they may react in some not very helpful ways. They may give bogus reassurance, make fun, or become contemptuous and angry. But other, more experienced members of a group will effectively offset such reactions; and, even the worst that persons who are still "in hiding" can do to us when we become honest is not nearly as bad as what is almost certain to happen if we, ourselves, persevere in deceit and scapegoating. Besides, there is always the possibility that our honesty will make others less satisfied with their dishonesty.

Gossip is a calculated risk. But if the members of a group follow the policy of telling only their own story, the risk is minimal. Gossip, in general, represents an attempt to explain and understand otherwise unintelligible situations. If one makes a deliberate attempt to "get by" with something, others have a right to form their own conjectures—and, incidentally, to set up indirect social controls. Thus, the surest way to avoid gossip is to make our lives so open that there *is* no mystery, nothing for anyone to conjecture or be concerned about.

One of the arguments for "professional help" is that a doctor or priest can be relied upon not to reveal secrets. That is true; but, unfortunately, professional persons also discourage one from revealing secrets to anyone but them. Today it is a common practice for physicians, when consulted by persons in deep distress of soul, to say: "Here, take a pill and keep still. No one else should know anything about this." There is steadily mounting evidence that nothing provides such radical relief as having no secrets, at least no shameful ones, *from anybody.*

The next objection one is likely to encounter is this: "Granted that you may be safe in making an intimate disclosure to the ordinary people in your life, do you have any *right* to do this? Although the disclosure may make *you* feel better, isn't there the possibility that, in the process, you will hurt other persons quite unnecessarily?"

In September, 1964, one of our popular magazines carried an article entitled "The Limits of Intimacy," in which a great deal was made of this point. The author had consulted a number of psychiatrists, clinical psychologists, and marriage counselors; and they all agreed that if one has done something reprehensible, it is better to "talk it out" with a detached, objective professional person than to bother members of one's family or close friends.

Where did we get the idea that merely *talking*, to anyone, was sufficient restitution for bad behavior?

There are, admittedly, complications when one tries to deal with mistakes and the ensuing guilt in the context of ordinary interpersonal relations. If, for example, a man confesses infidelity to his wife, it will almost certainly be the occasion for her to do some systematic soul searching. And if the man deliberately tries to evade responsiblity for his conduct by blaming his wife, much of the benefit of the confession is, of course, lost. In this event it becomes less a confession than an accusation, and attack. And, until the man can approach his wife in a different frame of mind, he will probably do well to keep his silence. But even when a disclosure is made in all sincerity, consideration, and humility, it will put pressure upon the wife to ask herself what contributions, if any, *she* has made to the estrangement, loss of communication and trust, and the final infidelity. The chances are, of course, that the wife already knows there is something wrong with the marriage; and the husband's avowal makes it possible for her, at long last, to begin thinking, talking, and acting relevantly.

There are, of course, some circumstances in which one cannot confess without "hurting" others—although, even here, the effect may in the end be salutary. Consider, for example, the case of an adolescent girl who accepts the advances of a lecherous father and is then overcome by her guilt. Confession of the wrong she has committed obviously cannot be made without implicating "the other person." But the question is: Does he, in this instance, have any right to "santuary," any basis for really expecting the daughter to "protect" him? He has already betrayed *her* and forfeited any claim to loyalty on her part. And surely no one would seriously censure the girl for exposing both herself and her father under the circumstances. Even if the daughter has been somewhat provocative, the father still has little ground for expecting her to shield him. He manifestly should have "known better" than to enter into such a relationship; and even though there was an element of seductiveness on the girl's part (motivated perhaps by the wish to neutralize her father as a moral authority and source of control in her life), the father can claim little consideration. If we were more prepared to be "hurt" by others when we behave in an unworthy manner with respect to them, it might have a decidedly helpful effect on our conduct.

But, in general, it is probably true that we ought to tell our own story and not take anyone else's "inventory." For example, when a husband confesses infidelity to his wife, she will harm herself far more than she harms her husband if, out of resentment, she extends the "confession" for him. There are very likely other persons *he* needs to tell, but as long as he accepts the responsibility for what he has done and does not try to place the blame upon his wife, the problem is his, and he should be allowed to handle it as such.

"But," someone is almost certain to interject, "isn't confession likely to be psychologically dangerous? Regardless of how others react, isn't there a question of what the individual himself may do? What about the possibility of suicide or psychosis?"

This question gains substance from the fact that many psychiatrists, and even general practitioners, can cite instances in which someone has admitted serious misbehavior more or less openly, to relatives or friends, and then become so disturbed that hospitalization was necessary. On the face of it, such confession, far from being "good for the soul," has just the reverse effect. Much depends, it seems, upon the expectation of the person making the confession, and the persons receiving it.

If there is a naive belief that confession, itself, is enough, there is almost certain to be trouble, perhaps very serious trouble. And those who hear the confessions of others and hasten, forthwith, to assure them of forgiveness and acceptance, either human or divine, are performing a very doubtful service. Confession is not enough! It is a beginning, an essential first step; but it is not the last one. Voluntary penance, restitution, and amendment of life are also necessary. And anyone who believes or is led to believe that confession alone will suffice is likely to undergo "unconscious" (i.e., conscience-inflicted, "involuntary") penance of one type or another.

Suppose one could do anything, no matter how despicable and base, eventually confess it, and "go scot free." What deterrence would there be for *any* form of immorality or crime? In recent times, both psychology and theology have given very bad advice in this connection.

In order to encourage confession in wayward, alienated persons, a social system ought to show some tendency toward mercy and clemency in the event of confession, and usually it does; but the notion that one can be suddenly delivered from responsibility for his misdeeds by merely *talking* about them, either in a religious, psychological, or legal context, is a grave misconception and the source of much confusion and avoidable suffering. Psychiatrists and psychologists who are in "private practice," despite the general ambiguity of their situation, have a wry advantage here: their "therapy" is not free. In other words, if one "confesses" to them, it usually *costs* something, sometimes quite a lot, thereby providing a kind of built-in penance, which does not, of course, have to be mentioned by name to serve this deeply "moral" function. If one clearly recognizes the realities of this type of situation, can one not choose one's own penances and objects of "charity" to better effect?

The policies and practices of Alcoholics Anonymous are particularly instructive on this score. The heart of AA is its Twelve-Step Program, of spiritual and moral progress. Here there is much reference to confession and restitution, and not one word about "forgiveness." Here it is assumed that each member is going to have to *work out* his own salvation "with fear and trembling," and that there is going to be no "justification by faith only."

Finally, let us consider some related, minor questions:

1. "When has one confessed enough?"

In a general sense, the answer to this question is: Whenever there is no felt need for further confession, but no fear of having anyone else know the truth about oneself. We continue, all our lives, to make mistakes and to need the discipline of group experience; and when it is useful to other persons, as an encouragement to them in their own efforts to become honest, then one should be willing to "share his story," again and again. Practically speaking, however, one rarely feels that anything about himself is much of a "secret" if upwards of half a dozen other persons know it.

2. "Isn't there danger of overdoing confession, of getting to the point of 'boasting' about one's sins?"

If confession is not directly and explicitly associated with a program of restitution, there is indeed a danger of "overdoing" it, because confession, alone and of itself, never does enough. But I have yet to see anyone, who has *acted* as well as talked about his sins, talk too much or inappropriately. If, in our groups, someone seems to be dwelling unduly upon a past misdemeanor, he is likely to be asked: "What have you *done* about it?" Or, "What *else* do you need to talk about?"

3. "Should one start confession with an individual or in a group?"

In general, it is easier to begin with one person, who will then gradually "sponsor" one into the open fellowship of a group. But when there are painful problems to be worked through with a marital partner, it is sometimes desirable to have at least one other person present, sometimes a full-fledged group. This provides a kind of "center of gravity," which keeps issues in clearer focus, and helps each of the partners to behave with restraint and fairness.

4. Then we are often asked: "To *whom* shall I talk, confess—everyone I meet, or only a few? And how are *they* to be selected?"

Most people aren't that interested. So the question is one of pertinence, relevance. Tell it to whom you would most dread having know your story. Painful? Of course, but liberating in a way which nothing else could be. What a terrible waste of time it is seeing a "counselor" who never counsels one to do anything but to continue talking *to him*! And group therapy, while an improvement over most individual counseling, can also fall short of full effectiveness if it becomes ingrown and does not encourage its members to reach out to, and often incorporate in the group, "significant others."

5. And then there is the question: "*What* shall I confess?"

Not long ago a professional psychologist observed (through a one-way mirror, which the patients all know about) one of our hospital groups in action. Later he said: "There were two young women in that group whom I found very 'sexy'. If I had been participating in the group, would I have been expected to confess my thoughts and fantasies about those girls?"

The question was: Had this man *done* anything wrong, and did he have anything about which to feel guilty? Our position, in general, is this. One cannot entirely control the thoughts that pass through one's head, but one *can* keep from dwelling upon them or "acting out" with respect to them. If one simply notes that a given person, of either sex, is attractive, and then passes on to other things, what is there to "confess"? And precious little time is spent in our groups with conversations of this kind. But if one deliberately encourages sexual fantasies and perhaps subsequently uses them as the basis for inappropriate sexual behavior, then that is a very different matter; and the best way of bringing an end to it is to submit oneself to the discipline of absolute candor. (I think our position would also be much the same with respect to "feelings of hostility," although this too is a problem which, in practice, doesn't often arise. We find that if one deals with one's self-anger, that is, guilt, the occasion to be enraged with others is dramatically reduced.)

Because of the infinite variety and richness of group experience, it is, of course, impossible to anticipate *all* the questions and problems that may arise in this connection. What has been said here is intended, at most, as a rough guide.

Stuttering as Simultaneous
Admission and Denial

Since the following chapter concludes with a summary, there is no need to provide one in this introduction. Nor do I find anything in the text itself which calls for special comment—so will make none.

This paper was originally published in the Journal of Communication Disorders *(1967, 1, 46–50), and was reproduced in Hugo H. Gregory's* Learning Theory and Stuttering Therapy *(Evanston, Ill.: Northwestern University Press, 1968).*

The reader should be forwarned, at the outset, that this paper is almost wholly speculative—or, perhaps more precisely, inferential, deductive. That is to say, the point of view which will be set forth herein is but a special case or application of an overarching conception of psychopathology in general. The author (and his students) have, to be sure, had stutterers as patients; but this has been relatively rare, and the results, again relatively speaking, modest. However, the intractability of the symptom, as will be indicated later, may be a confirmation of the proposed explanation, rather than the reverse.

Freud and the Freudians have long emphasized the "biphasic" nature of symptoms. Due to the excessive counterforce of moral scruple (i.e., the superego), some impulse (such as sex or aggression) has, they hold, been "repressed," in the sense of being not only denied overt expression and gratification, but of also being excluded from representation in consciousness. As long as the repression is maintained, the repudiated impulse will, of course, continue to clamor and strive for satisfaction, but satisfaction will be possible only if it is *disguised*, and also accompanied by *suffering*. Thus, the Freudians have held that symptoms involve both an element of distorted ("displaced") instinctual

201

pleasure *and* "moral" pain. But since the pain is fully explicit and the gratification much less so, the symptom is seen as primarily painful, and therefore mysterious. If the symptom is as painful as the patient reports, *why* does it persist? Freud's conjecture was that the motivating force behind a symptom is always instinctual, in the way already indicated. And the element of gratification, he maintained, is also always present; but it is more or less camouflaged to begin with, and is then overlaid by suffering to make is further acceptable. The "symptom" thus persists because, in balance, it is rewarding.[1]

Perhaps it is thus legitimate to say that Freud "discovered the unconscious," but it is far less certain that he ever understood what is *in it*. Efforts to alleviate symptoms, prevent "neurosis," and provide sound guidance to the good life which have been predicated on Freudian assumptions have, by and large, borne bitter fruit; and at this juncture we have, it would seem, no choice but to search for more felicitous conceptions.

There is today mounting experimental as well as clinical evidence (Mowrer 1961, 1964, 1965, 1967) for believing that in "neurosis" the instinctual pleasure which is causing the trouble is not a mere "dangerous" *wish* which may be gratified in the future, but a grim reality, a *fact* of the past. It is quite astonishing how completely would-be therapists and other clinical investigators have, in our time, looked for subtle indications of repressed impulses, and systematically ignored a long history of socially inappropriate *impulse satisfaction*. And the result of such a life style is *guilt*, which, as a good first approximation, can be defined as a chronic fear of being found out and punished (as would have happened if the individual had been "caught in the act").

Immediately, of course, an important distinction has to be made, between individuals who, because of poor character, can experience only "sociological" or "objective" guilt, that is, the fear of being caught and punished by others, and individuals who, because of basically good character, are subject to the judgment and harassment of that inner tribunal we call conscience. The first type of individual is, of course, the *sociopath*; and the second type is the "neurotic" or, more appropriately, *psychopath* (if the word had not previously been used for the sociopath), because the trouble is now psychic, in the intra- rather than interpersonal sense.

---

[1] However, Freud resolved this horn of the dilemma only to find himself impaled upon the other one: if, as he maintained, the moral fears which impede normal, direct impulse expression are excessive and unrealistic, why do these fears not spontaneously extinguish? In other words, the question is: Why are not all "neuroses" self-correcting?

Thus, for the person of poor character, wrongdoing leads to conflict only if he is caught and confronted by others; whereas, in the person of good character, wrongdoing sets up an *inner* conflict, regardless of whether he is socially apprehended or not. In this type of person, society has, so to say, a "secret agent" or "representative in residence" and the "crime" does not have to be known on the outside for outside standards to start having an effect. (This, of course, is the reason we try to give all children a conscience: so they will have inner controls, and, hopefully, not get into "trouble with the law," in the objective sense of the term.)

Ordinarily, when we behave in a way which is socially (morally) inappropriate but not yet externally known, conscience, as we say, "speaks to us," "protests." Now the individual faces a critical decision: Will he do the behest of conscience, confess, make restitution and amend his ways? Or will he *ignore* conscience, and persevere in a policy of duplicity and "hardness of heart"? If the individual chooses the latter course of action (and here we are assuming that human beings do have choice in such matters, Cherbonnier 1955), what *then* is conscience to do? What, we may ask, would an "ambassador" in the international sphere do in such an instance? Manifestly he would try to get "word" back to the country he represents, in the hope of getting "outside" assistance. But now let us further suppose that the offending "foreign" country decides to close all "diplomatic channels" and not let the damaging report or criticism "get out."

The personal condition we ambiguously call "neurosis" is, I submit, analogous. Conscience begins to try to get the "report" out, but the individual (in Sullivan's sense of "ego system") resolves to suppress it. For a time, there may be a sort of stalemate, reflected only by lowered personal efficiency, since the individual must now spend so much time guarding against a "slip" or "leak" of some sort. But eventually, if conscience is reasonably strong and persevering, it manages to interfere with or distort ongoing action in such a way as to make the individual's behavior very strange and suspicious. Anyone can then see that something is manifestly "wrong" with the afflicted person, but he continues to try to keep the exact nature of his "problem" from being known. This "compromise formation"—between a desire (on the part of conscience) for communication and a desire (on the part of the ego) for concealment—is, I believe, the essential dynamism of all neurotic symptoms.

Now we must ask: Is stuttering a "symptom"? Because of its common intractability to conventional "therapeutic" approaches, many writers have maintained that it is not; and I am not here prepared to argue very forcibly otherwise. All I ask is that we be willing to *consider* it in the light of the conception of neurosis which has just been sketched. And if we do this, we see that stuttering (as well as other "functional speech disorders") has a special status among symptoms: it is an especially *good* one, in that conscience has succeeded in getting its message into the individual's *main communication channel* in such a way that, if the message itself cannot be clearly transmitted, it can at least "jam" and distort what the ego or self-system is trying to say. That is, although the ego stubbornly refuses to let conscience tell its story directly, conscience can, if strong and clever enough, seriously interfere with what the ego is trying to "tell the world," and thus provide a broad hint that something on the "inside" is not as it should be.

When conscience is able to produce only "bodily" symptoms, its message is inchoate and only remotely intelligible. But when it manages to get into the nervous centers controlling speech, this is extraordinarily good from the standpoint of conscience—and very bad, very dangerous, as far as the self-system is concerned.

At the outset of this paper, I say that stuttering has proved intractable to therapeutic efforts which have been predicated on this kind of thinking. I now realize that "intractable" is not quite the correct term. What I should say instead is that, without exception so far as I can recall, stutterers who have sought this type of therapy (without perhaps understanding what they were getting into), have not continued. Several instances immediately come to mind, in which the patient simply disappeared as soon as the therapist began to "hear" what his speech impedement was "saying." For example, I recall a Jewish college boy from a devout family who said, quite frankly, that he would rather stutter a little (his incapacity was indeed relatively slight) than tell his parents (a) that he had long made a practice of pilfering small amounts of money from his father's wallet and (b) that he now occasionally joins his fraternity brothers in a junket to a house of prostitution in a nearby town. The embarrassment of not being able to *talk properly* was, apparently, sufficient atonement to prevent this young man from becoming seriously "decompensated." And we may also conjecture that conscience in this instance felt (if one may speak in such a vein) that, in producing such an "obvious" symptom as stuttering, it had already done its duty, and it was now up to others to "get the message," and decide what should be done about the situation.

My surmise is that if a stutterer could be *kept* in "therapy" of this kind, he could be "cured." If this is not true, either the whole conception of psychotherapy which has here been delineated is invalid, *or* stuttering is not, after all, a "neurotic symptom." Flanagan, Goldiamond, and Izrin (1959) have suggested that stuttering is a "habit" which, like any other habit, has come into existence, not because of any such complicated reasons as suggested here, but because of a history of systematic positive reinforcement; and in support of this thesis these investigators report that verbal nonfluency can be reliably increased in otherwise normal speakers by standard behavior-shaping (Skinnerian) methods. What are the implications of this finding for the hypothesis suggested in the foregoing pages? This hypothesis, it should be said, is not without adumbrations in the clinical literature on stuttering. Wischner (1950) and Sheehan (1953) have both published related suggestions; and I am sure that anyone who is more conversant with the "speech" literature than I am could find other instances of related theorizing. The present paper, as indicated at the outset, is very "schematic," and claims empirical support only indirectly, i.e., as a special case of a general conception of psychopathology which seems to be gradually gaining in credibility.

Summary

There is considerable evidence for the view that neurotic symptoms arise, not because of repressed instincts (as psychoanalysis maintains), but because of unacknowledged real guilt, arising from inappropriate, hidden impulse satisfaction. On the assumption that one of the functions of conscience is to bring about acknowledgment of secret wrongdoing, symptoms in general may be seen as a compromise formation between an impulsion (from conscience or superego) to speak the truth, and a conscious (ego-mediated) effort to maintain the concealment. Stuttering may thus be interpreted as a conflict between these two tendencies, operating within the verbal communication channel rather than in a nonverbal channel. This interpretation is valid only if stuttering is a bona fide neurotic symptom, rather than a "mere habit."

References

Cherbonnier, E. L. B. *Hardness of heart*. New York: Doubleday, 1955.

Flanagan, B., Goldiamond, I., & Izrin, N. H. Instatement of stuttering in normally fluent individuals through operant procedures. *Science* 1959, *130*, 979–981.

Mowrer, O. H. *The crisis in psychiatry and religion*. Princeton, N. J.: Van Nostrand, 1961.

Mowrer, O. H. *The new group therapy*. Princeton, N. J.: Van Nostrand, 1964.

Mowrer, O. H. Learning theory and behavior therapy. In B. Wolman (Ed.), *Handbook of clinical psychology.* New York: McGraw-Hill, 1965.

Mowrer, O. H. (Ed.). *Morality and mental health.* Chicago: Rand McNally, 1967.

Sheehan, J. G. Theory and treatment of stuttering as an approach-avoidance conflict. *Journal of Psychology,* 1953, *36,* 27–49.

Wischner, G. J. Stuttering behavior and learning: A preliminary theoretical investigation. *Journal of Speech and Hearing Disorders,* 1950, *15,* 324–355.

Social Alienation and Reintegration: History and Contemporary Implications

I do not recall the circumstances under which the following paper was written; but for some time it remained unpublished, in mimeographed form, until I received a request for a brief manuscript from the editor of the Journal of Psychological Researches, *which is sponsored by the Madras (India) Psychology Society. The manuscript was accepted for publication and appeared in the January, 1970, issue of this periodical (14, 1–3).*

The paper touches upon certain historical aspects of the problem of deception, its consequences, and its management not otherwise covered in previous chapters.

Some 20 years ago I recall having heard the psychologist, Kurt Lewin, make the statement that a man cannot today understand his own personality or the world around him unless he knows two thousand years of history. At the time I confess that this remark did not have much meaning for me. I knew very little history, and most of my fellow psychologists seemed to be about as uninformed and uninterested in this area as I was. However, during the intervening years I have become increasingly concerned with a problem which is indeed intelligible only if one approaches it historically.

My own decision to enter psychology as a profession dates back to high school, and came, in considerable measure, from the fact that I was then suffering from certain personality problems which I did not at all understand. For a number of years after I completed my formal training in psychology, I worked in quite unrelated areas, namely, physiological psychology and learning theory. But during World War II, I was in a branch of government service which required that I function as a clinical psychologist. Since that time I have been increasingly concerned with the urgent and baffling problem of so-called "mental illness" and mental health. And it is here, specifically, that I have found the historical dimension so essential and illuminating.

Today it is widely recognized that in former times the problems of psychiatry (which literally means, the care or cure of souls) were handled largely within the sphere of religion. And the indications are that during the first few centuries of the Christian era, the church was extraordinarily competent in this regard. Religious "congregations" were then not the large and relatively impersonal masses of people which today make up the membership of so many of our churches. Instead, they were little bands or groups (sometimes called "house churches") whose members knew each other intimately and who deeply shared their life experiences.

Today we are finding that the essence of psychopathology lies in the fact that the afflicted person is socially alienated, out of community, estranged. Characteristically, and quite understandably, he is uncomfortable with and afraid of people, and the tendency to withdraw from human contact is an almost universal "symptom." In early Christian times, such wayward or "lost" souls were encouraged to join a little community or group of persons who called themselves, not Christians, but simply People of the Way. And this "way" was specifically designed to lead the lost and estranged back into authentic, fulfilling human existence. This was the essence of "salvation," healing.

And how, exactly, was this end accomplished? First of all, there was a theory, an assumption as to what was wrong with soul-sick persons. They had *sinned*, and then *hidden* their sin. As a result, they were afraid that other persons would see through them, fathom their guilty secrets, and punish them; hence the tendency to withdraw from human contact. But in such a retreat, a man carries a piece of the community with him in the form of conscience; and this "inner voice" continues to "bother" him, not because it hates and wants to hurt him, but because it loves him and wants to bring him back to community— motivate him to rise up and return to his "father's house," as the story of the Prodigal Son puts it.

The Early Christians understood all this well. And the first step in the restoration of the wayward was a procedure known as *exomologesis*, namely, a deep, thoroughgoing, unreserved form of self-disclosure, perhaps first to one or two individuals, and then to a small group. After this the individual placed himself "under the judgment" of the group.

The group responded to his confession of past wrong-doing with love and compassion, and rejoiced at his newfound honesty and courage. But "forgiveness" was not automatic. The individual, depending upon the nature and extent of his misdeeds, was expected to make restitution, do penance. And when this was accomplished, the person's self-respect returned, his apprehension and fear vanished, and he was restored to community, healed.

But this powerful and effective form of "psychiatry" was to undergo a strange fate. In 325, the Roman Emperor Constantine called the Council of Nicaea, and there made the Christians a remarkable offer. If they would give him a consistent, monolithic description of their faith and functions, he would not only end the persecution in which he and his predecessors had engaged; he would make Christianity the State Religion (and thus, hopefully, stop the impending disintegration of the Roman Empire). Understandably, the Church Fathers who assembled at Nicaea accepted Constantine's proposal. But this action was disastrous. The church now had to be popular, had to have a universal appeal, with the result that "salvation" became progressively easier— and less and less genuinely effective. By the twelfth century, confession was no longer made to a congregation or group, but to a priest, in secret; and penance also became trivial and irrelevant.

By the sixteenth century, the church had, in this way, so far lost its original power and purpose that a revolution took place—the so-called Protestant Reformation. But instead of restoring the highly effective psychological and social practices of the early church, the Reformers "sealed" the confession still further. The one remaining representative of the human community, the priest, was eliminated; and the faithful were admonished to take their sins directly to God in *silent* prayer. The result was that the church now became even less effective in dealing with sick souls than it had previously been. The "insane" were said to be possessed of the Devil, and were not uncommonly beaten, thrown into prison, and otherwise abused.

What is sometimes called the First Psychiatric Revolution involved a reclassification of the psychically disabled. No longer were they regarded as evil, but *ill*. Their abode changed from dungeons to hospitals; and instead of being punished, they were to be helped, treated. Despite abundant good intentions, this movement was also not successful. There was no very explicit theory of "mental illness," and treatment was accordingly diffuse and ineffective. People went to mental hospitals, and stayed there. They did not recover. And the belief grew that "insanity" was essentially incurable, untreatable.

The Second Psychiatric Revolution was introduced, around the turn of the present century, by Sigmund Freud. He, at long last, gave psychiatry a theory, and the attendant method of treatment he called psychoanalysis. The "sick" person, he thought, had repressed some of his "instincts," notably those of sex and aggression. And the cure consisted of helping him undo these repressions and learn to be freer, more expressive. But now, after half a century of energetic application of this approach, the situation is still critical, and many believe that we are today caught up in a third revolution. This is variously called social psychiatry, community mental health, or group therapy. But, in any case, the underlying assumption is that people get into emotional difficulties because they have been deviant and dishonest, that is, *out* of community. And "therapy" calls for a return to community, through improved communication with significant others, and commitment to a more responsible and mature style of life.

The language which is thus being used is obviously different from that of the Early Christians (who often spoke of having been lost and then found, dead and brought to life, etc.); but the underlying principles and operations are strikingly similar. And if the church, by proceeding along these lines, was once effective, there is reason to believe that modern psychology and psychiatry can also be. Here, interestingly, science and religion seem to be coalescing. The term "religion" comes from the Latin word *ligare,* which is also the root of our words "ligament" and "ligature." Thus, religion means, literally, a reunion, rebinding, reintegration. And when conceived in this way, the objectives of religion become virtually identical with those of social psychiatry and group therapy. Seen in historical perspective, the problem of personality disorder, which for a long time has been dogged by confusion and failure, is once again being approached in a way which justifies at least guarded optimism and hope.

_____ *IV*

Epilogues

As indicated in the Preface, it seemed desirable to have this volume end with a contemporary survey of the field of psycholinguistics which would update the contents of Parts I, II, and III, all of which were written a decade or more ago. Dr. Kurt Salzinger graciously agreed to undertake this assignment, which is reproduced here as the first chapter in Part IV. As the reader will discover, Dr. Salzinger's paper draws heavily on psycholinguistics, as it has been influenced by the psychology of B. F. Skinner, with only passing reference to Parts I, II, and III of this book. Although the Salzinger chapter is a valuable addition, it gives scant attention to the *cognitive* developments in psycholinguistics which have occurred in the past two decades, and the author feels reluctant to have the volume end on such a noncognitive note.

In the meantime, Anees A. Sheikh started a publication entitled the *Journal of Mental Imagery*, and invited the author to submit a paper, entitled "Mental Imagery: An Indispensable Psychological Concept" (1977, *2*, 303–326). I anticipated so little interest in this article that I ordered no reprints, only to be deluged by requests for them from many persons in this country and abroad. Although not explicitly concerned with psycholinguistics, this paper provides a systematic counterbalance to the heavy Skinnerian emphasis provided by the Salzinger chapter. The editor of this volume, Dr. R. W. Rieber, has generously agreed to the inclusion of this "imagery" chapter, as the second chapter in Part IV, which is quite congruent with developments in the book as a whole, thus avoiding a one-sided concluding emphasis on either behavioristic or cognitive psychology.

The final planning and organization of this book has involved a good deal of very pleasant interaction with Robert Rieber and Harvey Graveline, Production Editor—and some quite delightful surprises. Perhaps the most remarkable of these was an invitation to include, at the end of this book, "your complete bibliography, if you would like that." Since the list of my publications has not been published elsewhere, I happily assented to this suggestion. Hence, Chapter 16.

The Concept of the Behavioral
Mechanism in Language

Kurt Salzinger

Tracing the contributions of scientists to their intellectual siblings and descendants is at best a risky business. It should be done a long time after both the contributors and recipients have done their major work, so that one can do the analysis with the required cool calculating gaze that yields objective conclusions. We cannot indulge in that luxury in psychology, however. Psychologists, it is said, unlike scientists in the physical sciences who stand on the shoulders of their ancestors, step in their faces; changes in theories of psychology take place so fast that constant evaluation of influences is not only not possible, but is not even particularly useful in taking full advantage of whatever contributions are made.

O. H. Mowrer's contributions are in a number of different areas, and each of these will have to be reviewed separately. It will be the burden of this chapter that Mowrer's major contribution to the psychology of language is a conceptual one: that learning theory, or more generally behavior theory, is capable of proposing mechanisms to explain the important aspects of how language functions—how it is acquired, how maintained, and how dissolved or interfered with when things go wrong physiologically, psychologically, or sociologically.

We shall define a behavioral mechanism to be a description of the means—the particular operations—by which some particular behavioral act is accomplished.

That such a concept as the behavioral mechanism is valuable has been shown best in the area of psychopharmacology (Thompson & Boren, 1977). In that area, scientists have asked in what way a particular drug acts to produce its characteristic effect: Does it do so, for

213

example, by reducing or enhancing the salience of certain stimuli so that they exert their discriminative control with a greater strength? Does the drug affect the energy level of the organism so that the rate of response is directly reduced or enhanced? Does the drug affect the state of hunger of the organism so as to reduce the reinforcing strength of the consequence of the responses?

I have recently shown (Salzinger, in press) that the concept can equally effectively be applied to the area of abnormal psychology in which one is trying to find the behavioral mechanism that explains behaviors society characterizes as bizarre or antisocial. A number of questions are answered by the appropriate application of the concept. In some cases, the critical mechanism is the reaction of society to the person's behavior; in some cases, the critical mechanism is the degree to which discriminative stimuli exert their control over the person's behavior; in other cases the basic problem is paucity of reinforcing stimuli; and so on. In each case, an understanding of the behavioral mechanism suggests a way of locating and describing individuals who form groups in accordance with the behavioral mechanism that is at fault, and points in the direction of a possible treatment site.

Cognitively oriented psycholinguists have used different kinds of concepts to gain an understanding of language behavior. Particularly interested in verbal behavior in children, they have posited the language acquisition device (Chomsky, 1965). It refers not to behavior, nor to a kind of behavioral control, but rather to a "thing" ostensibly located in the brain of every child; that "thing" separates the nonsentences from the sentences, acting like a kind of sieve. This kind of concept reifies and promotes questions about the structure of the "thing" rather than about the behavior or its control. It is also related to another "thing" concept, competence, which contains within it all the important verbal behaviors lying dormant until the speaker or hearer becomes ready to use them. We find the promotion of research about the structure of competence rather than about the function of language behavior (viz., Salzinger, 1975) to which, in the end, it must be related. Glucksberg and Danks (1975) point out that the language acquisition device, which suggests that competence consists of a universal prewired grammar in the brain, was adopted as a reasonable possibility because no evidence could be found that adults could acquire anything but the simplest syntactic rules in artificial miniature languages. What the cognitive psycholinguists forgot is that actual language is not acquired in this way either. Language—and this would come as no surprise to a layperson—is acquired through its meaning or its effect on the learner of the language, either directly in problem solving or indirectly in communication. Nevertheless, as George Miller said (quoted in Glucksberg & Danks, 1975), there were only two tenable theories of language acquisition: one of them impossible (learning theory), and the other a miracle (the innate language acquisition device). It is good to see that the innate language acquisition device is viewed by one of the pioneers in psycholinguistics as a miracle theory. I obviously concur with that. However, the characterization of behavior theory as impossible, fails to examine the contributions that behavior theory could make, namely, hypothesizing the behavioral mechanisms by means of which language is acquired, emitted in communication, applied to problem solving, produced to influence others, etc.

In this respect, Mowrer's contributions are given grudging respect even in some psycholinguistics books that hold close to the cognitive approach, which they consider to be antithetical to behaviorism. Clark and Clark (1977), to take a recent example of a cognitively oriented psycholinguistics book, refer to Mowrer's autism theory of language acquisition. Essentially that theory (see Chapter 4, in this book) states that speech is acquired through the mechanism of conditioned reinforcement. The caretaker (mother, father, or someone else) talks to the baby while feeding it and otherwise reinforcing it positively with various primary reinforcers, such as food and body contact. The speech, because of its association with primary reinforcement, becomes a conditioned reinforcer. In addition, the baby emits noises in imitation of the caretaker, or possibly just in the same way that it thrashes about in the carriage, that is, by way of general activity. These noises resemble the speech and noises produced by the caretaker of the child, with the interesting consequence of the child itself producing the very sound that has acquired conditioned reinforcer value; the child participates in its own training process of language acquisition. All that babbling, and other self-directed speech when it becomes that, according to Mowrer's autism theory provides what I am going to call a behavioral mechanism for explaining one source of language acquisition. We must add here, as Mowrer himself says elsewhere in this book, that this particular hypothesis has not fared well when directly tested with respect to birds (Grosslight & Zaynor, 1967). But the important point here is not whether any one hypothesized mechanism actually works, but rather that behavior theory is capable of generating possible mechanisms. We will return to consideration of this particular behavioral mechanism below.

Mowrer has suggested still another behavioral mechanism in explaining language behavior: the sentence as a conditioning device. He discussed it at length in his presidential address (of the American

Psychological Association, 1954) and does so in this book too (Chapter 7). His concern here was the acquisition of meaning. He proposed the sentence as a conditioning device in promoting the transfer of meaning from predicate to subject; the role of the predicate is esentially to elicit the reactions typically brought forth by the unconditional stimulus, while the subject acts in the role of the conditional stimulus. Information is passed from speaker to listener and from author to reader through the sentence as conditioning device. A great deal of criticism has been heaped on this particular idea of Mowrer's, particularly the one of simplicity. Nevertheless, while admittedly inadequate by itself as a complete account, it very clearly points to a kind of conditioning that undoubtedly exists. Anecdotal evidence abounds in everyday conversation about people who are characterized by speakers as "making their blood boil" when their names are mentioned, or as making them "feel good all over" when others are discussed. Associate unknown people with those known to elicit much emotion and watch the transfer of "meaning." We do get to like or dislike people and things, at least in part, through their juxtaposition with other people and things that we already like or dislike. None know this better than our advertising experts, who change people's behavior by this very method.

The particular mechanism also has been mentioned, albeit too often with a sneer, in various books in psycholinguistics, namely, Palermo (1978), who does so just before launching into a well-deserved longer explanation of Osgood's theory of meaning. Of course, Osgood (1979) has gone on from a simple explication of measures of meaning based on mediational learning theories to considering a whole theory of language. His work was no doubt much encouraged by Mowrer's writings along similar lines.

The scientist who most directly applied Mowrer's notion of the sentence as a conditioning device was Staats (1968, 1975). He set up a series of experiments that deliberately and forthrightly showed the juxtaposition of words to result in the change of meaning just as predicted by Mowrer. Staats, like the rest of us, went on to argue that one must make use of both operant and respondent conditioning paradigms, a point of course made by Mowrer and also by Skinner (1957), although the latter stressed operant conditioning. Staats showed quite graphically that a sentence could be a conditioning device; in his experiments he accomplished that result by merely pairing words in what might appear to be fairly artificial situations. If it could work there, it certainly could work in sentences. As to questions of the role of the grammatical structure of the sentences, here too we have at least partial answers within a behavior-theory framework. Indeed, Razran conducted a series of ingenious experiments (1936, 1949, 1961, 1971) quite early on, varying the structure of sentences and demonstrating that the insertion of a "not" would elicit a different response from the subject than when the sentence was presented minus that critical word. His basic technique was the use of the semantic generalization paradigm, according to which subjects were conditioned to salivate to certain sentences, and were then tested with others resembling the initial conditional-stimulus sentence. Razran's experiments essentially showed a transfer of meaning from one sentence to others. The primary variable was quite clearly the "meaning" of the sentence rather than its structure—in other words, his experiments, like those done by Staats, showed the viability of the behavioral mechanism suggested by Mowrer.

It is the intention of this chapter to suggest other behavioral mechanisms that might fruitfully be applied to the study of language in the same spirit in which Mowrer suggested them, although it is clearly too difficult to be equally ingenious. I should point out here also that the behavior theory I will follow comes from Skinner (1957, 1974). The interested reader is referred to two other papers in which I have made explicit the more recent experiments and the old ones that encourage me to follow that theory (Salzinger, 1979a, b).

A word of caution before we proceed. The listing and explication of separate behavioral mechanisms to explain the various phenomena of language behavior do not imply that any one of the mechanisms alone controls or accounts for the language phenomenon discussed. On the contrary, I submit, as does Skinner (1957), that language behavior is multiply determined. It is only in the quiet of the study where the investigators hold forth from an armchair that they can afford the luxury of exploring single mechanisms. Nevertheless, it is by making explicit what the individual mechanisms are that puts us in a position to explain language in general. We hope that this will be at least in partial answer to Miller and Johnson-Laird (1976):

> We assume that there is more than one kind of learning and that the kinds required for mastering language are still poorly understood. What is needed is a theory of learning adequate to account for language acquisition, but such a theory is not likely to emerge until we know a great deal more about what it is that has to be acquired. (p. 692)

The point of this chapter is to show that there are, according to behavior theory (a term that includes learning theory but transcends it, since the problem is not only to account for how something is acquired, but also for how it is maintained), a number of different mechanisms working in concert to produce the complexities found in language behavior. As to the second part of the Miller and Johnson-Laird quotation, it is not at all clear that examination of what is learned will lead to the most general statements we can construct. In language behavior, what is learned must be expressed in terms of function, and that includes grammatical structure as well as meaning. Miller and Johnson-Laird's stress of perception is very much in agreement with the behavior-theory approach to language. In fact, it implies that we must cease searching for the controlling variables of language behavior within language alone. In addition, we must find out, not only what is learned, but also *what need not be learned.* Given the redundancy of stimulus control, neither the speaker nor the listener need pay attention to all the structural aspects of language; in fact, with the propensity toward doing what is easiest, the speaker/listener is likely to be controlled by the simplest stimuli around. What are these stimuli? They are the environment—physical and social. The recent realization by students of language that this is true has propelled the area of sociolinguistics into the forefront of research (e.g., Hymes, 1974; Searle, 1975). It is what has convinced me to use the name ecolinguistics (Salzinger, 1979b) to describe the behavioral approach to language study, a name that includes not only the usual behavioral and environmental terms, but also takes into account the influence of physiological factors in determining language behavior—neurolinguistics, another area of research that must be included to furnish a full description of language behavior and its controlling variables. Osgood (1979) makes the point that the need to include nonlinguistic factors in an Abstract Performance Grammar (which he seeks to develop in this work) means that any merely linguistic constructs and rules must, by definition, be inadequate to account for any language behavior—although, to be sure, Osgood does not reject out of hand the need for a competence grammar, for he feels that it must still be included in a complete account. With these words of introduction, let us survey some behavioral mechanisms to account for language.

First we will look at acquisition of language in detail; then we will speak briefly about adult language.

Acquisition of Language

The Classical Conditioning Mechanism

We have already mentioned Mowrer's autism theory as one candidate for a behavioral mechanism for the acquisition of language.[1] It is

---

[1] Mentioning Mowrer's autism theory under the heading of the "classical conditioning mechanism" does not negate the fact that the theory involves operant conditioning as well; it calls attention to its unique contribution, namely that of using classical conditioning to explain a part of the acquisition of language.

the classical conditioning paradigm that is the mainspring of the action here. As already explained, since speech by the mother or other caretaker is paired with the unconditional stimuli (US) of food, body contact, and other such stimuli, we can expect the speech itself (CS) eventually to elicit conditional responses similar to those elicited by the unconditional stimuli. The consequence of this procedure is that the child, in addition to learning to love the mother or other caretaker, also acquires the first set of conditioned reinforcers—namely the mother's speech, which in turn sets the stage for the next mechanism described below.

Stimulus-Generalization Mechanism

Since the child is also capable of emitting speech which to some degree resembles the speech and other vocalizations caretakers make to children, the classical conditioning mechanism is followed by stimulus generalization to the child's sound production. The child's emission of sounds similar to those of the caretaker produces further conditional stimuli for the child, although without the unconditional stimuli presented by the caretaker. Since intermittent pairing of CS and US produces greater resistance to extinction than continuous pairing (e.g., Notterman, Schoenfeld, & Bersh, 1952), it follows that the child's sound production will increasingly elicit the same reaction as the US. As to why the child makes the initial sounds, there are various and sundry reasons. Various reflex responses are elicited from infants—as for sound production, there is crying because of discomfort, and burping because of gas. The point is that the operant level for sound production is not zero, but on the contrary it occurs with some frequency in all babies.

Modification-of-the-Environment-as-Reinforcer Mechanism

Mere change in the environment has been shown to be an effective reinforcer with respect to a number of different animals (Kish, 1966); the effect is not very strong, but it is significant. Furthermore, it stands to reason, given the relatively little energy output involved in sound production and the rather large consequences, that the child might well be endowed genetically to be responsive to those self-produced sounds. In other words, another possible behavioral mechanism for the increase and maintenance of sound production is that the change produced in the environment is a primary reinforcer in the operant conditioning paradigm, just as food and contact are.

Imitation Mechanism (Early and/or Innate)

There are now data to suggest that imitation takes place as early as 12 days of age (Meltzoff & Moore, 1977).[2] The authors believe that imitation is a behavioral mechanism of matching visual and proprioceptively received information which is built in. The fact that facial grimaces and manual gestures are rather easily imitated by infants less than one month of age, lays the foundation for the possibility of much learning's taking place subsequently. Imitation is a very important mechanism for the acquisition of new responses in the course of the life of the individual. If there is a series of mechanisms either individually powerful or powerful in concert because all of them move in the same direction, then there certainly is no need to assume that language itself is built in. Apparently, what is built in is a series of mechanisms to make the acquisition of language relatively easy or comparatively fast. Note that the early imitation described by Meltzoff and Moore (1977) requires no reinforcement, at least according to the paper cited. The mechanism of imitative learning at a later stage under the control of reinforcement will be taken up among the mechanisms of operant conditioning.

Operant-Conditioning Mechanisms

Operant conditioning provides a number of mechanisms, but we shall, for the sake of exposition, deal with them under one heading. The critical concept here is the reinforcement contingency, which states that in the presence of some stimuli (the discriminative stimuli) a class of responses will be reinforced, that is, will be followed by a consequence that strengthens the occurrence of such responses under similar circumstances. The reinforcer is either positive—that is, by occurring, it strengthens the response that produces it, or negative—that is, by being eliminated by the response, it strengthens the response that so eliminates it. Every part of the reinforcement contingency is important. Much misunderstanding about behavior theory would be avoided if this concept were completely understood. To take but some of the examples of misunderstanding, let us look at the following.

Greespoon's experiment (1955) showed that one can, by means of simple surreptitious vocalizations, reinforce positively or negatively an arbitrary verbal response class. Subsequently, a number of review papers (e.g., Holz & Azrin, 1966; Krasner, 1958; Salzinger, 1959,

---

[2] The results are being disputed by Moshe Anisfeld who claims that a reanalysis of the data does not bear out Meltzoff and Moore's conclusions.

1969). discussed some interesting variables in the verbal conditioning experiment, response class (Salzinger, 1967) and response unit, which Skinner very carefully showed to be a matter of functional considerations, and which this author reviewed (Salzinger, 1973) to show how arbitrary unit size can get one just so far in learning about language behavior. The review papers were followed by a series of experiments best explained perhaps as a compulsion ritual in which the attempt was to simplify increasingly until the subject's task was merely to pair one of three pronouns with one verb. Thus the notion of response class was reduced to a size of one member; the problem of response unit was reduced to an arbitrary and identical size from one response to the next.

In addition, most of these experiments took no account at all of nonverbal determinants. The discriminative stimuli were verbal; most of the time, the subjects had the task of scanning a series of words and selecting from among them; and finally the reinforcers too were exclusively verbal. Although some of us in this area did make an effort to deal with a free operant situation, as in a series of monologue studies that came from our laboratory (Salzinger, Portnoy, & Feldman, 1964; Salzinger, Portnoy, Zlotogura, & Keisner, 1963), where we used such broadly defined response classes in context as the classes consisting of statements describing one's emotional attitude which we called self-referred affect statements, most did the simple experiments, and those were the ones that attracted attention. As a consequence, a lot of investigators who might otherwise have been intrigued by the operant conditioning approach were not, and turned to cognitive approaches. What did the verbal operant conditioning literature add up to? It showed over and over again that verbal reinforcement influenced verbal behavior: it could increase or decrease it. The awareness battle was waged in the experiments that made the whole conditioning process so obvious that awareness—in the sense that subjects must have said to themselves, "Every time I do such and such he (or she) says 'good,'"—was inevitable. The awareness that was elicited consisted of subvocal behavior, none unfortunately as simple as the investigators tried to make their experiments; they generally examined the awareness of their subjects by conducting interviews after the experiments.

These awareness interviews, ironically enough, completely ignored the very findings that some of us working in the area of verbal operant conditioning showed to be exemplary of the reinforcement effects (Salzinger & Pisoni, 1958, 1960, 1961); in other words, having conducted some rather artificial verbal-behavior experiments, the experimenters then conducted interviews which made no attempt to control for such variables as the reinforcement normally given in the course of that technique. But what did the awareness studies (see also Krasner, 1967) show? They showed essentially that the typical college sophomore has been conditioned to solve problems when confronted with a psychological experiment; this meant the subject would indulge in some subvocal behavior relevant to the conditioning experiment. That subjects provide themselves with instructions, especially when the experimenter presents a paucity of them, should not have been of any great surprise. All in all, these experiments turned out to be a great tribute to the discriminative stimuli, especially the ones that subjects present to themselves. In problem solving, what one teaches is to make the problem solvers as aware of their responses as possible, so that they can be efficient; college students proved themselves to have been apt pupils.

Another source of verbal operant conditioning was the need to deal with cases of muteness or bizarre speech. Salzinger, Feldman, Cowan and Salzinger (1965), and Lovaas (1977) showed in children, and Isaacs, Thomas, and Goldiamond (1960), and Sherman (1965) in adults, that one can instate speech in subjects who either ceased speaking or who never learned to speak. These experiments for the most part made use of edible reinforcers, and in this way also tended to provide the outsider with still another peculiar picture of the conditioning model when applied to verbal behavior. As a result of these experiments, a large number of people now talk about the M & M [the chocolate candy] method of producing speech in children, missing, unfortunately, the significance of producing speech in persons who are not speaking, and whose speech is eventually largely but by no means exclusively (as in normals) controlled by verbal and other social reinforcers.

Despite all of the specializations that took place and that were not integrated (the transfer–mediation paradigm of Jenkins and Palermo, 1964, is still another discussed in Salzinger, 1979a, b) to produce a coherent argument for the usefulness of the behavior theory model to explain how speech is acquired, I maintain that all of this work did show quite clearly that speech is increased or reduced depending on the consequence of that speech; in much of our verbal behavior the only consequence is verbal, although not just "mmhm" or "yeah" as such reinforcers are conveniently used in experiments with normal adults or children. Very often our speech is reinforced by the simple occurrence of other speech, or the keeping of someone's attention, or the possibility of making a sale, or a sexual conquest, or an intellectual convert, or food, etc. Surely, what these experiments have shown is that reinforcers are critical in language acquisition. They have also shown, if one looks somewhat more carefully into the literature, that the discriminative stimulus cannot be ignored, that verbal response classes are not merely increased in frequency in general but that they are increased (or for that matter decreased) in the presence of certain stimuli that we call discriminative.

Having discussed some of the misunderstandings of this literature, let us now return to consideration of another behavioral mechanism for the understanding of the acquisition of language. In the first mechanism, we showed that speech itself may become a conditional stimulus; since the unconditional stimulus with which it is normally paired is a positive primary reinforcer such as food, it stands to reason that children are in a position to reinforce themselves for emitting sounds. As in the case of classical conditioning, intermittent reinforcement of speech is such as to make it more resistant to extinction than does continuous reinforcement, and therefore the behavior is likely to be maintained. The conditional stimulus of the first behavioral mechanism along with the generalization mechanism, produces the conditions for making more reinforcement available for the child's learning of speech than would otherwise be possible.

Another operant-conditioning mechanism we have already examined is the sensory reinforcer, which, because sound production constitutes such a significant modification in the environment for the infant, will, along with the other reinforcers, increase vocalization on the part of the infant, which in turn will provide the increased opportunity for the caretaker to respond to the infant as well, providing the conditioned reinforcement.

This brings us to the most important reinforcer in the operant conditioning mechanism for language acquisition, namely, the reinforcing behavior of the caretaker. We have already explained how caretakers provide not only the obvious primary reinforcers such as food, contact, and other comforts, but because of their association with those primary reinforcers how their very presence and other behaviors, including speech and other sound production, become conditioned reinforcers. This means that the caretaker is in a position to reinforce a good deal of behavior on the part of the infant. We must remember that, although the infant does not have much control over its shaping of sounds, sound production itself, by comparison to other responses (with the possible exception of smiling, which by the way is originally elicited by gas, and is then reinforced as an operant response through the caretaker's responses), has a very high operant level, thus presenting a special opportunity for reinforcement by being so noticeable.

An important misunderstanding here is the notion that somehow, for operant conditioning to work, it must be done under the precise conditions of the laboratory and, worse yet, that it must be done on a continuous reinforcement basis. Nothing could be further from the truth. The unpredictable conditions of intermittent reinforcement in real life, it turns out, are more conducive to stability of response than are the fully predictable conditions of continuous reinforcement of the laboratory. Skinner (1938) made the discovery of intermittent reinforcement many years ago. Its greater resistance to extinction has been demonstrated enough times with enough different species, including the human one, so that its effect is unassailable.

Many people conceive operant conditioning to require a formal learning situation. It does not. The continued and erroneous practice of some high school teachers of teaching a foreign language formally through the almost exclusive teaching of grammatical rules, does not result in successful language learning. The commercial foreign language teachers, on the contrary, try very hard to simulate the real-life conditions that characterize the typical situation in which people talk to one another. As everyody knows, it is in the real-life situation that people learn the most of a foreign language. Why? Speaking and understanding speech take place in the presence of the relevant discriminative stimuli. Nonverbal discriminative stimuli evoke responses often at the same time as the verbal ones do; what's more, they sometimes are the only controlling stimuli, with the verbal stimuli never acquiring that power, but simply being present. When a child learns, quite early on, a name for milk, a multitude of conditions lead that child to acquire that response. The caretaker says it, and the child has a propensity to imitate; the caretaker has a tendency to reinforce imitation; society at large reinforces the caretaker with the most verbal child, so that the caretaker regularly stimulates the child so as to be able to reinforce it; the child has a high operant level for vocalization because it is reinforced by the attention of the caretaker; when the child is in a room alone, nobody knows when the child is awake and ready for feedings or a diaper change or whatever unless that child vocalizes, with the result that once more it is reinforced for vocalizing. Finally, the child's vocalization need not be very close to the "correct" pronunciation of the desired word for milk, mommy, or daddy, since caretakers accept approximations to the correct responses, especially when regularly emitted by the child on the same occasion. When accepting the response because it is "cute," the caretakers reinforce it by hugging the child, by making other vocal responses, by staying with the child longer than otherwise, etc. Note how important is the variety of reinforcers that impinge on the child's behavior. Returning to the point that learning of the behavior is informal, we must add to this that the caretaker will not reinforce the behavior each and every time, thus providing the conditions of intermittent reinforcement which we have already said maintain behavior best.

Where does imitation come into all of this? The child is surrounded by speech under normal circumstances, and, as we have already pointed out, the propensity for imitation is there at a very young age. Eventually, whatever the original source of imitation control, it is controlled by operant reinforcement contingencies. In this case, that contingency is simply that reinforcement is forthcoming, provided the response of the infant matches that of the adult. The degree of matching varies from caretaker to caretaker and changes as the child becomes older and more capable of matching on a greater number of the characteristics of speech.

Of course, something else is involved in the process of reinforcing better and better approximations to adult speech, namely shaping, or the reinforcement of ever closer approximations to the desired response. For a number of years, the cognitively oriented psycholinguists maintained that such shaping either does not take place, or, if it does, that it is unsuccessful. I have commented on these experiments elsewhere (Salzinger, 1979a, b), and shown that they are particularly unrepresentative of what actually takes place. A number of studies have shown that the caretakers do indeed reinforce their children in appropriate ways (Moerk, 1974, 1976). The parents have also been demonstrated to modify their reinforcing behavior depending on what the child does at a particular time. This means that no parent would require a child to repeat a long complicated sentence when that child was still struggling with short ones. Furthermore, the parents and other caretakers do modulate their verbal behavior (Moerk, 1974, 1976) depending on the age and other characteristics of the child, so that when a child is described as mentally retarded, their speech is modified to make it more understandable than for a "normal" child. Society approves of the reinforcing behavior of caretakers by its theories and practices, such as whether a child should or should not be speaking in different ways at different ages, for example. Thus all of these factors produce a situation in which shaping is done without the caretakers' having to learn the principles of operant conditioning. It is only when something goes wrong, as in children who have reached the age of four and not yet learned to speak, that special training procedures must be invoked in an explicit fashion to produce speech.

This discussion of the reinforcement of speech brings us to the question of what is learned by the child. The answer must be in terms of the reinforcement contingency: The child learns to make responses that are reinforced on particular occasions. We must add to this that all

characteristics of responses are not critical in satisfying the reinforcement contingency; thus, whether a child speaks loudly or quietly, as
long as the speech is audible but not so loud as to be aversive, the reinforcement would not depend on that characteristic. This is not to say
that nonessential response characteristics are not *also* conditioned by a
reinforcement contingency. In fact, the pulling along of nonessential (in
terms of the reinforcement contingency) response characteristics is what
we often refer to as "style" in speaking and writing, and of course
accounts for the individual differences in communications. Why are
these idiosyncratic response characteristics produced if they are not part
and parcel of the reinforcement contingency? Because they happen for
unrelated reasons, for example, because a particular word (intonation,
pronunciation, loudness, etc.) was just heard, or a particular nonverbal
stimulus happened to be there at the time without bearing any intrinsic
relationship to the reinforcement contingency.

What about grammar? That is always thrown up as a challenge to
behavioral approaches. The question is: How do you account for a
child's "knowing" a particular complicated structure? The test is traditionally carried out in a situation devoid of any nonverbal discriminative
stimuli, and the response made by the younger child is traditionally
interpreted to signify knowledge only of the simpler grammatical structure. As already suggested, however, that result can also be explained
by the grammatical structure of the speech that surrounds the child at
various ages. If the responses describable as having more complex structures are acquired at a later age, then so are the verbal stimuli presented
at a later age, and, perhaps even more important, so are the relevant
nonverbal discriminative stimuli and reinforcement contingencies that
make it possible for the child to learn the meaning of that more complex
structure. Children respond to verbal stimuli that are directed at them,
using all the information (including nonverbal stimuli and particularly
those studied in sociolinguistics) available at the time. In addition, they
also make use of their past reinforcement history. Thus, when they are
asked to "throw a chair," they simply do what they have learned in the
past one does with a chair: they sit on it (Kramer, 1973) rather than
follow the patently absurd direction. When a message is difficult to
"interpret," they respond in the ways in which they have been trained
to respond in the past.

But what about the syntax which, in one way or another, children
do eventually acquire? To answer that question it is most important to
realize that syntax is not an end in communication; with the exception
of the work of linguists or that of writers intent on producing a
particular effect on the reader, syntax is not part of the reinforcement

contingency, except at the extreme where it interferes with communication. A "badly" phrased sentence is not followed by reinforcement, because it may be misunderstood, and the hearer may therefore not reinforce that particular manner of speaking, that is, a manner that gives rise to a particular grammatical analysis. Incorrect use of grammar may, short of leading to misunderstanding, nevertheless lead to the caretaker's responding to the grammar, rather than to the content of the message; although such response is not always the case in child–caretaker conversations, it occurs more frequently than psycholinguists had supposed (Moerk, 1974, 1976). The point is that the syntax of a verbal response is similar to the manner of the rat's pressing the bar; in some cases the manner of pressing the bar may result in less reliable activation of the food magazine, and therefore less likelihood of achieving reinforcement; furthermore, as the rat becomes more and more efficient at its task, certain aspects of the response that postpone reinforcement drop out, so that the response becomes more effective at producing reinforcement. An interesting instance of this was observed by Salzinger and Waller (1962), who reinforced barking in dogs. One of the dogs whose barking response had to be shaped began by standing in one part of the box, moved his tail three times from side to side, then moved his head three times from side to side, and then finally started to bark. Eventually, the extra responses of tail wagging and head moving dropped out, and a kind of natural shaping procedure took place. No doubt a similar kind of process takes place in the child's acquiring language; the greater the degree to which the child approximates adult speech, the greater the likelihood of understanding by others, and therefore the greater the likelihood of being reinforced. Syntax, then, is reinforced, but only to the extent that it is critical in the reinforcement contingency for communication.

I briefly mentioned the problem of understanding of language before. Psycholinguists assume a very close relationship between understanding and producing language, especially with respect to grammatical properties. We must note here, however, that a child correctly following an instruction may be responding to a number of stimuli, not the least of which is the environment where the instructions are given, modified by the child's past reinforcement history as to what those stimuli are generally occasions for, when they are a part of another more familiar stimulus complex than the one currently being presented. We must also add that responding to stimuli in particular ways does not mean "understanding" them in the way that psycholinguists assume, namely, ability to construct the verbal responses which are responded to as stimuli. It is quite possible, and is done with great reliability, to dis-

criminate the complex stimuli of the music of Beethoven from those of
Tschaikowsky without being able to write music or even understand
basic scales, and without being able to play any one of the instruments,
never mind being able to sound like the orchestra in either instance; the
same argument can be made about paintings and other art forms. It
seems, therefore, arbitrary and superfluous to assume that, at any level,
hearers must be able to produce the stimuli to which they are being subjected in order to "understand" them; understanding must be defined
generally to mean that the hearer is able to make a response in a reliable fashion which is appropriate for the situation; clearly, for the linguist, that response is more often one of doing a grammatical analysis,
but for most mortals the language behavior of another individual is the
stimulus for quite different responses. In general, we may well have difficulty repeating verbatim what someone has just said, but still can
convey our understanding of that utterance by responding to it appropriately. When the verbal behavior of others is the discriminative
stimulus to which we respond, we circumvent its complexity by
responding to those stimuli for which our reinforcement history has prepared us. The well-learned lesson by the experienced psychologists is
that a stimulus is not what the experimenter presents, but rather what
the subject responds to.

     These, then, are the mechanisms that a behavioral point of view
leads us to posit for the acquisition of language. These mechanisms are
not mysterious; there need be no postulation of a special acquisition
device for a nervous system that we know achieves complexity through
combinations and permutations of chemical and neuronal reactions. The
basic idea of the behavioral mechanisms is that complexity in behavior
is achieved, not through a mirrored complexity in the nervous system,
but rather by a combination of the simpler behavioral processes acting
in concert. It was, in fact, the analysis of language into its behavioral
mechanisms that resulted in even the lowly chimpanzee's achieving language (Gardner & Gardner, 1978; Premack, 1970, 1976; Rumbaugh,
1977, Rumbaugh & Gill, 1976).

Adult Language

     We have already talked about the two other processes that are so
important in language behavior, namely, production, and perception or
understanding of language behavior. The stimuli by means of which we
acquire speech and writing are similar to those that maintain our
behavior in later years. It is certainly true that more and more of our

language behavior comes to be controlled by verbal stimuli as we grow older; nevertheless, a substantial amount of stimulus control over our language behavior comes from nonverbal stimuli, whether they be discriminative or reinforcing. Response-produced stimuli also become increasingly more important in governing our language behavior as we mature; we engage in what we call thinking and problem solving, in which our subvocal and often our written language behavior governs what we do, and where, interestingly enough, the solutions of problems constitute reinforcers for problem-solving behavior. Here is a form of self-reinforcement that we have not sufficiently investigated but which no doubt plays an important role in much of our lives.

A current behavior therapy technique, behavioral rehearsal, bears a close resemblance to such problem-solving activity. Here the therapist prompts the subject to make certain verbal responses so that they will eventually be evoked by the troublesome situation which the patient is seeking aid in handling and understanding. The therapist not only prompts the responses but reinforces them when the patient emits them. The importance of self-regulation was carefully investigated by Luria (1967) some years ago. He showed that the degree of stimulus control of verbal responses first emitted by others, and then by the children themselves, changes with age, no doubt at least in part because of training.

Without taking the time to develop the particular mechanisms in as great detail as the other ones, we can say that language behavior acts not only as a response for the speaker, and as a discriminative stimulus for the hearer (along with whatever nonverbal stimuli are there), and as a reinforcer for the hearer, but also as a discriminative stimulus for further verbal and nonverbal behavior on the part of the speaker, as well as in some fortunate moments as a reinforcer for the speaker's behavior, as happens in arriving at solutions to problems as one responds verbally, whether vocally or subvocally.

Conclusion

By sketching out a number of behavioral mechanisms in an explicit fashion, one can outline the conditions necessary to explain the acquisition of language as well as its maintenance and understanding. Once the behavioral mechanisms are so outlined, the construction of the experiments to validate their role becomes, if not a trivial task, then at least a straightforward one.

Acknowledgment

The author wishes to thank R. S. Feldman for editing this paper.

References

Chomsky, N. *Aspects of the theory of syntax.* Cambridge: M.I.T. Press, 1965.

Clark, H. H., & Clark, E. V. *Psychology and language.* New York: Harcourt Brace Jovanovich, 1977.

Gardner, R. A., & Gardner, B. T. Comparative psychology and language acquisition. In K. Salzinger & F. Denmark (Eds.), *Psychology: The state of the art. Annals of the New York Academy of Sciences,* 1978, *309,* 37–76.

Glucksberg, S., & Danks, J. H. *Experimental psycholinguistics.* Hillsdale, N. J.: Lawrence Erlbaum, 1975.

Greenspoon, J. The reinforcing effect of two spoken sounds on the frequency of two responses. *American Journal of Psychology,* 1955, *68,* 409–416.

Grosslight, J. H., & Zaynor, W. C. Verbal behavior and the mynah bird. In K. Salzinger & S. Salzinger (Eds.), *Research in verbal behavior and some neurophysiological implications.* New York: Academic, 1967.

Holz, W. C., & Azrin, N. H. Conditioning human verbal behavior. In W. K. Honig (Ed.), *Operant behavior: Areas of research and application.* New York: Appleton-Century-Crofts, 1966.

Hymes, D. *Foundations in sociolinguistics.* Philadelphia: University of Pennsylvania Press, 1974.

Isaacs, W., Thomas, J., & Goldiamond, I. Application of operant conditioning to reinstate verbal behavior in psychotics. *Journal of Speech and Hearing Disorders,* 1960, *25,* 8–12.

Jenkins, J. J., & Palermo, D. S. Mediation processes and the acquisition of linguistic structure. In U. Bellugi & R. Brown (Eds.), *The acquisition of language. Monographs of the Society for Research in Child Development,* 1964, *29,* No. 1, 141–169.

Kish, G. B. Studies of sensory reinforcement. In W. K. Honig (Ed.), *Operant conditioning: Areas of research and application.* New York: Appleton-Century-Crofts, 1966.

Kramer, P. E. Young children's responses to commands differing in length, structure, and meaning. Unpublished doctoral dissertation, Yeshiva University, 1973.

Krasner, L. Studies of the conditioning of verbal behavior. *Psychological Bulletin,* 1958, *55,* 148–170.

Krasner, L. Verbal operant conditioning and awareness. In K. Salzinger & S. Salzinger (Eds.), *Research in verbal behavior and some neurophysiological implications.* New York: Academic, 1967.

Lovaas, O. I. *The autistic child.* New York: Wiley, 1977.

Luria, A. R. The regulative function of speech in its development and dissolution. In K. Salzinger & S. Salzinger (Eds.), *Research in verbal behavior and some neurophysiological implications.* New York: Academic, 1967.

Meltzoff, A. N., & Moore, M. K. Imitation of facial and manual gestures by human neonates. *Science,* 1977, *198,* 75–78.

Miller, G. A., & Johnson-Laird, P. N. *Language and perception.* Cambridge: Harvard University Press, 1976.

Moerk, E. L. Changes in verbal child–mother interactions with increasing language skills of the child. *Journal of Psycholinguistic Research,* 1974, *3,* 101–116.

Moerk, E. L. Processes of language teaching and training in the interactions of mother–child dyads. *Child Development,* 1976, *47,* 1064–1078.

Mowrer, O. H. The psychologist looks at language. *American Psychologist,* 1954, *9,* 660–694.

Notterman, J. M., Schoenfeld, W. N., & Bersch, P. J. Partial reinforcement and conditioned heart rate response in human subjects. *Science,* 1952, *115,* 77–79.

Osgood, C. E. *Psycholinguistic papers.* The Hague: Mouton, 1979.

Palermo, D. S. *Psychology of language.* Dallas: Scott, Foresman, 1978.

Premack, D. A functional analysis of language. *Journal of the Experimental Analysis of Behavior,* 1970, *14,* 107–125.

Premack, D. *Intelligence in ape and man.* Hillsdale, N. J.: Lawrence Erlbaum, 1976.

Razran, G. Salivating and thinking in different languages. *Journal of Psychology,* 1936, *1,* 145–151.

Razran, G. Semantic and phonetographic generalizations of salivary conditioning to verbal stimuli. *Journal of Experimental Psychology,* 1949, *39,* 642–652.

Razran, G. The observable unconscious and the inferable conscious in current Soviet psychophysiology: Interoceptive conditioning, semantic conditioning, and the orienting reflex. *Psychological Review,* 1961, *68,* 81–147.

Razran, G. *Mind in evolution.* Boston: Houghton Mifflin, 1971.

Rumbaugh, D. M. (Ed.), *Language learning by a chimpanzee.* New York: Academic, 1977.

Rumbaugh, D. M., & Gill, T. V. Language and the acquisition of language-type skills by a chimpanzee (PAN). In K. Salzinger (Ed.), *Psychology in progress. Annals of the New York Academy of Sciences,* 1976, *270,* 90–123.

Salzinger, K. Experimental manipulation of verbal behavior: A review. *Journal of General Psychology,* 1959, *61,* 65–94.

Salzinger, K. The problem of response class in verbal behavior. In K. Salzinger & S. Salzinger (Eds.), *Research in verbal behavior and some neurophysiological implications.* New York: Academic, 1967.

Salzinger, K. The place of operant conditioning of verbal behavior in psychotherapy. In C. Franks (Ed.), *Behavior therapy: Appraisal and status.* New York: McGraw-Hill, 1969.

Salzinger, K. Some problems of response measurement in verbal behavior: The response unit and intraresponse relations. In K. Salzinger & R. S. Feldman (Eds.), *Studies in verbal behavior: An empirical approach.* New York: Pergamon, 1973.

Salzinger, K. Are theories of competence necessary? In D. Aaronson & R. W. Rieber (Eds.), *Developmental psycholinguistics and communication disorders. Annals of the New York Academy of Sciences,* 1975, *263,* 178–196.

Salzinger, K. Language behavior. In A. C. Catania & T. A. Brigham (Eds.), *Handbook of applied behavior analysis.* New York: Irvington/Naiburg, 1979. (a)

Salzinger, K. Ecolinguistics: A radical behavior theory approach to language behavior. In D. Aaronson & R. W. Rieber (Eds.), *Psycholinguistic research: Past, present, and future.* Hillsdale, N. J.: Lawrence Erlbaum, 1979. (b)

Salzinger, K. The behavioral mechanism to explain abnormal behavior. *Annals of the New York Academy of Sciences,* in press.

Salzinger, K., & Pisoni, S. Reinforcement of affect responses of schizophrenics during the clinical interview. *Journal of Abnormal and Social Psychology,* 1958, *57,* 84–90.

Salzinger, K., & Pisoni, S. Reinforcement of verbal affect responses of normal subjects during the interview. *Journal of Abnormal and Social Psychology*, 1960, *60*, 127–130.

Salzinger, K., & Pisoni, S. Some parameters of the conditioning of verbal affect responses in schizophrenic subjects. *Journal of Abnormal and Social Psychology*, 1961, *63*, 511–516.

Salzinger, K., & Waller, M. B. The operant control of vocalization in the dog. *Journal of the Experimental Analysis of Behavior*, 1962, *5*, 383–389.

Salzinger, K., Portnoy, S., Zlotogura, P., & Keisner, R. The effect of reinforcement on continuous speech and on plural nouns in grammatical context. *Journal of Verbal Learning and Verbal Behavior*, 1963, *1*, 477–485.

Salzinger, K., Portnoy, S., & Feldman, R. S. Experimental manipulation of continuous speech in schizophrenic patients. *Journal of Abnormal and Social Psychology*, 1964, *68*, 508–516.

Salzinger, K., Feldman, R. S., Cowan, J. E., & Salzinger, S. Operant conditioning of verbal behavior of two young speech-deficient boys. In L. Krasner & L. P. Ullmann (Eds.), *Research in behavior modification*. New York: Holt, Rinehart & Winston, 1965.

Searle, J. R. Speech acts and recent linguistics. In D. Aaronson & R. W. Rieber (Eds.), *Developmental psycholinguistics and communication disorders. Annals of the New York Academy of Sciences*, 1975, *263*, 178–196.

Sherman, J. A. Use of reinforcement and imitation to reinstate verbal behavior in mute psychotics. *Journal of Abnormal Psychology*, 1965, *70*, 155–164.

Skinner, B. F. *The behavior of organisms*. New York: Appleton-Century-Crofts, 1938.

Skinner, B. F. *Verbal behavior*. New York: Appleton-Century-Crofts, 1957.

Skinner, B. F. *About behaviorism*. New York: Knopf, 1974.

Staats, A. W. *Learning, language, and cognition*. New York: Holt, Rinehart & Winston, 1968.

Staats, A. W. *Social behaviorism*. Homewood, Ill.: Dorsey Press, 1975.

Thompson, T., & Boren, J. J. Operant behavioral pharmacology. In W. K. Honig & J. E. R. Staddon (Eds.), *Handbook of operant beavior*. Englewood Cliffs, N. J.: Prentice-Hall, 1977.

Mental Imagery: An Indispensable Psychological Concept[1]

As an undergraduate at the University of Missouri (1925–1929), I majored in psychology of a radically behavioristic type. Under the relentless insistence of Professor Max F. Meyer, we students were taught that all behavior consisted of reflexes, innate or conditioned, and that it was quite inadmissible to mention *any* "mentalistic" concept or phenomenon whatever, "images" being, of course, a salient case in point. Meyer, in his native Germany, had been trained as a physicist, so it was perhaps natural for him to adopt a highly mechanistic approach when, as a result of an extraordinary set of circumstances (Mowrer, 1976), he found himself head of a psychology department. In this respect he antedated John B. Watson by several years. Although he wrote the first psychology text with "behavior" in the title (Meyer, 1911), he did not, however, as Watson (1914, 1919, 1924) was later to do, use the term "behaviorisim;" and, again unlike Watson, he did not establish a "school" and attract a large number of followers. But it was nevertheless under him that I received my "baptism by fire" in systematic behaviorism.

Rudimentary Research on Reaction–Time Measurement—with Some Private Reservations

Since I was majoring in psychology and wanted to go on to graduate school, I tried to be a "good boy" and therefore talked and wrote as Meyer wished. But from the outset, I remember having some misgivings, which, however, I was careful to keep to myself. I liked—in fact, idolized—Max Meyer personally and didn't wish to do anything to

[1] Reprinted by permission from the *Journal of Mental Imagery,* 1977, *2*, 303–326.

displease him. But it was a good thing he couldn't read my "thoughts," which, of course, we weren't even supposed to have! I knew for myself, experientially, and for Meyer, inferentially, that we both *had* thoughts; and one of the experiments that intrigued me most, in this connection, in our beginning laboratory course had to do with the measurement of reaction time under varying conditions. Here it was perfectly clear—or so it seemed to me—that "intervening variables" (mental processes) were involved. If you started the simple but accurate reaction-time apparatus without warning, it was likely to take your lab partner (although he had his finger on the reaction key) .30 to .40 sec to respond; but if you said "Ready," and then shortly (but at slightly varying intervals) started the apparatus, he could respond in .15 or .20 sec. If we were "thinking about" something else when the timer started, we would not be ready, or "set," and our reaction time would be considerably slower. If we were machines, it was thus apparent that we were extraordinarily complicated ones, and not to be explained solely in terms of external stimulation and response, with no reference to internal processes ("using our head").

Our simple reaction-time device was also arranged so that one could measure the time of a response involving a "discrimination." I don't remember the exact details of this procedure, but I do recall that when one went from simple to discrimination reaction-time measurement, the response time was always longer. It was thus evident that the process of discriminating between the two stimulus circumstances was something that went on in one's head and could not be very well explained in simple S–R terms.

Certain aspects of response readiness, or preparatory set, can, of course, be explained in S–R terms. For example, in order to make a particular response to a specified stimulus or signal quickly, one must have adopted a particular bodily posture, called muscular or motor readiness. Also, one must have adjusted one's sensory receptors in such a way as to be maximally ready to receive the "go" stimulus. If this stimulus is, let us say, visual, one obviously doesn't want to be looking in the "wrong" direction to catch this stimulus immediately. But these motor and sensory adjustments can have been correctly made and yet, if one's *mind* or *attention* isn't on the task at hand, one's start will still be slow. So the question arises: what is the essence of "paying attention," being alert, *psychologically* ready? Even as an undergraduate it seemed to me that the essential consideration here is the mental act of holding *an image* of the "go" stimulus steadily in consciousness and not, as we say, letting one's "attention wander."

So it was, with my early experience with reaction-time measurement, that my interest was first focused, so to say "technically," on the concept of imagery. At that time, I wasn't yet familiar with the old controversy concerning "imageless thought," and did not seriously consider the possibility that attention might be mediated by subvocal language. I don't know any definitive way of ruling out this possibility but think my initial supposition about the role of imagery was probably nearer the truth.

Preparatory Set Encountered again in Work with Conditioning

As a result of fortuitous circumstances, I did my Ph.D. thesis on "The Modification of Vestibular Nystagmus by Means of Repeated Elicitation" (Mowrer, 1934), and a number of related studies while still in graduate school, all of which were concerned with vestibular or oculomotor reflexes, which seemed to be quite immune to and unrelated to consciousness. Moreover, I continued work along these same lines for two years (1932–1934) as a National Research Fellow (at Northwestern Univeristy and Princeton). Then, in the fall of 1934, I went to Yale for further study with Raymond R. Dodge, who had a long-standing interest in this area.

However, at Yale the Department of Psychology was then an integral part of the Institute of Human Relations (IHR); and here I soon found myself becoming, for the first time, directly concerned with the psychology of learning. It is true that, in my prior work, I had often seen the adaptation or habituation of vestibular reflexes as a result of repeated elicitation (especially under abnormal circumstances); but one would have been on tenuous grounds to have called this "learning" in any very conventional sense of the term, and I don't recall that I ever did (but see Mowrer, 1936). However, at Yale, especially under the pervasive and beguiling influence of Clark L. Hull, it seemed that just about everyone was interested in learning in one way or another, and I soon joined ranks. One of the first experiments which I undertook brought me face to face, again, with the phenomenon of preparatory set, or "expectancy," as I then began to call it. By this time it was well established that the galvanic skin reflex (GSR) could be "classically conditioned;" and at the IHR, we had elegant instrumentation for such work. So I decided to see if the GSR could be *instrumentally* learned, by having a setup in which the occurrence of the GSR as a conditioned response would prevent the unconditioned stimulus (a brief electric shock) from occurring. Here I can do no better than to quote from a paper, published in 1938, and entitled "Preparatory Set (Expectancy)— A Determinant in Motivation and Learning."

However, it soon became evident that it was useless to carry out the experiment as originally planned, for it was noted during the early stages of the study that the subjects almost always showed a sizable galvanic response to the light (i.e., the CS) on its *first* presentation, before the shock had ever been presented. Ordinarily such a reaction would merely be referred to as the "unconditioned response to the to-be-conditioned stimulus;" but the ineptness of this expression was soon demonstrated by the observation that the GSR to the first presentation of the light was either quite small or entirely absent *if the electrodes through which the shock was to be administrated to the subject were left unattached.* When, on the other hand, the electrodes were then attached to the subject, a vigorous "unconditioned" response made its appearance as soon as the light was again presented (p. 63).

These findings thus aroused the suspicion that not only the "unconditioned" response to the light but also the "conditioned" response which could be elicited after the light had actually been paired with the shock were largely dependent upon the subject's *state of expectancy or preparatory set, and did not reveal true learning.* (p. 64)

Further exploration showed that a "conditioned" GSR could be instantly "extinguished" in most subjects by simply telling them that, even though the shock electrodes were still attached, no more shock would be presented. Obviously, *cognitive factors* were at work here which were not a part of orthodox conditioning theory. In other words, if the conditioned stimulus in the situation just described caused subjects to expect, or *visualize,* the imminent occurrence of the unconditioned stimulus, a so-called conditioned response would occur; but if they did not expect, or visualize, such an occurrence, there was no "conditioned response," despite the occurrence of the "conditioned stimulus." In a paper entitled "There is No Convincing Evidence of Operant or Classical Conditioning in Adult Humans," William Brewer (1974) has reviewed a host of later investigations involving the GSR which consistently confirm my early findings; but I would not go so far as to take the extreme position implied by the title of the Brewer paper. However, the findings just reported certainly shattered any *simplistic* conception of conditioning that I may have formerly held. Also, it revived the interest in imagery which I had developed in connection with my undergraduate experiences with reaction time, nearly a decade before.

Preparatory Set in the Context of a Recurring Noxious Stimulus

Early on in the 1938 paper, partly on the basis of fragmentary laboratory observations and also common sense, I hypothesized that if

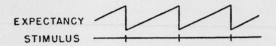

EXPECTANCY

STIMULUS

Figure 1. Hypothetical course of expectancy of a stimulus. This diagram, reproduced from an earlier study by the writer (Mowrer, 1938), represents the hypothetical course of expectancy between successive presentations of a psychologically significant stimulus. While admittedly schematic, the general shape of the upper line was suggested by the comments of subjects who had served in a study of the galvanic skin response to electric shock.

one were to present a momentary electric shock to human or animal subjects at regular (e.g., 30-sec) intervals, the subject's "expectation" of shock would follow a course similar to the one schematically represented in Figure 1. Here I remarked:

> In experiments with human subjects in which a momentary, painful stimulus is recurrently presented, the subjects commonly report that they begin to experience shortly after each presentation of the stimulus a mounting feeling of inner tension which they variously describe as "anticipation," "dread," "apprehension," "expectancy," "anxiety," etc. This subjective experience is reported as rising toward a maximum and then dropping suddenly with the actual occurrence of the noxious stimulus. Although individual differences, frequency and intensity of the stimulus, number of times it has previously been presented, etc., are undoubtedly influential here, this subjective, cyclic phenomenon, in general, follows the pattern shown in the diagram.
>
> Weaver (1930) working with cats, Upton (1929) with guinea pigs, and Schlosberg (1934) with rats have all reported objective evidence of the cyclic phenomenon just described. Curtis (1937, p. 3) has recently given an especially clear description of the phenomenon as it appears in the domestic pig. This writer reports that, following the presentation of the recurrent shock to the pig's front leg, there is a period "of several minutes of abnormal quiet, as shown by the regular breathing and smoothness of activity. Suddenly respiration becomes irregular, the pig begins to growl, crouch, brace the body, and the performance culminates in this case with a squeal and sharp flexion of the leg in about ten seconds—the same length of time which the normal reaction requires. But in this case, neither signal nor shock was given by the experimenter. The whole thing is what we have called with anthropomorphic enthusiasm a 'hallucinatory reaction,' although a better explanation probably is that the mounting tension which is to be released, trigger-fashion, by the anticipated shock signal, has grown so strong that the animal can no longer contain it. It is significant from this point of view that *the electric shock seems both in the pig and sheep to come as a relief, and is followed by a period of comparative relaxation before anticipatory behavior toward the next shock begins*" (pp. 72-73, italics added).
>
> If, as the foregoing observations indicate, a recurrently presented noxious stimulus of brief duration is characteristically preceded by a period

of heightened anticipatory tension, and if this tension is markedly reduced immediately following the occurrence of such a stimulus, one can think of escape from tension as providing no less appropriate conditions for the operation of the law of effect than does escape from hunger, escape from protracted electric shock, or escape from any other motivating stimulation. (pp. 72–73)

Much earlier Pavlov, working with the salivary reflex, had reported the phenomenon of *temporal conditioning* of this response; and other researchers, who were investigating the conditioning of motor responses, had often reported "interval," or "false," occurrences of these responses, i.e., their occurrence in the interval between stimulus presentations, and tended to interpret them, also, as instances of temporal conditioning. (See Hull, 1943, for a discussion of the phenomenon of "stimulus trace" as a possible basis for the occurrence of interval responses, in the absence of an external conditioned and/or unconditioned stimulus.) But one could hardly view the behavior between "trials" of Curtis's pig as instances of automatic, mindless temporal conditioning. In the first place, there was not just the specific leg retraction. The pig became restless, agitated, postured, and then "with a squeal [made] a sharp flexion of the leg." It seems clear that the pig ("dumb" though these creatures are usually thought to be) "had something on his mind." And who would doubt what it was: surely apprehension about the shock, imagining it in a progressively more vivid way? That such a perception of the situation was not uncongenial to Curtis himself, is indicated by his use, albeit in question marks, of the expression "hallucinatory reaction."

Also it is noteworthy (and not inherent in the concept of temporal conditioning) that immediately after Curtis's pig had made the leg flexion, it became very calm, relaxed, relieved. How should this phenomenon be explained? In the training procedure, the pig had learned that once the shock had occurred and it had flexed its leg, it was *safe* for several minutes. Could it be that responding anticipatorily also made the pig "feel better"? This relief would almost certainly have served to *reward*, in the Thorndikian sense, such a response. If Curtis had just omitted the next regularly scheduled CS and UCS (shock), he would undoubtedly have discovered the "Sidman effect" (Sidman, 1953), i.e., the pig would have continued to flex his leg periodically without any (or at least with very little) further external stimulation. (Early in the 1940s, Westbrook and I tried to produce this effect in albino rats in a revolving-wheel cage; but to our astonishment we did not succeed. I now think albino rats are too docile and stupid to show this kind of adaptive behavior; for, Keehn and I (1958) easily produced it years later in the same setup with hooded and Lashley-strain rats (which have some wild rat "blood" in them). A lot more was obviously going on in Curtis's experiment than either Pavlov or Hull ever envisioned (or at least admitted) in their postulations regarding temporal conditioning. Here we seemingly have to postulate *two* "intervening variables" of a kind not admissible in radical behaviorism parlance: *fear* and *imagery*. (See also Mowrer, 1947).

Further Evidence Emerges Serendipitously

Again we pick up on the discussion in the 1938 article, "Preparatory Set (Expectancy)—A Determinent in Motivation and Learning":

> Attention has already been called to the tendency of highly developed preparatory sets to go over into overt action (e.g., "jumping the gun" in athletic events or "premature" responses in the reaction-time experiment), before the actual occurrence of the expected, or prepared-for, stimulus; "coming forward" is a common characteristic of certain types of conditioning and again points to the probable connection between this phenomenon and set (cf. Spragg, 1936). In general, observations in this field have been restricted primarily to anticipatory, or false, *reactions,* which are easily observed and recorded, but the same principles seem also to be operative in connection with perception. In the quotation previously cited, Curtis has suggested that the anticipatory reactions made by his experimental animals might be interpreted as due to an "hallucinatory" perception of the shock stimulus. This was frankly only a surmise which could not be directly confirmed. However, in an experiment with human subjects, undertaken for quite a different purpose, the writer has recently obtained evidence which clearly supports Curtis' conjecture.
>
> In the investigation referred to, the subjects were instructed, as part of a more elaborate procedure, to press down a key with the index finger as soon as they felt a repeatedly presented electrical shock which started at zero intensity and gradually built up. In the preliminary stages of this study, it happened that apparatus difficulties occasionally necessitated delays of two or three minutes between the time when the shock was turned off and the time when it could again be build up. *During these delays the subjects would almost invariably push the key, indicating perception of shock when no shock whatever was present* [italics added]. Exploratory investigation [of this phenomenon] has shown (1) that false responses of this kind occur only after an interval greater than that normally existing between successive presentations of the actual shock [at threshold intensities]; (2) that there seems to be a positive correlation between the promptness of the occurrence of the false response and the general reactivity level of the subject; and (3) that the length of time which the false reaction persists shows individual variability. A photographic record of a typical false reaction of the kind here referred to is reproduced. (pp. 81–82)

Elsewhere (Mowrer, 1960a,b) I have suggested that an image may be regarded as a "conditioned sensation" (or perception). It seems that an image thus conceived can become so strong, or "vivid" (as the introspectionists used to say), that it can be misinterpreted as the real thing. Part of the meaning of many words is undoubtedly visual or imaginal; and when we "think," with the subvocal equivalents of words, there tends to be a constant byplay of images. But we normally do not confuse these associated images with their objective prototypes in the external world. An image goes over into an "hallucination" when this distinction breaks down, under experimental conditions such as described here, or in psychosis, where the basis for the confusion is probably biochemical.

Among the seven conclusions listed at the end of the paper under discussion, the following may be quoted as especially pertinent for present purposes:

> 1. Apparent conditioned responses can be suddenly established and equally suddenly abolished in human beings (and probably also in animals) merely by controlling the subject's state of expectancy or preparatory set.
> 2. Evidence from a variety of conditioning experiments suggests that many of the subsidiary facts discovered in this field are due simply to changes in the nature and extent of the subject's preparedness or readiness to make the particular response under investigation and have no relation to learning.
> 4. By acknowledging the mounting anticipatory tension (preparatory set) which precedes the presentation of a recurrent noxious stimulus as a form of motivation which is markedly reduced by the occurrence of the resulting response, it is possible to show that painful stimuli can be used to create and strengthen connections instead of weaken them.
> 6. The fact that anticipatory reactions, precipitated by an overdeveloped preparatory set, may be accompanied by an hallucinatory perception of the anticipated stimulus, points to a response theory of sensation and provides an approach to a stimulus–response analysis of suggestion. (p. 88)

Experiments Demonstrating Central (Mental) Elements in Preparatory Set

In 1940, the writer, in collaboration with Nelson Rayman and Eugene Bliss, published a paper entitled: "Preparatory Set (Expectancy)—An Experimental Demonstration of Its 'Central' Locus." At that time, intransigent behaviotists, who could not ignore the reality of preparatory sets, tried to keep them in a stimulus–response frame of reference by maintaining that they were all just a matter of muscular adjustment (as mentioned earlier in this paper). Although in the 1938 paper I had been able to cite some rather compelling evidence to the contrary, it was unsystematic and meager. We therefore began to design more formal and persuasive research. In the 1940 paper, three separate experiments were reported; the first of these was carried out as follows. Eighteen human subjects (Yale undergraduates) were put individually into an isolation chamber, seated at a low table on which there was a telegraph key, and instructed to hold the key down with their preferred hand and to *release it* as quickly as possible, whenever *either* a tone sounded or a small neon light, directly in their line of vision, came on. The same muscular adjustment served in both cases to provide response readiness, but only the tone stimulus was used. A series of reaction times was recorded (with the experimenter outside the chamber); and then the subjects were told to dismiss the possibility that the light might come on (which it had not) and to expect only the tone. Again a series of reaction times to the same number of tone presentations was recorded. Does anyone want to guess what the outcome was? With the second, uncomplicated set of instructions, the subjects reacted much faster than they had precisely to the same stimulus under the first set of instructions. Having to be *mentally* ready to respond to a light as well as to a tone obviously introduced complications not present when the subjects had to be set for only a tone, although in fact no stimulus but the tone ever occurred.

The second experiment involved 21 subjects who were put into the same experimental setting and told to be ready to respond as quickly as possible to either the tone or the light, and were then presented with a series of seven tones, nine lights, 14 tones, and 21 lights. Although the required response throughout was the same, the reaction time increased strikingly each time the stimulus modality was changed and then immediately became faster again. Having to shift attention (expectation, imagery), without warning, from one sensory modality to another clearly called for a mental readjustment, not a motor one, requiring a readily measurable amount of time.

Finally, it had been hypothesized that if subjects were presented with the tone and the light in a simple alternation pattern, reaction time would be increased if this pattern was broken and two tones were present in succession. Unaccountably this did not happen, but when the light was presented following the two successive tones, reaction time increased markedly, showing that the break in the established pattern of stimulus presentation had not been without "central" effect.

In short, these little experiments showed that the time required to make a motor response, such as releasing a telegraph key, can serve as a

quite sensitive index to events that are happening within the subject's
head and elude explanation in purely behavioristic terms.

In a paper by the writer, published in 1941 and entitled "Preparatory Set (Expectancy)—Further Evidence of Its 'Central' Locus," the
problem was experimentally approached with the same general
methodology but with new tasks or tests. The paper's summary follows:

> The purpose of the present study has been to obtain further evidence
> which would bear upon the validity of two rival hypotheses concerning the
> nature of preparatory set. These hypotheses are:
> A. That preparatory set necessarily involves both neural and muscular
> elements.
> B. That preparatory set, as an essentially neural phenomenon, may
> exist and vary independently of any muscular involvement.
> In an earlier study it was found that the quickness with which subjects
> could make the same, identical response (finger retraction) to two different
> stimuli varied according to whether the subjects more strongly "expected"
> (i.e., were better "set" for) one type of stimulus than the other. Since a
> given state of muscular tension in the responding bodily member would
> presumably be equally effective in facilitating reaction to either type of
> stimulus, the observed differences in promptness of reaction (which were
> taken to indicate differential sets) were interpreted as due to purely neural,
> or "central," factors.
> This interpretation has been challenged on the grounds that although
> differential muscular tensions in the responding bodily member admittedly
> cannot be regarded as responsible in the study cited for the results
> obtained, there remains the possibility that these results were due, not to
> purely central factors, but to differential sense-organ [particularly ocular]
> adjustments of a muscular nature. In the first three experiments here
> reported, the possibility of differential receptor adjustments has been
> severely minimized, if not entirely eliminated, by using stimuli which,
> although perceptively different, affected the same sense modality in such a
> way that the same receptor adjustment would be adequate for both types of
> stimuli. Under these conditions the effect referred to above did not appear,
> i.e., unexpected shifts from one type of stimulus to the other did not result
> in increased reaction times. This finding was regarded as ambiguous,
> neither proving nor disproving either Hypothesis A or B, since the absence
> of the phenomenon in question might have been due either to the absence
> of differential sense-organ adjustments or to the absence of cross-modality
> stimulation.
> In a fourth experiment, cross-modality stimulation was employed,
> involving the tactual and auditory senses. The phenomenon in question
> again appeared, and since there are no known muscles which specifically
> adjust the tactual receptors [or the ears] for optimal functioning,
> Hypothesis A is regarded as weakened by this finding and Hypothesis B
> strengthened.
> In a fifth experiment, two stimuli were again employed in the same
> (visual) sense modality, but they were of such a character as to demand
> (because of their divergent locations) markedly differentiated receptor

adjustments. The failure to obtain the phenomenon in question in this situation again suggests that it is dependent upon cross-modality stimulation rather than upon differential sense-organ adjustments and supports the neural rather than the neuro-muscular theory of set.

Incidental features of the experimental findings are briefly discussed, along with the question of the precise mechanism whereby set, as a purely neural phenomenon, is mediated. (p. 132)

Objective Methods of Measuring Preparatory Set (Expectancy)

A diagram (Figure 1) was reproduced above showing the hypothetical course of preparatory set, or expectancy, between recurrently presented stimuli calling for some specific response. A search through the literature revealed that a few earlier writers (Schilder, 1929; Woodworth, 1938) had also speculated regarding this question and constructed somewhat similar diagrams; but there were no "hard" data to support these hypothetical curves. In 1940, I published a *Psychological Monograph* entitled "Preparatory Set (Expectancy)— Some Methods of Measurement." This study was reproduced in my 1950 book, *Learning Theory and Personality Dynamics,* with a prefatory note reading, in part, as follows:

> Earlier writers had commonly subsumed under the term *attention* many of the phenomena here discussed. Behaviorists, eschewing such mentalistic concepts, tended to speak instead of *posture, sense-organ orientation,* and other *motor equivalents.* The present paper demonstrates the unreliability of purely muscular indices of secondary-drive sets and suggests instead the concept of *tension* [or, one might say, *at-tension*]. The tension concept is clearly related to that of secondary motivation and emotion [and, as previously noted, to perception and imagery]. (p. 28)

In the monograph's Introduction appears this passage:

> Academic psychologists have been aware of the forward-looking functions of the human mind [even Pavlov, as a result of animal research, spoke of the *signaling* function of conditioned stimuli], but the successful scientific investigation of a phenomenon involves more than mere recognition of its reality. Lindner (1938) has recently reviewed the attempts of the early introspectionists to analyze the anticipatory processes and concludes that the work of these writers "nets us very little" (p. 225). On one point, however, these writers were in fair agreement, namely, that anticipation or expectancy is commonly accompanied by a feeling of "strain" which they sought to localize in the skeletal musculature. Lange (1888), carrying this type of analysis a step further, reached the conclusion that, as James (1890) has rephrased it, "ideational preparation itself is a consequence of muscular adjustment, so that the latter may be called the essence of the atten-

tive process throughout" (p. 444). If, as this view held, anticipation of an impending event were not only accompanied by, but actually dependent upon, characteristic changes in the subject's motor apparatus, all that would be needed to make this phenomenon objectively identifiable and measurable (and thus lay the foundation for its scientific study) would be the development of refined methods of detecting minute muscular changes. Within the past two decades such technical progress has been made in this connection that virtually any type of muscular activity, however subtle, can be detected and recorded. But application of these improved methods has not confirmed the assumption of a necessary connection between anticipation and muscular activity. Woodworth (1938) has reviewed some of the major attempts that have been made to demonstrate a muscualr basis for quickness of simple reaction time (which is known to be a function of anticipation) and shows that the results have been distinctly unsatisfactory. The negative findings of Hathaway (1935), who used action-current recording, are especially noteworthy in this connection (pp. 30–31. These page references are to *Learning Theory and Personality Dynamics*, not to the original monograph.)

The findings just cited come as no surprise in light of the two studies on the central locus of preparatory set reviewed in the preceding section of this paper. By 1940, everything was thus dovetailing very nicely around evidence for the "mental" as opposed to "motor" nature of preparatory set or, to use the subjective term, expectancy. At this juncture the writer felt that the only really important job remaining in this field was, as noted above, to find objective ways of measuring this phenomenon. In the monograph here under consideration, several objective indices of preparatory set are described and documented with data; but the neatest evidence of all came, once again, from the use of the reaction-time measurement. The whole story of the experimental procedure at issue here is told in two graphs, reproduced here as Figures 2 and 3, which, with their legends, are largely self-explanatory. Only one or two additional comments are pertinent.

It will be noted that we did not sample for expectancy (i.e., test reaction time) at less than three sec after the last reaction had been elicited. Thus we do not know what the average reaction time for our 100 subjects would have been if tested more immediately after the preceding reaction, let us say, at one sec or even half a sec. It would presumably have been very long, because, with a standard 12-sec interval between stimulus presentations, expectancy of a stimulus almost immediately after the preceding one would have been very low. So, extrapolating on the basis of this reasoning, the reaction-time curve (Figure 3) presumably rises very *high* as it approximates the ordinate, and the expectancy curve sinks very *low* as it likewise extends back toward the ordinate. However, we have actual data only for tests at the

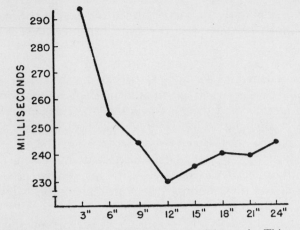

Figure 2. Reaction times at expected and unexpected intervals. This curve represents the average reaction time (in milliseconds) of 100 male college students as a function of the interval between successive presentations of the reaction stimulus (tone). The standard interstimulus interval was 12 seconds, but occasionally the stimulus occurred at one of the "test" intervals indicated along the abscissa.

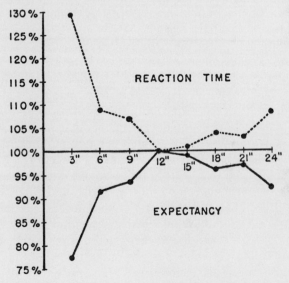

Figure 3. Method of translating reaction times into an expectancy curve. The dotted-line curve shows the extent (in terms of percentages) by which the average reaction time of 100 male college students on "test" presentations of the reaction stimulus (tone) at the intervals indicated along the abscissa exceeded the average reaction time of the same subjects on the three standard-interval presentations of the stimulus that immediately preceded each "test" presentation. The solid-line curve is the reciprocal of the dotted-line curve and is assumed to represent the course of "expectancy."

three-, six-, and nine-sec intervals; and it looks as if the rise in expectancy from three to twelve sec (the standard interstimulus interval) is roughly linear.

Now when the response stimulus was given at the usual 12-sec interval and a reaction (key press) occurred, expectancy presumably always dropped abruptly, as postulated in Figure 1; but one does not see this in Figure 3, and the reason is that the extension of the expectancy curve beyond the 12-sec interval was derived from the speed of reactions occurring at test intervals *longer* than the standard 12-sec intervals, i.e., at 15, 18, 21, and 24 sec. It is interesting to note how precisely expectancy of the reaction stimulus peaked at the standard 12-sec interval and then gradually decayed during the following 12 sec when the standard stimulus was withheld.

In rereading the section *Implications* in the monograph under consideration, I am struck by the fact that I was here concerned exclusively with the way in which the discovery of the motivating and rewarding power of the tension involved in "attention" ("expectancy") and its reduction could improve our systematic understanding of the psychology of learning and its application in respect to education. As we shall presently see, the importance of these considerations is not to be underrated. However, what is of greatest cogency here is the fact that the line of investigation thus far reviewed in this paper shows that even so rudimentary a phenomenon as variation in reaction time under certain conditions powerfully supports recognition of "mental life," including such phenomena as expectation and imagery. This work, if I may say so, drove a deep wedge into the arbitary semantic armor of behaviorism, and was one of the developments that laid the basis for the resurgence of *cognitive psychology* which is today so much in evidence.

But at the time I received scant thanks for my efforts. My work on preparatory set received only a little more attention than had my earlier research on vestibular and oculomotor reflexes, and there was meager indication in 1940 that I would ever become the sixth most cited member of the American Psychological Association (Myers, 1970). In fact, while I was at Yale and doing the reaction-time work, Clark Hull, who was extraordinarily influential at that time and with whom I enjoyed the most cordial of personal relations, once told me that he did not find my notions about "expectancy" at all "useful" and saw no future for this line of inquiry. In recent years, I have occasionally purchased some of the many new books on cognitive psychology, but, being preoccupied with other matters, have not read a word in any of them. Just now, however, it occurred to me to wonder if my earlier (pre-Skinnerian) discoveries regarding the "indispensability" of certain

cognitive processes are cited in this new literature or have been for-
gotten. The only two such books that I have conveniently at hand are
Cognition and the Symbolic Processes, edited by Weimer and Palermo
(1974), and W. K. Estes's two-volume *Handbook of Learning and
Cognitive Processes* (1975). In the author index of the first book I find
two citations, consisting of two sentences on page nine and a bib-
liographic citation on page 38 of the 1938 study first mentioned in the
present paper. In the Estes volumes I do a little better, with a total of
11 references. But zounds! I find that all of the Estes references are to
my later work on learning and make not a single allusion to my work in
the 1930's on cognitive problems. Offhand, the only reference to the
1940 monograph, of which I am aware, appears in Shaffer (1976).
What a vein of pure gold these latter-day writers on cognition appear to
have missed!

However, there was one respect in which the preparatory-set
studies paid off handsomely. They made me aware of the tension in
attention and soon led to a recognition of the enormous and undeniable
importance of *fear* as a secondary drive and reinforcement. Along with
Neal Miller (1948), I was able to show in a number of experiments
reported in *Learning Theory and Personality Dynamics* (Mowrer,
1950) that one can produce a variety of behavioral phenomena in laboratory rats that are inexplicable unless one posits fear, the *emotion* of
fear, as an "intervening variable" between external stimuli and
responses. When I was an undergraduate, Max Meyer referred to emotions as "wasted reactions"—he might as well have called them "useless
reactions." They were, and of course still are, an embarrassment to all
behaviorists. But they now have a great volume of experimental findings
before them which they don't know how to handle, without violating
their "scientific objectivity." The best that the Skinnerians have been
able to do in this connection is to resort to a transparent semantic ruse.
Instead of saying that a CS which has been associated with a noxious
UCS acquires the capacity to *arouse fear* in the subject, they say, disin-
genuously and ambiguously, that the CS has "become aversive." The
implication, which is patently absurd, is that the *stimulus* has changed,
not the organism. That there has been no change in the CS itself is
easily proven by subjecting another, "naive" sugject to is, who finds it
not at all "aversive."

Behavior modification is, and for some years has been, the biggest
thing in both academic and pop psychology; but it is very far from
being simon-pure *Behaviorism.* At most, it is a form of neo- or quasi-
behaviorism, shot through with caveats and heresies in wondrous
variety. To cite a single example: in one very famous form of behavior

therapy, namely, "systematic desensitization," the subjects are unabashedly encouraged to make use of *imagery* in the treatment process. Considerable knowledge of teaching and learning has been around for a long time. How else would cultures, both simple and complex, have been so successfully transmitted? But here again the beguiling attraction of novel terminology—behavior modification instead of simply teaching and learning—is manifest.

Sytematic Learning Theory and Imagery

During the period when I was working on preparatory set (1935–1940), I was also becoming increasingly immersed in the psychology of learning; and after that period, for a good 20 years, I was almost exclusively concerned with this field (and its relationship to language). In 1947, I published a long paper entitled "On the Dual Nature of Learning—A Reinterpretation of 'Conditioning' and 'Problem Solving'" (reproduced as Chapter 9 in Mowrer, 1950). Here I reviewed and systematized both theory and empirical evidence for believing that there are two basic, and basically different, types of learning, but that, in the ongoing behavior of living organisms, there is a constant interplay and coordination of the two. I am referring, as the title of this paper indicates, to *conditioning* (of responses mediated by the autonomic nervous system) in the tradition of I. P. Pavlov, and habit formation and elimination (involving responses mediated by the central nervouse system), as E. L. Thorndike conceived these processes. But, by acknowledging the reality and importance of *both* of these types of learning and their interaction, one could considerably extend the scope and power of learning theory to include two previously neglected sources of secondary reward, namely, *relief* and *hope,* and two sources of secondary punishment, *fear onset* and *frustration* or *disappointment.*

For the detailed ramifications of this particular treatment of conditioning and extinction and habit learning and unlearning, the reader is referred to the 1947 paper; for we now want to move on to developments which were not fully reported until the publication of my two books, *Learning Theory and Behavior* (1960a) and *Learning Theory and the Symbolic Processes* (1960b). As is well known, Edward Thorndike thought learning by conditioning was inconsequential, or even nonexistent; whereas Ivan Pavlov regarded conditioning as the only *true* form of learning, from which so-called habits could be derived. In support of this position, he published, in 1932, a paper entitled "The Reply of a Physiologist to Psychologists," wherein he gave an illustration of how habits can be reduced to a concatenation of conditioned reflexes. However, the phraseology was awkward and the argument hard to follow, and the paper attracted little attention. But, by a course of developments which I shall briefly delineate, I eventually came to believe that Pavlov's 1932 paper, however ineptly expressed, was valid.

The first development in this connection came about in relation to the phenomenon of punishment. Thorndike was a self-styled *connectionist,* believing that habits come into existence under the influence of reward, which strengthens the neural pathway between a particular stimulus or situation and a particular response or series of responses and that, conversely, habits are weakened or obliterated by punishment, because it weakens the neural pathways which mediate them. Everyone knows, on the basis of common sense if not laboratory observations with animals, that an act which is consistently followed by punishment involving noxious stimulation, such as electric shock, or secondary punishments (fright or frustration), is very likely to be inhibited. But there is a way, other than the one put forward by Thorndike, of explaining this effect. The conditioning of fear, in both human beings and lower animals, to any *external* stimulus closely associated in time with a painful event of almost any nature is commonplace. Moreover, it is well established that behavioral acts themselves produce *internal* (e.g., proprioceptive) and also quite possibly external (e.g., visual) stimuli. Hence, if such an act is followed by punishment, one would expect fear to become associated with these response-associated stimuli, thus producing a conflict between the fear, conditioned to response-associated stimuli, and whatever other motivation (e.g., hunger) had initiated the response. That is to say, if a response is punished one or more times, it is likely to stop occurring, not because some neural pathways have been "stamped out" (as Thorndike was wont to say), but because the initiation of the response aroused stimuli which now cue off fear, which can be eliminated only by cessation of the response producing these stimuli.

Thus one can rather easily derive a conditioning theory of habit inhibition, in agreement with Pavlov's position, except that Pavlov was never much interested in habit inhibition by means of punishment and restricted his 1932 article to an attempt to show that conditioning can be used to account, not for the inhibition of habits, but for their establishment. Having shown how easy it is to derive a conditioning explanation of habit elimination, let us therefore see if the same logic can be used, more simply than Pavlov did in his paper, to account for habit formation. Here we have as a point of departure the well known fact that if an external stimulus is closely associated in time with the occurrence of a pleasant or rewarding state of affairs (such as food for a hungry animal), the subject will develop a *liking* for or a *positive* "attitude" (Freud spoke of "cathexis") with respect to this stimulus, as manifested in numerous ways, such as eagerly watching for its recurrence, approaching it, and displaying certain appetitive responses (such as salivation or sexual excitement). In short, such a stimulus takes on *secondary reinforcement* properties; and all one has to do to derive a conditioning explanation of habit formation is to note, again, that the stimuli that are inherently associated with a response which results in primary reinforcement will also take on secondary reinforcement properties, thus powerfully facilitating, rather than inhibiting, the recurrence of this response. Ergo, it is possible to explain habit formation without recourse to the "stamping in" of any specific stimulus-response neural pathways as Thorndike conceived them.

When I first clearly saw the possibility of thus deriving a conditioned-response explanation of habit formation, as well as of habit inhibition, I was greatly heartened to discover in a book entitled *Conditioned Refelexes and Neuron Organization*, published in 1948 by the distinguished Polish neurophysiologist, Jerzy Konorski, that he had quite independently arrived at essentially the same "cybernetic" or "feedback" conception of behavior facilitation and inhibition. Moreover, as I reread Pavlov's 1932 article, I realized that what he was trying, rather ineptly, to say about the dependence of habit formation on conditioning was also fully congruent with this way of thinking about the development of so-called habitual responses.

But, unhappily, it soon became apparent that there was "a fly in the ointment." The feedback (conditioning) theory of response inhibition (as opposed to Thorndike's connection "stamping out") offers no problem; and once a response is in progress, the feedback theory of habit blocking works quite nicely. The rub comes when we have to answer the question: How does a habitual response get *selected and started* in the first place—since there can be no sensory feedback with reinforcing power until this happens? If one accepts Thorndike's connectionistic, or "bond," theory of habit, this difficulty does not arise, but his theory has other difficulties, and no one today seems to take it very seriously. So we must, in some way, answer the foregoing question, or also abandon the feedback conception of habit. Here is the only solution which seemed viable when I wrote the 1960 books, and which, to me, still seems highly tenable:

> At this point we face an expositional dilemma. The writer believes there is an eminently satisfactory solution to the problem just posed; but it has been arrived at in a rather circuitous and unexpected manner and cannot be convincingly described at this juncture without a major digression.

Therefore, what we shall do is deliberately postpone full discussion of this problem until later (1960b, see especially Chapters 6 and 7). . . .

In other words, the relevance of *cognitive* as well as *affective* processes is being recognized in systematic theory; and the solution to the problem of response selection and initiation hinges, quite specifically it seems, upon the reality of *imagery* (or *memory*), which is a cognitive phenomenon, pure and simple. . . . Therefore, as already indicated, our plan will be to hold discussion for the balance of this volume at a level such that cognitive considerations can be side-tracked and then, subsequently, returned to for detailed treatment. (1960a, pp. 251–252)

A hungry boy who has never before eaten an apple sees one and samples it. It is pleasant tasting and satisfies his hunger. Conceivably the sight, smell, and taste of the apple and the other sensations (proprioceptive and the like) associated with the act of eating become *conditioned to the hunger drive,* so that when the hunger subsequently recurs, the boy will "think of" apple eating, i.e., he will have *images* derived from the earlier experience. The hope (secondary reinforcement) which was conditioned to the sensations will now generalize to the images; and, lacking conflicting impulses, the boy will start trying to find another apple. Here we are making a number of assumptions which are highly unorthodox as far as conventional learning theory is concerned, but they may nonetheless be valid. Thorndike by-passed any such thinking on the premise that, in the situation described, a bond is forged directly between hunger and apple-seeking and apple-eating behavior. The difficulties inherent in this view are well known. In Pavlovian parlance, one might speak of some reaction elicited by the apple (e.g., salivation) getting conditioned to some stimulus experienced just before (or as) the apple was eaten (e.g., the sight or smell of the apple); but one would *not* be inclined to think of the *hunger drive* becoming a conditioned stimulus. This is precisely what the foregoing analysis presupposes, that the hunger becomes the conditioned stimulus for arousing an image of apple and apple eating, to which has also been conditioned the emotion of hope which, for reasons previously considered in this book, would put the individual into more or less appropriate action. In section VII of this chapter, some importance has already been attached to the concept of "reference level," image, or standard toward which an error-actuated servo-system always moves. Perhaps if images (of objects and actions) get conditioned to drives, the program of "scansion" and "search" is solved. Moreover, there is already a considerable literature suggesting a relationship between drive, or need, and imagery. (1960b, pp. 286–287)

As already indicated, Jerzy Konorski published a book in 1948 supporting the view that habits (i.e., "voluntary responses") are dependent, both for their initiation and inhibition, upon the positive and negative reinforcement (respectively) of the sensory feedback from such responses. This view was based in considerable measure upon the results of early research which indicated that if one of the legs of a laboratory animal (dog or cat) is deafferentated so that proprioceptive and related sensations of movement in the leg are eliminated, and if the animal is in a hammock, or sling, which keeps it from seeing this leg, habitual, or voluntary, responses cannot be effectively initiated. However, later research contradicted the earlier findings. It showed that a laboratory animal can initiate and execute voluntary (habitual) responses without sensory feedback therefrom, but that the response in question will lack the precision it would normally have. In his magnum opus, *Integrative Activity of the Brain: An Interdisciplinary Approach*, Konorski (1967) expressed this altered view thus:

> The important conclusion which can be inferred from our concept is that when a set of gnostic units representing a definite kinesthetic pattern has been established, it can be thrown into operation through the associative way independently of the sensory input from the limb concerned. In other words, a given movement can be programmed and executed even if the kinesthetic feedback is impaired or abolished. This is why a subject who has sustained a cerebellar operation does not lose either the programming of purposeful movements or the ability for their execution. The impairment concerns only the precision of a movement and its smooth character, because sensory feedback is indeed necessary in the course of the performance of motor acts, particularly when they are complex and serial. (pp. 195–196)

What Konorski means by "our concept" is made clear in the following paragraphs which occur a few pages earlier:

> Now, the problem of first importance arises as to the physiological mechanism of this downward stream of messages leading *from* the kinesthetic gnostic units to the executive organs.
>
> We think that we can give a reasonable solution of this problem on the basis of our general ideas concerning the functional organization of the afferent systems. (pp. 191–192)
>
> As far as the psychological evidence is concerned, we know that imaging a certain movement leads either to its overt performance or at least to its latent performance, manifested by the EMG [electromyogram] record. That the image of a movement is an agent eliciting that movement was clearly stated by James (1890), who called this phenomenon "ideo-motor action," and who provided evidence to show that it is true. It is worthwhile to cite some of his own statements concerning this problem:
>
> "An anticipatory image, then, of sensorial consequences of a movement plus (at certain occasions) that fiat [intention or command] that these consequences shall become actual, is the only psychic state which introspection lets us discern as the forerunner of our voluntary act." (op. cit. p. 501)
>
> "Sometimes a bare idea is sufficient, but sometimes an additional conscious element, in the shape of a fiat, a mandate or express consent has to intervene and precede the movement. The cases without a fiat constitute the more fundamental, because the more simple, variety." (op. cit. p. 522)
>
> "We may therefore lay it down for certain that every representation of a movement awakens in some degree the actual movement which is its object; and awakens it in a maximum degree whenever it is not kept from so doing by an antagonistic representation present simultaneously to the mind." (op. cit. p. 526)

These quotations show how clearly James saw the mechanism of voluntary movement, a mechanism at which he had arrived on the basis of astute introspection. It is most encouraging to know that we have come to exactly the same concept by quite different considerations—namely, through the physiological analysis of movements.

No less conclusive seems to be the neurological evidence based either on the effects of injuries of the cortex or of its stimulation in unanesthetized subjects. (pp. 193–194)

Although in the context of the earlier quotation from pages 286–287 of *Learning Theory and the Symbolic Processes,* I did not cite James's ideomotor theory of voluntary (habitual) behavior, I did cite his anticipation and remarkable appreciation of what has become known as cybernetics (Wiener, 1948) and error-actuated systems. In this connection James (1890) said:

So in acquiring any art or voluntary function, the marksman ends by thinking only of the exact position of the goal, the singer only of the perfect sound, the balancer only of the point of the pole whose oscillations he must counteract. The associated mechanism has become so perfect in all these persons that each variation in the thought of the end is functionally correlated with the one movement fitted to bring the latter about. (p. 497)

To which I added the following comment:

But despite the shrewdness of these observations (and of similar ones by Dewey), they fell among stones and were not to get a congenial hearing for more than half a century. Why, one must ask, was this the case? The answer undoubtedly is complex; but we may conjecture that one important element in the situation was the lack, in James' account, of a proper emphasis upon motivation or dynamics. If our analysis is sound, a particular course of behavior is selected, or "willed," because its image or anticipated occurrence arouses hope; whereas, its nonoccurrence or incorrect occurrence arouses no hope, or even fear. (1960b, p. 286)

Konorski's conversion to the "ideomotor" theory was published, as previously noted, in 1967, whereas the publication of my own espousal of this hypothesis occurred in 1960. Konorski knew of my work, he visited my laboratories and I visited his, and he also knew of the two 1960 books. But in *Integrative Activity of the Brain,* he cited only *Learning Theory and Behavior,* and that critically as propounding the "claim that the proprioceptive feedback of the performed movement is essential for instrumental conditioning as a sort of secondary reinforcement" (p. 415). How could he have failed to note my own reservations on this score, briefly expressed in the first of the 1960 books (see earlier quotation from pages 251–252), and my full elaboration in the second of the books of the same alternative position he had come to advocate? Let us hope that he had not read either of my books really carefully, and had *quite independently* arrived at this position, thus giving it additional credibility and force (cf. Mowrer, 1976).

Carol McMahon to the Rescue

Learning Theory and Behavior (1960a) and *Learning Theory and the Symbolic Processes* (1960b) were the culmination of more than 20 years of work, and I had high hopes with respect to their reception in psychology and related disciplines. Both of them were favorably, but not exactly enthusiastically, reviewed (Amsel, 1961; Jeffrey, 1961); and for a few years they sold moderately well. But in about 1970, the publisher said that his company was going to let *Learning Theory and the Symbolic Processes* go out of print, and a year or so later I received the same news regarding *Learning Theory and Behavior* (a blow that was somewhat softened, however, by a subsequent letter from Mr. Robert E. Krieger, who informed me that he had purchased the "plates" of this book and was going to reprint it—see Mowrer, 1973). All this was, of course, disappointing, but perhaps inevitable. With the publication of these two books, in 1960, I abandoned virtually all further research and writing with respect to the psychology of learning, didn't keep up with the current literature, and had no interest in trying to revise or update these volumes. So, in 10 years' time, they were "old books," and scores of newer ones were inundating the field. In the meantime, I had become engrossed in another field (see, for example, Mowrer, 1972), and it was not too difficult for me soon to regard the work on learning as a closed chapter. Obviously the 1960 books were not destined for immortality (despite my continued faith in them), and I bowed to the seemingly inevitable.

But then a remarkable thing happened. Carol E. McMahon, in 1973, published in the *American Journal of Psychology* a superb article entitled "Images as Motives and Motivators: A Historical Perspective." Her Abstract reads as follows:

An extremely influential theory of motivation is traced from its inception in Aristotle's thinking to the form it has assumed in contemporary work. The ancient theory—that mental images of goal objects serve as motives by providing energization and direction—seemed to succumb to the Darwinian revolution in the nineteenth century, despite William James' attempt to save it, but then surreptitiously reappeared in behavioristic systems and has since openly surfaced in Mowrer's theory. Its treatment in contemporary physiological and cognitive psychology obviates the problems that led to its earlier abandonment.

Fortis imaginatio generat causum
(A strong imagination begets the event itself)
                                        —Scholastic axiom

And the opening paragraph of the McMahon paper is no less
cogent:

> As they are traditionally construed, the problems of motivation are
> those of the activation and direction of behavior. Both of these aspects were
> directly linked to mental imagery in Aristotle's extremely influential theory
> of motivation. His theory was that the image serves as the source of activa-
> tion and that it guides and directs behavior by representing the goal object.
> After thriving vigorously for two thousand years, the theory has not been
> heard of for nearly fifty years and has not been properly accepted or dis-
> cussed for close to one hundred years. (p. 465)

There then follows an engaging review of Aristotle's general
psychological position, with especial emphasis upon his repeated allu-
sions to the importance of imagery, and a discussion of how Aristotle's
work has been interpreted and evaluated through the ages. So refresh-
ing, informative, and "contemporary" is all this that I would like to see
the entire McMahon paper republished in the *Journal of Mental
Imagery*. But for immediate purposes the following paragraphs are the
pertinent ones:

> O. Hobart Mowrer deserves the credit for having been the first in
> contemporary psychology to unabashedly use the term "imagery" in the
> context of motivation and for giving the image a place of such prominence
> as to make it indispensable to his system. Of course, as in other neo-
> behavioristic drive theories, he did not think of the "primary motivation,"
> or driving force, as inherent in the cognitive processes; but neither did
> Aristotle.
>
> The image enters Mowrer's theory as a mechanism of self-regulation
> and of the direction of behavior. Action, he argues, is guided or directed by
> "hopes" and "fears" that have become conditioned to "response-correlated
> stimuli," which later are simply "good and bad images," and all behavior
> is a form of searching or exploration in which the image serves as a stand-
> ard or ideal of some sort—as a "thermostat." His analogy of the function
> of the image with that of a thermostat can be exemplified by Miller,
> Galanter, and Pribram's (1960) TOTE model, which stands for the
> sequence: test, operate, test, exit. The test determines whether or not
> things are as they should be; if they are not, some operation is performed
> to remedy the situation, and a further test determines the effectiveness of
> the operation. The sequence is repeated until the test shows a satisfactory
> outcome, at which point the organisms exists from the behavior pattern.
> Mowrer's thermostatic image provides the standard; that is, the informa-
> tion necessary for the organism to know whether or not things are as they
> should be. Whenever there is a discrepancy between the actual and the

ideal (in both senses of that last word), the organism is motivated to take
action to correct the discrepancy. When the product of its operation is in
agreement with the image (i.e., when the thermostat registers normal), the
organism exits to new behavior. The motive, therefore, is eliminated when
the goal is obtained.

Note the similarity between Mowrer's thinking and Condillac's
contention that we are moved only after comparison of past pleasant sensations, in imagery form, with present unpleasant sensations. In further
agreement with old thought, Mowrer describes fear as "an image of pain"
and hope as "an image of pleasure or gratification." However, he also
insightfully extends these principles to the animal level, with the
phenomenon described by Muenzinger (1938) as "vicarious trial and
error," for "as the rat symbolically samples, successively, the probable consequences of one course of action as opposed to another [a right turn or a
left turn at the choice point in a T-maze], he is not experiencing mere
cognitions but actual *motivating states*" (Mowrer 1960b, p. 216). The
image in Mowrer's system thus serves its traditional function of guiding
and directing behavior and, in addition, provides a mechanism for the
maintenance of homeostasis. (pp. 484–485)

I do not follow the new cognitive psychology literature closely
enough to know what sort of reception McMahon's salient paper has
had, but as far as I am concerned it is right "on target," and provides a
far better historical context and even a more vivid and clearer formulation than I was able to give to my conception of the role of imagery in
Learning Theory and the Symbolic Processes. Thank you, Carol
McMahon!

Somehow the story got back to me that during the late 1960s
Richard Bugelski, of the Department of Psychology of the State
University of New York at Buffalo, was conducting a learning seminar,
and in the course of a discussion of *Learning Theory and the Symbolic
Processes* he remarked: "When Mowrer says it's time to start taking
imagery seriously, it's time to start taking mental imagery seriously." In
the most recent APA biographical membership directory, I find that
Carol McMahon took her undergraduate degree at SUNY at Buffalo in
1970, then did graduate work at the University of Pennsylvania, and in
1974 joined the psychology faculty back at her old Alma Mater. Could
it be that she was in Bugelski's seminar and heard, and took to heart,
his remark about the neglected significance of imagery? If so, I also
want to say, Thank you, Dick Bugelski![2]

[2] Since the above was written, I have received the first issue (Vol. 1, No. 1) of the
Journal of Mental Imagery, and find that it contains a seminal paper by Professor
Bugelski, entitled "Imagery and Verbal Behavior." Apparently not only his former
student, Carol McMahon, but Richard himself is indeed "taking imagery seriously."

Miscellaneous Observations

In this paper the indispensability of the concept of imagery has been stressed only in relation to the problem of giving an adequate account of voluntary (habitual) behavior. Of comparable importance is the role of imagery in the psychology of language, especially in relation to the problem of the *meaning* of words and the role of meanings as "mediators" in both thought and overt behavior. But I have gone into all this at great length in *Learning Theory and the Symbolic Processes* (see especially Chapters 2, 3, and 4), and there is no need to discuss again, even synoptically, that material here (cf. also Mowrer, 1954).

It is interesting to note that even members of the Association for the Advancement of Behavior Therapy are now increasingly referring to images and imagery. Reference has already been made to the use of imagery or fantasy in "systematic desensitization," and in glancing over the program of the December, 1975, meeting of AABT (in San Francisco), I noted with special interest the titles of two workshops: "Cognitive and Behavioral Management of Clinical Depression" and "Cognitive-Behavior Modification." Also, as typical of this trend, one notes two articles in a recent issue of *Behavior Research and Therapy* with the word "imagery" in their titles (McLemore, 1976; Weinstein, 1976).

Under date of January, 1977, I received a letter from Donald L. King, Associate Professor of Psychology at Howard University, which began with these words:

> I read your recent article in *American Psychologist* [Mowrer, 1976] with great interest. It galvanized me into writing to you about my own *image approach to conditioning* [italics added].
>
> My work most closely relates to yours in its use of a feedback theory to account for the increase or decrease in the probability of the instrumental response. I am indebted to both you and N. Wiener for my reliance on feedback theory.

With the letter, Professor King included the following published or mimeographed papers: "An Image Theory of Classical Conditioning" (1973); "Perception, Binocular Fusion, and an Image Theory of Classical Conditioning" (1974a); "An Image Theory of Instrumental Conditioning" (1974b); "Learned and Perceived Reinforcer Response Strengths and Image Theory" (1976); and "Bring-about-Stimulus and Closed-Loop Theories of Learning" (1977). Also included was a synopsis of a recently completed undergraduate textbook entitled,

Introduction to Conditioning: An Image Approach[3]. I had not previously known of this recent work and was pleased to learn that it is so much in line with the approach delineated in my 1960 books. Thank you, Donald King.

Dalbir Bindra, of McGill University, now has in mimeographed form a paper in which he reviews and successively discards as inadequate a long series of theories of learning, the next to last of which is what we may here term the "ideomotor" theory (of Aristotle, James, and others). Bindra (1977) says this theory is also unworkable, despite its time-honored status and acceptance. The last theory in Bindra's series is the one which he has constructed and finds freest from objections; but I, personally, am not able to understand it. I do not propose, therefore, to make any judgment regarding its validity, and commend it to readers, both as a critique of ideomotor theory and as a possible improvement (or replacement) thereof. However, as McMahon has usefully demonstrated, ideomotor theory (and the role of imagery) has a long and impressive history that is not going to be easily dismissed.[4]

References

Amsel, A. Hope comes to learning theory. *Contemporary Psychology,* 1961, *6,* 33–36.

Bindra, D. *A critique of theories of learning.* Mimeographed, 1977.

Brewer, W. F. There is no convincing evidence for operant or classical conditioning in adult humans. In W. B. Weimer & D. S. Palermo (Eds.), *Cognition and the symbolic processes.* Hillside, N. J.: Lawrence Erlbaum, 1974.

Bugelski, B. R. Imagery and verbal behavior. *Journal of Mental Imagery,* 1977, *1,* 39–52.

Curtis, Q. F. *The experimental neurosis in the pig.* Paper presented at the meeting of the American Psychological Association, Minneapolis, September, 1937.

---

[3] See King, D. L. *Conditioning: An image approach.* New York: Gardner Press, 1979.

[4] In response to a letter to Dr. Bindra regarding above matters, I received, under date of June 21, 1977, a gracious and informative reply. I quote in part: "For the past several years I have been following your general line of argument and trying to see how, in detail, one might go about explaining instrumental learning in terms of classical conditioning concepts. I enclose a reprint of each of two recent papers (*Psychological Review,* 1974, *84,* 199–213; *Canadian Journal of Psychology,* 1976, *30,* 157–173). But the full argument I have developed in my recent *A theory of intelligent behavior* (Wiley, 1976), which, incidentally, is reviewed in this month's *Contemporary Psychology.* In this volume I have tried to put together a neuropsychological account of behavior, and, even from this viewpoint your general approach comes out to be essentially on the right track." Unable to examine these treatises by Professor Bindra before this paper goes to press, I look forward to becoming better versed with respect to his work in the near future.

Estes, W. K. *Handbook of learning and cognitive processes* (Vol. 2). New York: Wiley, 1975.

Hathaway, S. R. An action-potential study of neuromuscular relations. *Journal of Experimental Psychology*, 1935, *18*, 285–298.

Hull, C. L. *Principles of behavior*. New York: Appleton-Century-Crofts, 1943.

James, W. *The principles of psychology* (Vol. 2). New York: Henry Holt, 1890.

Jeffrey, W. E. To complete Hobart Mowrer. *Contemporary Psychology*, 1961, *6*, 358–361.

King, D. L. An image theory of classical conditioning. *Psychological Reports*, 1973, *33*, 403–411.

King, D. L. An image theory of instrumental conditioning. *Psychological Reports*, 1974, *35*, 1115–1122. (a)

King, D. L. Perception, binocular fusion, and an image theory of classical conditioning. *Perceptual and Motor Skills*, 1974, *39*, 531–537. (b)

King, D. L. Learned and perceived reinforcer response strengths and image theory. *Bulletin of the Psychonomic Society*, 1976, *7*, 438–441.

King, D. L. *Bring-about-stimulus and closed-loop instrumental conditioning*. Department of Psychology, Howard University, Washington, D.C., 1977 (mimeographed).

Konorski, J. *Conditioned reflexes and neuron organization*. Cambridge: Cambridge University Press, 1948.

Konorski, J. *Integrative activity of the brain*. Chicago: University of Chicago Press, 1967.

Lange, N. Beiträge zur Theorie der sinnlichen Aufmerksamkeit und der activen Apperzeption. *Philosophishe Studien*, 1888, *4*, 390–422.

Lindner, R. M. An experimental study of anticipation. *American Journal of Psychology*, 1938, *51*, 253–261.

McLemore, C. W. Factorial validity of imagery measures. *Behaviour Research and Therapy*, 1976, *14*, 399–408.

McMahon, Carol E. Images as motives and motivators: A historical perspective. *American Journal of Psychology*, 1973, *86*, 465–490.

Meyer, M. F. *The fundamental laws of human behavior. Lecturers on the foundations of any mental or social science*. Boston: R. G. Badger, 1911.

Miller, N. E. Studies of fear as an acquirable drive. I. Fear as motivation and fear-reduction as reinforcement in the learning of a new response. *Journal of Experimental Psychology*, 1948, *38*, 89–101.

Miller, G. A. Galanter, E. H., & Pribram, K. H. *Plans and the structure of behavior*. New York: Holt, Rinehart & Winston, 1960.

Mowrer, O. H. *The modification of vestibular nystagmus by means of repeated elicitation. Comparative Psychology Monographs*, 1934, *9*, No. 45, p. 48.

Mowrer, O. H. "Maturation" vs. "learning" in the development of vestibular and optokinetic nystagmus. *Journal of Genetic Psychology*, 1936, *48*, 383–404.

Mowrer, O. H. Preparatory set (expectancy)—A determinant in motivation and learning. *Psychological Review*, 1938, *45*, 61–91.

Mowrer, O. H. *Preparatory set (expectancy)—Some methods of measurement. Psychological Monographs*, 1940, *52*, No. 2, p. 43.

Mowrer, O. H. Preparatory set (expectancy)—Further evidence of its "central" locus. *Journal of Experimental Psychology*, 1941, *28*, 116–133.

Mowrer, O. H. Inter-trial responses as "rehearsal": A study of "overt thinking" in animals. *American Journal of Psychology*, 1947, *60*, 608–616.

Mowrer, O. H. *Learning theory and personality dynamics*. New York: Ronald, 1950.

Mowrer, O. H. The psychologist looks at language. *American Psychologist*, 1954, *9*, 660–694.

Mowrer, O. H. *Learning theory and behavior*. New York: Wiley, 1960. (a)

Mowrer, O. H. *Learning theory and the symbolic processes*. New York: Wiley, 1960. (b)

Mowrer, O. H. Integrity groups: Principles and procedures. *The Counseling psychologist*, 1972, *3*, 7–32.

Mowrer, O. H. *Learning theory and behavior*. Huntington, N. Y.: R. E. Krieger, 1973.

Mowrer, O. H., "How does the mind work?" Memorial address in honor of Jerzy Konorski. *American Psychologist*, 1976, *31*, 843–857. (a)

Mowrer, O. H. The present status of behaviorism. *Education*, 1976, *94*, 4–23. (b)

Mowrer, O. H., & Keehn, J. D. How are inter-trial "avoidance" responses reinforced? *Psychological Review*, 1958, *65*, 209–221.

Mowrer, O. H., Rayman, N. N., & Bliss, E. L. Preparatory set (expectancy)—An experimental demonstration of its "central" locus. *Journal of Experimental Psychology*, 1940, *26*, 357–372.

Muenzinger, K. F. Vicarious trial and error at a point of choice. I. A general survey of its relation to learning efficiency. *Journal of Genetic Psychology*, 1938, *53*, 75–86.

Myers, C. R. Journal citations and scientific eminence in contemporary psychology. *American Psychologist*, 1970, *25*, 1141–1148.

Pavlov, I. P. The reply of a physiologist to psychologists. *Psychological Review*, 1932, *39*, 91–127.

Schilder, P. Conditioned reflexes. *Archives of Neurology and Psychiatry*, 1929, *22*, 425–443.

Schlosberg, H. Conditioned responses in the white rat. *Journal of Genetic Psychology*, 1934, *45*, 303–335.

Shaffer, L. H. Intention and performance. *Psychological Review*, 1976, *83*, 375–393.

Sidman, M. Two temporal parameters of the maintenance of avoidance behavior in the white rat. *Journal of Comparative and Physiological Psychology*, 1953, *46*, 253–261.

Spragg, S. D. S. Anticipatory responses in serial learning by chimpanzees. *Comparative Psychology Monographs*, 1936, *13*, 62.

Thorndike, E. L. *The fundamentals of learning*. New York: Teachers College, Columbia University, 1932.

Upton, M. The auditory sensitivity of guinea pigs. *American Journal of Psychology*, 1929, *41*, 412–421.

Watson, J. B. *Behavior: An introduction to comparative psychology*. New York: Holt, 1914.

Watson, J. B. *Psychology from the standpoint of a behaviorist*. Philadelphia: Lippincott, 1919.

Watson, J. B. *Behaviorism*. New York: Norton, 1924.

Weimer, W. B., & Palermo, D. S. (Eds.), *Cognition and the symbolic processes*. New York: Wiley, 1974.

Weinstein, D. J. Imagery and relaxation with a burn patient. *Behaviour Research and Therapy*, 1976, *14*, 481–483.

Weaver, E. G. The upper limit of learning in the cat. *Journal of Comparative Psychology*, 1930, *10*, 221–233.

Wiener, N. *Cybernetics—or control and communication in the animal and the machine.* New York: Wiley, 1948.

Woodworth, R. S. *Experimental psychology.* New York, 1938.

_____*16*

Complete List of Author's Publications

1. Head movements and eye functions of birds. *Journal of Comparative Psychology*, 1930, *11*, 99–113. (With Knight Dunlap.)
2. Concerning the normal function of the vestibular apparatus. *Annals of Otology, Rhinology, & Laryngology*, 1932, *41*, 412–422.
3. A note on the effect of repeated hypnotic stimulation. *Journal of Abnormal and Social Psychology*, 1932, *27*, 60–62.
4. A note on the relationship between nystagmus and thyroid condition. *Endocrinology*, 1932, *16*, 431–433.
5. A comparison of the visual function of nictitation and blinking. *Journal of Comparative Psychology*, 1933, *15*, 75–94.
6. A device for numerically recording either rotary or linear movements of an oscillatory character. *Journal of General Psychology*, 1933, *9*, 251–254.
7. An analysis of the effects of repeated bodily rotation, with special reference to the possible impairment of static equilibrium. *Annals of Otology, Rhinology, & Laryngology*, 1934, *43*, 367–387.
8. The effect of general anaesthesia upon the experimental reduction of vestibular nystagmus. *Journal of General Psychology*, 1934, *11*, 133–144.
9. The influence of "excitement" on the duration of post-rotational nystagmus. *Archives of Otolaryngology*, 1934, *19*, 46–54.
10. The modification of vestibular nystagmus by means of repeated elicitation. *Comparative Psychology Monograph*, 1934, *9*, No. 45, p. 48.
11. A device for studying eye-hand coordination without visual guidance. *American Journal of Psychology*, 1935, *47*, 493–495.
12. The electrical response of the vestibular nerve during adequate stimulation. *Science*, 1935, *81*, 180–181.
13. The nystagmic response of the pigeon to constant angular acceleration at liminal and supraliminal intensities. *Journal of Comparative Psychology*, 1935, *19*, 177–193.

14. Some neglected factors which influence the duration of post-rotational nystagmus. *Acta Oto-Laryngologica*, 1935, *22*, 1–23.

15. A comparison of the reaction mechanisms mediating optokinetic nystagmus in human beings and in pigeons. Dodge Commemoration Number, *Psychological Monographs*, 1936, *47*, 294–305.

16. The corneo-retinal potential difference as the basis of the galvanometric method of recording eye movements. *American Journal of Physiology*, 1936, *114*, 423–428. (With T. C. Ruch and N. E. Miller.)

17. An experimental analysis of the vestibular pointing test. *Annals of Otology, Rhinology, & Laryngology*, 1936, *45*, 1–25. (With R. M. Dorcus.)

18. "Maturation" vs. "learning" in the development of the vestibular and optokinetic nystagmus. *Journal of Genetic Psychology*, 1936, *48*, 383–404.

19. The influence of vision during bodily rotation upon the duration of post-rotational vestibular nystagmus. *Acta Oto-Laryngologica*, 1937, *25*, 351–364.

20. Enuresis—A method for its study and treatment. *American Journal of Orthopsychiatry*, 1938, *8*, 436–459.

21. Apparatus for the study and treatment of enuresis. *American Journal of Psychology*, 1938, *51*, 163–166.

22. Determinants of the perceived vertical and horizontal. *Psychological Review*, 1938, *45*, 300–323. (With J. J. Gibson.)

23. Some research implications of the frustration concept as related to social and educational problems. *Character and Personality*, 1938, *7*, 129–135.

24. The meaning and management of crying. *Child Study*, 1938, January, 1–5. (With Willie Mae Mowrer.)

25. Preparatory set (expectancy)—A determinant in motivation and learning. *Psychological Review*, 1938, *45*, 61–91.

26. Animal studies in the genesis of personality. *Transactions of the New York Academy of Sciences*, Series II, 1939, 3, 1–4.

27. Authoritarianism vs. "self-government" in the management of children's aggressive (anti-social) reactions as a preparation for citizenship in a democracy. *Journal of Social Psychology*, S. P. S. S. I. Bulletin, 1939, *10*, 121–126.

28. *Frustration and aggression.* New Haven: Yale University Press, 1939, (With J. Dollard, L. W. Doob, N. E. Miller, and R. R. Sears.)

29. A stimulus-response analysis of anxiety and its role as a reinforcing agent. *Psychological Review*, 1939, *46*, 553–565.

30. Anxiety-reduction and learning. *Journal of Experimental Psychology*, 1940, *27*, 497–516.

31. An experimental analogue of "regression" with incidental observations on "reaction-formation." *Journal of Abnormal and Social Psychology*, 1940, *35*, 56–67.

32. Preparatory set (expectancy)—An experimental demonstration of its "central" locus. *Journal of Experimental Psychology*, 1940, *26*, 357–372. (With N. N. Rayman and E. L. Bliss.)

33. Preparatory set (expectancy)—Some methods of measurement. *Psychological Monographs*, 1940, *52*, No. 2, 1–43.

34. The tumbler pigeon. *Journal of Comparative Psychology*, 1940, *30*, 515–533.

35. Motivation and learning in relation to the national emergency. *Psychological Bulletin*, 1941, *38*, 421–431.

36. Preparatory set (expectancy)—Further evidence of its "central" locus. *Journal of Experimental Psychology*, 1941, *28*, 116–133.

37. Avoidance conditioning and signal duration—A study of secondary motivation and reward. *Psychological Monograph*, 1942, *54*, No. 5, 1–35. (With R. R. Lamoreaux.)

38. A multi-purpose learning-demonstration apparatus. *Journal of Experimental Psychology*, 1942, *31*, 163–171. (With N. E. Miller.)

39. A cumulative graphic work-recorder. *Journal of Experimental Psychology*, 1943, *33*, 159–163.

40. Educational considerations in making and keeping the peace. *Journal of Abnormal and Social Psychology*, 1943, *38*, 174–182.

41. Extinction and behavior variability as functions of effortfulness of task. *Journal of Experimental Psychology*, 1943, *33*, 369–386. (With Helen M. Jones.)

42. Habit progression and regression—A laboratory study of some factors relevant to human socialization. *Journal of Comparative Psychology*, 1943, *36*, 229–252. (With J. W. M. Whiting.)

43. "Culture and personality": A conceptual scheme. *American Anthropologist*, 1944, *46*, 1–29. (With Clyde Kluckhohn.)

44. Education and collective security. *Harvard Educational Review*, 1944, March, 105–117.

45. Dynamic theory of personality. In J. McV. Hunt (Ed.), *Personality and the behavior disorders*. New York: Ronald, 1944, Chapter 3. (With Clyde Kluckhohn.)

46. Language and learning: An experimental paradigm. *Harvard Educational Review*, 1945, January, 35–48. (With Peter Viek.)

47. Time as a determinant in integrative learning. *Psychological Review*, 1945, *52*, 61–90. (With A. D. Ullman.)
48. Habit strength as a function of the pattern of reinforcement. *Journal of Experimental Psychology*, 1945, *35*, 293–311. (With Helen M. Jones.)
49. Fear as an intervening variable in avoidance conditioning. *Journal of Comparative Psychology*, 1946, *39*, 29–50. (With R. R. Lamoreaux.)
50. The law of effect and ego psychology. *Psychological Review*, 1946, *53*, 321–334.
51. On the dual nature of learning—A reinterpretation of "conditioning" and "problem-solving." *Harvard Educational Review*, 1947, *17*, 102–148.
52. A method of measuring tension in written documents. *Journal of Abnormal and Social Psychology*, 1947, *42*, 3–32.
53. Discussion of Dr. Hebb's paper "Spontaneous Neurosis in Chimpanzees." *Psychosomatic Medicine*, 1947, *9*, 16–19.
54. Discipline and mental health. *Harvard Educational Review*, 1947, *17*, 284–296.
55. Inter-trial responses as "rehearsal": A study of "overt thinking" in animals. *American Journal of Psychology*, 1947, *60*, 608–616.
56. Modern woman and the Harvard report. *An educational philosophy for exceptional children.* Proceedings of special conference on education and the exceptional child of the Child Research Clinic of the Woods Schools. Langhorne, Pa., May, 1947.
57. What is normal behavior? In L. A. Pennington & I. A. Berg (Eds.), *An introduction to clinical psychology*. New York: Ronald, 1948.
58. Individual learning and "racial experience" in the rat, with special reference to vocalization. *Journal of Genetic Psychology*, 1948, *83*, 29–43. (With Florence Palma and Marjorie D. Sanger.)
59. An experimental analogue of fear from a sense of helplessness. *Journal of Abnormal and Social Psychology*, 1948, *83*, 193–200. (With Peter Viek.)
60. Learning theory and the neurotic paradox. *American Journal of Orthopsychiatry*, 1948, *18*, 571–610.
61. *Exploring personality* (O. H. Mowrer, editor), 3 volumes. Chicago: the Delphian Society, 1949.
62. Frustration and aggression. In V. C. Branham & S. B. Kutash (Eds.), *Encyclopedia of Criminology*. New York: Philosophical Library, 1949.

63. Biological vs. moral "frustration" in personality disturbances. *Progressive Education*, 1949, *26*, 65–69.
64. Review of N. R. F. Maier, *Frustration—The study of behavior without a goal. Science*, 1950, *111*, p. 434.
65. *Learning theory and personality dynamics*. New York: Ronald, 1950.
66. Implications of a two-factor learning theory. *Psychological Service Center Journal*, 1950, *2*, 116–122.
67. Pain, punishment, guilt, and anxiety. In P. H. Hoch & J. Zubin (Eds.), *Anxiety*. New York: Grune & Stratton, 1950.
68. Two-factor learning theory: Summary and comment. *Psychological Review*, 1951, *58*, 350–354.
69. Conditioning and conditionality (discrimination). *Psychological Review*, 1951, *58*, 196–212.
70. Training in psychotherapy. *Journal of Consulting and Clinical Psychology*, 1951, *15*, 274–277.
71. *Introduction*. In Swami Akhilananda, *Mental health and Hindu psychology*. New York: Harper, 1951.
72. Anxiety theory as a basis for distinguishing between counseling and psychotherapy. In R. R. Berdie (Ed.), *Concepts and programs of counseling*. Minneapolis: University of Minnesota Press, 1951, 7–26.
73. Motivation. In G. P. Stone, (Ed.), *Annual review of psychology*. Stanford: Annual Reviews, Inc., 1952.
74. The autism theory of speech development and some clinical applications. *Journal of Speech and Hearing Disorders*, 1952, *17*, 263–268.
75. Neurosis and its treatment as learning phenomena. In L. Abt (Ed.), *Progress in clinical psychology*. New York: Grune & Stratton, 1952, 312–323.
76. Learning theory and the neurotic fallacy. *American Journal of Orthopsychiatry*, 1952, *22*, 679–689.
77. Learning theory. *Review of Educational Research*, 1953, *22*, 475–495.
78. *Psychotherapy—Theory and Research* (Ed.). New York: Ronald, 1953.
79. *Current theory and research in motivation. A symposium*. Lincoln: University of Nebraska Press, 1953. (With J. S. Brown, H. F. Harlow, L. J. Postman, V. Nowlis, & T. M. Newcomb.)
80. Some philosophical problems in mental disorder and its treatment. *Harvard Educational Review*, 1953, *23*, 117–127.

81. Neurosis: A disorder of conditioning or problem solving? *Annals of the New York Academy of Sciences*, 1953, *56*, 273–288.
82. All the neurotic needs is "courage." *Bulletin, American Protestant Hospital Association*, 1953, *17*, 1–3.
83. Freedom and responsibility: A psychological analysis. *Journal of Legal Education*, 1953, *6*, 60–78.
84. Ego psychology, cybernetics, and learning theory. In *The Kentucky symposium on learning theory, personality theory, and clinical research*. New York: Wiley, 1954.
85. Learning theory and identification. *Journal of Genetic Psychology*, 1954, *84*, 197–199.
86. Learning theory: Historical review and reinterpretation. *Harvard Educational Review*, 1954, *24*, 37–58.
87. The psychologist looks at language. *American Psychologist*, 1954, *9*, 660–694.
88. Contiguity vs. drive-reduction in conditioned fear: Temporal variations in conditioned and unconditioned stimulus. *American Journal of Psychology*, 1954, *67*, 26–38. (With E. G. Aiken.)
89. Contiguity vs. drive-reduction in conditioned fear: The proximity and abruptness of drive-reduction. *American Journal of Psychology*, 1954, *67*, 15–25. (With L. N. Solomon.)
90. Two-factor learning theory reconsidered, with special reference to secondary reinforcement and the concept of habit. *Psychological Review*, 1956, *63*, 114–128.
91. Behavior theories and a counseling case. I. Neo-Analytic theory. *Journal of Counseling Psychology, 1956, 3,* 108–111. Reprinted, in Japanese, in *Counseling*. Tokyo: Seishin Shobō, 1962, pp. 372–411.
92. Some philosophical problems in psychological counseling. *Journal of Counseling Psychology*, 1957, *4*, 103–110.
93. Conditioning of fear: A function of the delay of reinforcement. *American Journal of Psychology*, 1957, *70*, 69–74. (With D. J. Mason and J. R. Davitz.)
94. Symbolic transformation—In two keys. *Contemporary Psychology*, 1957, *2*, 57–59. (A review.)
95. Relations between religion and mental health. *American Psychologist*, 1958, *13*, 577–579.
96. Hearing and speaking: An analysis of language learning. *Journal of Speech and Hearing Disorders*, 1958, *23*, 143–152.
97. Introduction to "A new theory of schizophrenia" (Anonymous). *Journal of Abnormal and Social Psychology*, 1958, *57*, 226–236.

98. How are intertrial "avoidance" responses reinforced? *Psychological Review*, 1958, *65*, 209–221. (With J. D. Keehn.)

99. Psychoanalysis: Lion or lamb? *Contemporary Psychology*, 1958, *3*, 60–61. A review of *The invisible curtain* (Joseph Anthony) and *The death and rebirth of psychology* (Ira Progoff).

100. The dean of American psychology takes a stand. (A review of Woodworth's *Dynamics of behavior*). *Contemporary Psychology*, 1959, *4*, 129–133.

101. The unconscious re-examined in a religious context. In O. Strunk, Jr. (Ed.), *Readings in the psychology of religion*. Nashville: Abingdon, 1959.

102. Miscellaneous commentary. In S. W. Standal & R. J. Corsini (Eds.), *Critical incidents in psychotherapy* Englewood Cliffs, N. J.: Prentice-Hall, 1959.

103. Changing conceptions of the unconscious. *Journal of Nervous & Mental Disease*, 1959, *129*, 222–234.

104. Comments on Trude Weiss-Rosmarin's "Adler's psychology and the Jewish tradition." *Journal of Individual Psychology*, 1959, *15*, 128–129.

105. Judgment and suffering: Contrasting views. *Faculty Forum*, 1959, No. 10, 1–2.

106. *Learning theory and behavior.* New York: Wiley, 1960.

107. *Learning theory and the symbolic processes.* New York: Wiley, 1960.

108. Footnotes to a theory of psychopathology. In L. E. Abt & B. F. Riess (Eds.), *Progress in Clinical Psychology*, Vol. IV. New York: Grune & Stratton, 1960.

109. "Sin," the lesser of two evils. *Contemporary Psychology*, 1960, *15*, 301–304.

110. Some constructive features of the concept of sin. *Journal of Counseling Psychology*, 1960, *7*, 185–188.

111. The new challenge to our churches and seminaries. *Foundations*, 1960, *3*, 335–347.

112. Basic research methods, statistics, and decision theory. *Occupational Therapy*, 1960, *14*, 119–205.

113. Relations between speech and psychology: Accomplishment and aspiration. *Central States Speech Journal*, 1961, *12*, 165–169.

114. Review of M. Rokeach, *The open and closed mind*. *Review of Religious Research*, 1961, *62*, 86–87.

115. Review of *Psychology—A study of science. Study I: Conceptual and systematic. Vol. 1: Sensory, perceptual, and physiological*

foundations. (S. Koch, editor). Review in: *Philosophy of Science,* 1961, *28,* 307–317.

116. The rediscovery of moral responsibility. *The Atlantic Monthly,* 1961, *208,* 88–91.

117. The "new" psychological liberty. *The Christian Scholar,* 1961, *44,* 206–222.

118. *The crisis in psychiatry and religion.* Princeton: Van Nostrand, 1961.

119. Guilt in the social sciences, or The conflicting doctrines of determinism and personal accountability. In H. Schoeck & J. W. Weaver (Eds.), *Psychiatry and Responsibility* Princeton: Van Nostrand, 1962.

120. The Almighty's unmighty ministers. *The Christian Century,* 1962, *79,* 1252–1254.

121. The quest for community. Occasional Paper No. 8. Rock Island, Ill.: Augustana College Library, 1962.

122. "But the peer group says . . ." *Journal of the National Association of Women Deans and Counselors,* 1962, *25,* 112–117.

123. Some philosophical problems in psychological counseling (previously published). In H. J. Peters (Ed.), *Counseling—Selected Readings* Columbus, Ohio: Charles E. Merrill Books, 1962.

124. The image of man and the psychology of learning. *Selected Papers, American Catholic Psychological Association.* New York: Fordham University, 1962.

125. A psychologist views (with alarm) the mathematical concepts of "multiplication" and "division." *The Arithmetic Teacher,* 1962, *9,* 3–9.

126. Cognitive dissonance or counterconditioning? A reappraisal of certain behavioral "paradoxes." *Psychological Record,* 1963, *13,* 197–211.

127. Payment or repayment? The problem of private practice. *American Psychologist,* 1963, *18,* 577–580.

128. Science, religion, and student values. *Christian Century,* 1963, *80,* 1200–1202.

129. Learning theory and pedagogical practice. In V. E. Herrick (Ed.), *New horizons for research in handwriting.* Madison: University of Wisconsin Press, 1963, pp. 95–110.

130. Freudianism, behaviour therapy and "self-disclosure." *Behavior Research and Therapy,* 1964, *1,* 321–337.

131. Science, sex, and values. *Personnel and Guidance Journal,* 1964, *42,* 746–753.

132. Pornography—Realism or illusion? *Concern,* 1964, *6,* 10–13.

133. Truth in communication. *Journal Business Communication*, 1964, *2*, 18–23.

134. The loss and recovery of personal identity. *Journal of the National Association of Women Deans and Counselors*, 1964, *27*, 77–82.

135. *The new group therapy*. Princeton: Van Nostrand, 1964.

136. Sigmund Freud: Psychopathologist or "theologian"? *Psychiatric Digest*, 1965, *26*, 39–47.

137. Integrity therapy. *Faculty Forum*, 1965, May, 1–3.

138. Alcoholics anonymous and the "third" reformation. *Religion in Life*, 1965, *34*, 383–397.

139. Learning theory and behavior therapy. In B. B. Wolman (Ed.), *Handbook of Clinical Psychology*, New York: McGraw-Hill, 1965.

140. Alcoholism, a metabolic or moral problem? *Kerygma*, 1965, *2*, 14–18.

141. As ye live (Review of *Counseling the dying*, by Bowers, Jackson, Knight, & LeShan). *Contemporary Psychology*, 1965, *10*, 426–427.

142. Symptoms of development. (Review of *Positive disintegration*, by K. Dabrowski), *Contemporary Psychology*, 1965, *10*, 538–540.

143. Stage-fright and self-regard. *Western Speech*, 1965, October, 197–201.

144. Models of man. *The Humanist*, 1965, November/December, 257–259.

145. Abnormal reactions or actions? An autobiographical answer. In J. A. Vernon (Ed.), *Introduction to Psychology: A self-selection textbook*. Dubuque: William C. Brown, 1966.

146. Some philosophical problems in mental disorder and its treatment. In C. E. Beck (Ed.), *Guidelines For Guidance*. Dubuque: William C. Brown, 1966.

147. Integrity therapy: A self-help approach. *Psychotherapy: Theory, Research and Practice*, 1966, *3*, 114–119.

148. The basis of psychopathology: Malconditioning or misbehavior? *Journal of the National Association of Women Deans and Counselors*, 1966, *29*, 51–58. (Reprinted from C. D. Spielberger (Ed.), *Anxiety and Behavior*. New York, Academic, 1966).

149. The behavior therapies, with special reference to modeling and imitation. *American Journal of Psychotherapy*, 1966, *20*, 439–461.

150. The theory of positive disintegration: Commentary. *International Journal of Psychiatry*, 1966, *2*, 247–249.

151. Stuttering as simultaneous admission and denial. *Journal of Communication Disorders*, 1967, *1*, 46–50.
152. A revolution in integrity? *Voices*, 1967, *3*, 26–33.
153. Civilization and its malcontents. *Psychology Today*, 1967, *1*, 48–52.
154. Communication, conscience, and the unconscious. *Journal of Communication Disorders*, 1967, *1*, 109–135.
155. Existentialism and integrity therapy. *Psychologia*, 1967, *10*, 109–117.
156. The psychologist looks at language. Reprinted in L. A. Jakobovitz & M. S. Miron (Eds.), *Readings in the psychology of language*. Englewood Cliffs, N. J.: Prentice-Hall, 1967.
157. Christianity and psychoanalysis: Is a new synthesis needed? In J. C. Feaver & W. Horosz (Eds.), *Religion in philosophical and cultural perspective*. Princeton: Van Nostrand, 1967.
158. Learning theory and the neurotic fallacy. Reprinted in L. Y. Rabkin & J. E. Carr (Eds.), *Sourcebook in Abnormal Psychology*. Boston: Houghton Mifflin, 1967.
159. *Morality and mental health—A book of readings*. Chicago: Rand McNally, 1967.
160. A clearing of ground. (Offer, D., & Sabshin, M., *Normality: Theoretical and clinical aspects*. New York: Basic Books, 1966). *Contemporary Psychology*, 1967, *12*, 184–185. Reproduced in *Psychiatric and Social Science Review*, 1967, *1*, 7–10.
161. Religious "therapy" in a secular culture. (Wood, W. W., *Culture and personality aspects of the Pentecostal Holiness religion*. The Hague: Mouton, 1965). *Contemporary Psychology*, 1967, *12*, 212–214.
162. Review. (Stafford-Clark, D., *What Freud really said*. New York: Schocken, 1966) *Zygon*, 1967, *2*, 215–217.
163. Communication, conscience, and the unconscious. *Journal of Communication Disorders*, 1967, *1*, 109–135.
164. Introduction to K. Dabrowski, *Personality-shaping through positive disintegration*. Boston: Little, Brown, 1967.
165. Loss and recovery of community—A guide to the theory and practice of integrity therapy. In G. M. Gazda (Ed.), *Innovations to group psychotherapy*. Springfield, Ill.: Charles C Thomas, 1968.
166. New evidence concerning the nature of psychopathology. In M. J. Feldman (Ed.), *Studies in psychotherapy and behavior change*. Buffalo: University of Buffalo Press, 1968.

167. Foreword to R. M. Jurjevich, *No water in my cup*. New York: Libra, 1968.

168. A resume of basic principles of learning. In H. H. Gregory (Ed.), *Learning theory and stuttering therapy*. Evanston: Northwestern University Press, 1968.

169. Stuttering as simultaneous admission and denial; *or* What is stuttering "saying"? In H. H. Gregory (Ed.), *Learning theory and stuttering therapy*. Evanston: Northwestern University Press, 1968.

170. *The new group therapy*. (Introduction by Fusako Murashima Baba. Translation by Ichiro Kamisato.) Tokyo: Seishin Shobo, 1969.

171. Too little and too late. *International Journal & Psychiatry*, 1969, *7*, 536–556.

172. New directions in the understanding and management of depression. In F. C. Frederick (Ed.), *The future of psychotherapy*. Boston: Little, Brown, 1969.

173. Psychoneurotic defenses (including deception) as punishment-avoidance strategies. In B. A. Campbell & R. M. Church (Eds.), *Punishment and aversive behavior*. New York: Appleton-Century-Crofts, 1969.

174. Critique of Patterson's article, "A current view of client-centered or relationship therapy." *The Counseling Psychologist*, 1969, *1*, 48–56.

175. A great opportunity not exploited. Review of D. Belgum, *Religion and medicine: Essays on meaning, values, and health*. Ames: Iowa State University Press, 1967. *Contemporary Psychology*, 1969, *15*, 531–532.

176. Conflict, contract, conscience, and confession. *Transactions*, Department of Psychiatry, Marquette School of Medicine, Milwaukee, 1969, *1*, 7–19.

177. The problem of good and evil empirically considered, with reference to psychological and social adjustment. *Zygon: Journal of Religion and Science*, 1969, *4*, 301–314. (Under the title of "A psychologist's view of good and evil and the church of the future," this article also appears in: Burhoe, R. W., *Science and Human Values in the 21st Century*. Philadelphia: Westminster Press, 1971.

178. *Frustration und Aggression* (with J. Dollard, L. W. Doob, N. E. Miller, & R. R. Sears). Berlin: Verlag Julius Beltz, 1970. (Translation of earlier work *Frustration and aggression*, 1939.

179. Bewusstsein und soziale Wirklichkeit. In O. W. Haseloff (Ed.), *Struktur und Dynamik des Menschlichen Verhaltens.* Berlin: Verlag W. Kohlhammer, 1970, pp. 54–69.

180. Civilization and its malcontents. In J. V. McConnell (Ed.), *Readings in social psychology today.* Del Mar, Calif.: CRM Publishing, 1970.

181. Social alienation and reintegration. *Journal of Psychological Researches* (Madras, India), 1970, *14,* 1–3.

182. Conflict, contract, conscience, and confession. *Mental Health Digest,* 1970, *2,* 23–26. (Abstract of a paper published in 1969).

183. The neurotic paradox. In W. S. Sahakian (Ed.), *Psychopathology today: Experimentation, theory, & research.* Itasca, Ill.: F. E. Peacock, 1970.

184. The moral model. In W. S. Sahakian (Ed.), *Psychopathology today: Experimentation, theory, and research.* Itasca, Ill.: F. E. Peacock, 1970. (From "'Sin' the lesser of two evils.")

185. No haven here. Review of E. V. Stein's *Guilt: Theory & therapy.* Philadelphia: Westminster Press, 1968. *Contemporary Psychology,* 1970, *15,* No. 12, 770–771.

186. An experimental analogue of "regression" with incidental observations on "reaction-formation." A republication in: S. G. M. Lee & H. Martin (Eds.), *Freud and Psychology.* Harmondsworth, England: Penguin, 1970.

187. Alexander's psychotherapy and learning theory: Critique and commentary. In A. R. Mahrer & L. Pearson (Eds.), *Creative Developments in Psychotherapy.* Cleveland: Case Western Reserve University Press, 1971.

188. Adler's basic concepts: Neurotic ambition and social interest. In A. G. Nikelly (Ed.), *Techniques for Behavior Change: Applications of Adlerian Theory.* Springfield, Ill.: Charles C Thomas, 1971.

189. Peer groups and medication, the best "therapy" for professionals and laymen alike. *Psychotherapy: Theory, Research and Practice,* 1971, *8,* 44–54.

190. Teach-In, May 7, 1970. *Journal of the National Association of Women Deans and Counselors,* 1971, *34,* 68–71.

191. *Conscience, contract, and social reality.* (Edited, with R. C. Johnson and P. Dokecki). New York: Holt, Rinehart, & Winston, 1972.

192. Is the small-groups movement a religious revolution? *Pastoral Psychology,* 1972, *23,* No. 222, 19–22.

193. Critical notice. (Review of F. H. Kanfer and J. S. Phillips' *Learning foundations of behavior therapy.* New York: Wiley, 1970.) *Behavior Therapy,* 1972, *3,* 112–125.
194. Integrity groups: Principles and procedures. *The Counseling Psychologist,* 1972, *3,* 7–32.
195. Beyond bondage and regimentation. (Review of B. F. Skinner's *Beyond freedom and dignity.* New York: Knopf, 1971.) *Contemporary Psychology,* 1972, *17,* 469–472.
196. "Old wine in new bottles"—Blueprint for a humanistic ethic. In J. F. Adams (Ed.), *Human behavior in a changing society.* Boston: Holbrook, 1973.
197. Integrity groups today. In R. M. Jurjevich (Ed.), *Direct psychotherapy* Vol. II. Coral Gables, Fla.: University of Miami Press, 1973.
198. Group counseling in the elementary school: The professional vs. peer-group model. In M. M. Ohlsen (Ed.), *Counseling children in groups: A forum.* New York: Holt, Rinehart & Winston, 1973.
199. Stress, constitution, character, and Integrity Groups. *Psychotherapy: Theory, Research and Practice,* 1973, *10,* 265–269.
200. Commendation and a few questions. (Critique of "The concept of healthy personality: What do we really mean?" by Robert W. White.) *The Counseling Psychologist,* 1973, *4,* 21–22.
201. My philosophy of psychotherapy. *Journal of Contemporary Psychotherapy,* 1973, *6,* 35–42.
202. Is the small-groups movement a religious revolution? In R. H. Cox (Ed.), *Religious systems and psychotherapy.* Springfield, Ill.: Charles C Thomas, 1973.
203. Entries in B. B. Wolman (Ed.), *Dictionary of behavioral sciences.* New York: Van Nostrand Reinhold, 1973.
204. Commendation and a few questions. Invited commentary on "The concept of healthy personality: What do we really mean?" by R. W. White. *The Counseling Psychologist,* 1973, *4,* 21–22.
205. O. Hobart Mowrer. In G. Lindsay (Ed.), *The history of psychology in autobiography.* Vol. VI. Englewood Cliffs, N. J.: Prentice-Hall, 1974.
206. Strength and weaknesses of intentional communities, with special reference to the nuclear family. *Journal of Pastoral Care,* 1974, *7,* 5–9.
207. *Integrity groups—The loss and recovery of community.* (With A. J. Vattano, B. B. Baxley & W. M. Mowrer.) Urbana, Ill.: Integrity Groups, 1974.

208. "Cry comfort, cry repentance, cry hope." (Review of *Whatever became of sin?* by Karl Menninger.) *Contemporary Psychology*, 1974, *19*, 592–594.

209. Review of McGuigan & Lumsden's *Contemporary approaches to conditioning and learning. Behavior Therapy*, 1974, *5*, 576–579.

210. The "no-win" position of professional therapists for drug addicts. *The Counseling Psychologist*, 1975, *5*, 127–137.

211. New hope and help for the disintegrating American family. *Journal of Family Counseling*, 1975, *9*, 17–23.

212. Loss and recovery of community. Republished in J. Hudson & B. Galaway (Eds.), *Considering the victim: Readings in restitution and compensation* Springfield, Ill.: Charles C Thomas, 1975.

213. Integrity groups: A context for growth in honesty, responsibility, and involvement. (With A. J. Vattano.) *Journal of Applied Behavioral Sciences*, 1976, *12*, 419–431.

214. Enuresis—A method for its study and treatment (condensation). (With W. M. Mowrer.) In J. Willis & D. Giles (Eds.), *Great experiments in behavior modification* Indianapolis: Hackett, 1976.

215. The "self-help" or mutual-aid movement: Do professionals help or hinder? In A. Gartner & F. Riessman (Eds.), *Self-help and health: A report.* New Human Services Institute: Queens College/CUNY, 1976, pp. 45–56.

216. "How does the mind work?" Memorial Address in honor of Jerzy Konorski. *American Psychologist*, 1976, *31*, 843–857.

217. Therapeutic groups and communities, in retrospect and prospect. *Proceedings of the First World Conference on Therapeutic Communities* (Noss Köping, Sweden). P. Vamos & J. J. Devlin (Eds.). Montreal: Portage Press, 1976.

218. The present status of behaviorism. *Education*, 1976, *97*, 4–23.

219. Changing conceptions of "neurosis" and the small-groups movement. *Education*, 1976, *97*, 24–62.

220. Integrity Groups: A context for growth in honesty, responsibility, and involvement. (With A. J. Vattano.) *Journal of Applied Behavioral Science*, 1976, *12*, 419–431.

221. From the dynamics of conscience to contract psychology—Clinical theory and practice in transition. In G. Serban (Ed.), *Psychopathology of Human Adaptation.* New York: Plenum, 1976.

222. Mental imagery: An indispensable psychological construct. *Journal of Mental Imagery*, 1977, *1*, 303–325.

223. Integritätsgruppen. Ein context zur Förderung von Ehrlichkeit.

Verantwortung und Engagement. (With A. J. Vattano.) *Gruppendynamik: Forschung und Praxis.* Stuttgart: Klett, 1977.

224. Learning Theory, a will-o-the-wisp? *Behavioral and Brain Sciences,* 1978, *1,* 69–70. A commentary on D. Bindra, How adoptive behavior is produced. *Behavioral and Brain Sciences* 1978, *1,* 41–52.

225. Is much psychotheray still misdirected and misapplied? *Canadian Counselor,* 1979, *13,* 120–135.

226. Reflections and commentary: The pioneers. In W. Redd, A. L. Porterfield & B. L. Anderson (Eds.), *Behavior modification: Behavioral approaches to human problems.* New York: Random House, 1979, Part II, 18–21.

227. *Psychology of language and learning.* New York: Plenum, 1980.

228. Enuresis: The beginning work—What really happened. *Journal of the History of Ideas in the Social Science,* 1980, *16,* 25–30.

229. The mental health professions and mutual help programs: Co-option or collaboration? In A. J. Gartner & F. Riessman, *Mental health and the self-help revolution.* New York: Human Sciences Press, 1980.

230. *Learning theory and behavior*—this week's citation clasic. *Current Contents,* February 4, 1980, *12,* 16 (Institute for Scientific Information, University City Science Service, Philadelphia).

231. Integrity groups. In R. Herink (Ed.), *Handbook of psychotherapy.* New York: New American Library, 1980.

Author Index

279

Subject Index